SEASONAL
GUIDE
TO
THE
NATURAL
YEAR

Wearing leather jesses with attached bells on its legs, this peregrine falcon has been trained for falconry.

SEASONAL
GUIDE
TO

A MONTH BY MONTH GUIDE

Colorado, New Mexico, Arizona and Utah

TO NATURAL EVENTS

THE
NATURAL
YEAR

Ben Guterson

FULCRUM PUBLISHING
Golden, Colorado

Book design and original illustrations by Paulette Livers Lambert.
Except as noted otherwise, photographs courtesy of
the U.S. Fish and Wildlife Service.

Library of Congress Cataloging-in-Publication Data

Guterson, Ben.
    Seasonal guide to the natural year : a month by month guide to
natural events.   Colorado, New Mexico, Arizona and Utah / Ben
Guterson.
        p.   cm.
    Includes bibliographical references (p.   ) and index.
    ISBN 1-55591-153-6
    1. Natural history—Colorado—Guidebooks.   2. Natural history—
New Mexico—Guidebooks. 3. Natural history—Arizona—Guidebooks.
4. Natural history—Utah—Guidebooks.   5. Colorado—Guidebooks.
6. New Mexico—Guidebooks. 7. Arizona—Guidebooks. 8. Utah—
Guidebooks. 9. Seasons—Southwest. New—Guidebooks. I. Title.
QH104.5.S6G87   1994
508.978—dc20   94-17557
                                                                       CIP

Printed in the United States of America

0 9 8 7 6 5 4 3 2 1

Fulcrum Publishing
350 Indiana Street, Suite 350
Golden, CO 80401-5093
800/992-2908

For Rosalind, Jacob and Olivia

5

12

• STERLING

22
6

23

4

11

7   8
21   9 • DENVER
10

COLORADO

• 3
GRAND JUNCTION

26

16

• COLORADO SPRINGS

24

17

2

13

15   •
ROCKY FORD

27

25

18

20   19

1   • DURANGO

14

SEASONAL GUIDE TO
THE NATURAL YEAR

SITE LOCATOR MAP

—COLORADO—

N

LIST OF SITES
Colorado

1. Mesa Verde National Park
2. Billy Creek State Wildlife Area
3. Jackson Lake State Park
4. Radium State Wildlife Area
5. North Park
6. Rocky Mountain National Park
7. Golden Gate Canyon State Park
8. Prospect Park
9. Sloan Lake
10. Rocky Mountain Arsenal
11. Barr Lake State Park
12. Pawnee National Grassland
13. John Martin Reservoir
14. Comanche National Grassland
15. Apishapa State Wildlife Area
16. Mueller State Park and Wildlife Area
17. Arkansas Headwaters Recreation Area
18. Great Sand Dunes National Monument
19. Alamosa National Wildlife Refuge
20. Monte Vista National Wildlife Refuge
21. Goergetown
22. Illinois River
23. Kremmling
24. Parlin
25. San Juan Skyway
26. U.S. Air Force Academy
27. Yankee Boy Basin

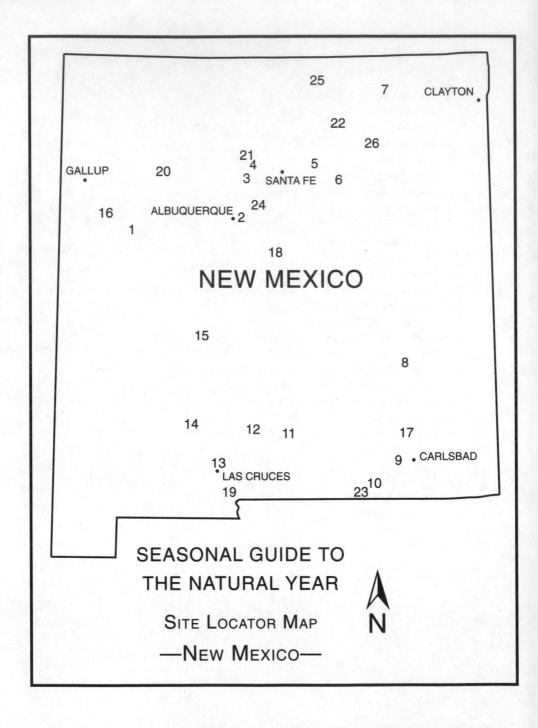

25

7

CLAYTON

22

26

21
4

5

GALLUP

20

3

SANTA FE

6

16

ALBUQUERQUE 2

24

1

18

NEW MEXICO

15

8

14

12

11

17

9 CARLSBAD

13

LAS CRUCES

19

23 10

SEASONAL GUIDE TO
THE NATURAL YEAR

SITE LOCATOR MAP

N

—NEW MEXICO—

LIST OF SITES
New Mexico

1. El Malpais National Monument
2. Rio Grande Nature Center
3. Cochiti Lake Dam
4. Bandelier National Monument
5. Sangre de Cristo Mountains
6. Las Vegas National Wildlife Refuge
7. Maxwell National Wildlife Refuge
8. Bitter Lake National Wildlife Refuge
9. Living Desert State Park
10. Carlsbad Caverns National Park
11. Oliver Lee Memorial State Park
12. White Sands National Monument
13. Dripping Springs Natural Area and Mimbres Resort Area
14. Percha Dam State Park
15. Bosque del Apache National Wildlife Refuge
16. Bluewater Lake
17. Brantley Lake State Park
18. Manzano Mountains
19. Mesilla Way
20. Mount Taylor
21. Pajarito Mountain Ski Area
22. Philmont Boy Scout Ranch
23. Rattlesnake Springs
24. Sandia Crest
25. Valle Vidal
26. Wagon Mound

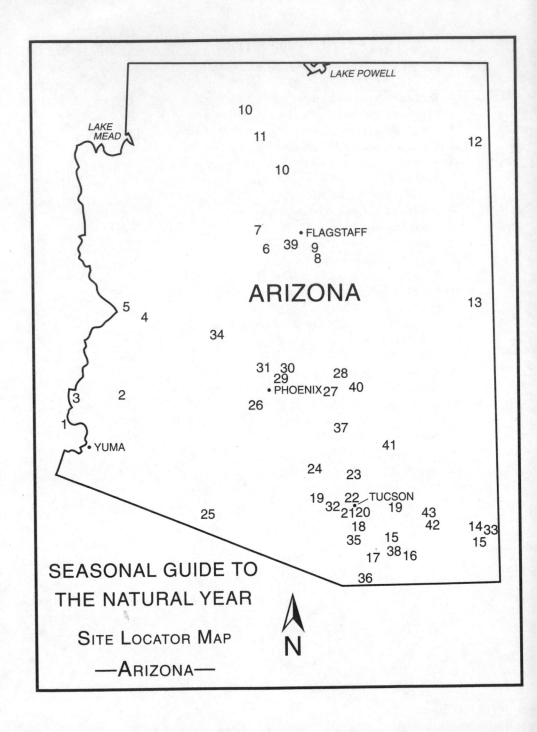

LAKE POWELL

LAKE
MEAD

10

11

12

10

7   • FLAGSTAFF
6   39   9
            8

ARIZONA

13

5
  4

34

31 30
  29   28
5   31 30
  • PHOENIX 27 40
26

37

41

24

23

19 32 22 TUCSON
      21 20   19   43
18   42 14 33
35   15   15
17 38 16
36

3

2

1
  • YUMA

25

SEASONAL GUIDE TO
THE NATURAL YEAR

SITE LOCATOR MAP

—ARIZONA—

N

LIST OF SITES
Arizona

1. Imperial National Wildlife Refuge
2. Kofa National Wildlife Refuge
3. Cibola National Wildlife Refuge
4. Havasu National Wildlife Refuge
5. Bill Williams Delta National Wildlife Refuge
6. Prescott National Forest
7. Coleman Lake
8. Mormon Lake
9. Upper and Lower Lake Mary
10. Kaibab National Forest
11. Grand Canyon National Park
12. Canyon de Chelly National Monument
13. Lyman Lake State Park
14. Rustler Park
15. Coronado National Forest
16. San Pedro Riparian National Conservation Area
17. Patagonia–Sonoita Creek Preserve
18. Santa Rita Experimental Range
19. Saguaro National Monument
20. Kitt Peak National Optical Astronomy Observatory
21. Sabino Canyon Recreation Area
22. Tohono Chul Park
23. Catalina State Park
24. Picacho Peak State Park
25. Organ Pipe Cactus National Monument
26. Phoenix South Mountain Park
27. Lost Dutchman State Park
28. Apache Trail
29. Desert Botanical Garden
30. Squaw Peak City Park
31. Phoenix North Mountain Park
32. Arizona–Sonora Desert Museum
33. Cave Creek Canyon
34. Joshua Forest Parkway
35. Madera Canyon
36. Pena Blanca Lake
37. Pinal Pioneer Parkway
38. Ramsey Canyon Preserve
39. Rogers Lake
40. Signal Peak
41. Pinaleno Mountains
42. Sulphur Springs Valley
43. Willcox Playa

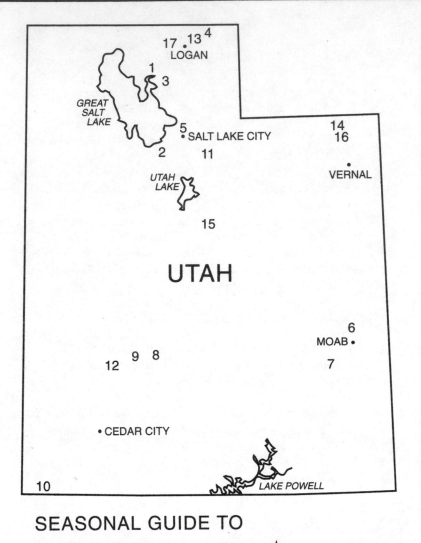

17 .13 4
LOGAN

1
3

GREAT
SALT
LAKE

5
. SALT LAKE CITY

2   11

14
16

UTAH
LAKE

VERNAL

15

UTAH

6
MOAB .

12   9 8   7

. CEDAR CITY

10   LAKE POWELL

SEASONAL GUIDE TO
THE NATURAL YEAR

SITE LOCATOR MAP

—UTAH—

N

LIST OF SITES
Utah

1. Bear River Migratory Bird Refuge
2. Ogden Bay Waterfowl Management Area
3. Harold S. Crane Waterfowl Management Area
4. Bear Lake State Park
5. Hardware Ranch
6. Arches National Park
7. Canyonlands National Park
8. Fremont Indian State Park
9. Fishlake National Forest
10. Joshua Tree National Landmark
11. Albion Basin
12. Big Flat
13. Logan Canyon
14. Lucerne Peninsula
15. Nebo Loop
16. Sheep Creek Geological Loop
17. Wellsville Mountains

Showing the large ears and black tails characteristic of the species, a mule deer buck and two does stand quietly in the autumn landscape.

CONTENTS

CONTENTS

List of Maps

ACKNOWLEDGMENTS

During the time in which this book was being written, it was my
good fortune not only to visit scores of outstanding wildlife sites
but to meet—over the phone, through the mail, and usually in
person—many generous individuals who are working to preserve
these places. I would like to thank the following people for
assisting me in the preparation of this book: Jeff Hogg, USDA
Forest Service, Albuquerque; David Hafner, New Mexico Mu-
seum of Natural History, Albuquerque; Don MacCarter, New
Mexico Game and Fish Department, Santa Fe; Andy Godfrey,
USDA Forest Service, Salt Lake City; Bill Romme, Fort Lewis
College, Durango; Terry Dunbar, Albuquerque Public Schools,
Albuquerque; Howard Lawler, Arizona–Sonora Desert Museum,
Tucson; Mark Dimmitt, Arizona–Sonora Desert Museum, Tucson;
Dave Krueper, Bureau of Land Management–San Pedro Riparian
National Conservation Area, Huachuca City, Arizona; Bob
Hernbrode, Colorado Division of Wildlife, Denver; Joe Pecor,
Sage Grouse Research, Gunnison; Bruce Anderson, Utah Division
of Wildlife Resources, Salt Lake City; Jack Rensel, Utah Division
of Wildlife Resources, Salt Lake City; Teral Fair, Photographer,
Crownpoint, New Mexico; Robert Heapes, Photographer, Parker,
Colorado; Allen Stokes, Professor Emeritus, Utah State University,
Logan; Scott Tolentino, Division of Wildlife Resources, Garden

City, Utah; Geoffrey LeBaron, National Audubon Society, New York; Christopher Rustay, National Audubon Society, Las Vegas, New Mexico; Ray Smith, National Audubon Society, Salt Lake City; Sonya Charley, Typist, Crownpoint. A special thank you to Gary Stolz of Bosque del Apache National Wildlife Refuge, Socorro, New Mexico, for assisting me in the field, reviewing several chapters, and providing the U.S. Fish and Wildlife Service photographs for use in this book. Another special thank you to Bob Tcherneshoff, Crownpoint, New Mexico, for his assistance in the field. Thank you to my wife, Rosalind, not only for drawing the maps in this book but for unfailing love and support. Many of the people listed above reviewed all or parts of many chapters, and I thank them for their tips and criticisms. Any errors that remain in the book are, of course, my own.

INTRODUCTION

Most of us exist in a world dominated by man-made, artificial time, a world in which clocks and calendars dictate our schedules even as they obscure the deeper rhythms of days and seasons. It is a wonderful thing to rediscover these more fundamental cycles, to directly experience a world impelled not by our wristwatches but by such things as temperature and length of day. In the Southwest, nature reveals herself throughout the year in an astonishing variety of guises, all delicately in tune with the seasons. At Carlsbad Caverns National Park, hundreds of thousands of Mexican free-tail bats swirl up from out of the main cave's mouth at dusk each evening throughout the summer. At but a single lake in the entire world, Bear Lake in northern Utah, the diminutive fish known as the cisco spawns in a wild, silvery flurry for only a few days in mid-January. The cheerful, sunny aspen sparkles like gold on mountain ridges throughout the Southwest for only two or three fleeting weeks in October; while the night-blooming cereus, a desert wildflower, blooms and dies in one day in early summer, opening after sunset and withering by early morning. Sage grouse strut on their ancestral mating grounds come sun or snow each morning throughout early spring. Rocky Mountain bighorn sheep smash heads amid the high, snowy mountains beginning each November. The eerie Joshua tree blooms in March, the rare elegant trogon can be heard calling in only a few canyons of southeastern Arizona in late spring and the mighty elk bugles in all its rut-crazed fury at dusk and dawn in September. The world unfolds in its own time. To appreciate wildlife, one must understand—and respect—its pace.

The guidebooks in the *Seasonal Guide to the Natural Year* series are designed to help the wildlife observer do just that. Instead of merely listing intriguing places to visit, *Seasonal Guide to the Natural Year: Colorado, New Mexico, Arizona and Utah* stresses the element of time: *when* to go is emphasized just as strongly as *where* to go. This book directs those who want to see some of the Southwest's most spectacular wildlife attractions to the likeliest spots in the likeliest months. Four unique viewing opportunities are offered for each month of the year, with the natural history of the species or event described and several suggested hotspots, or outstanding viewing sites, suggested. Breakout chapters focus on an especially interesting feature for that month. And finally, the shorttakes chapters within each section briefly list one or two additional wildlife events and likely viewing areas.

The four states included in this volume contain some of the most diverse habitats in North America. Everything from scorching deserts to frozen tundra can be found here, with the accompanying range of flora and fauna. The elevation along the Colorado River near Yuma is barely 100 feet above sea level, while Colorado's Mount Elbert, the highest point in the four-state region, tops out at 14,433 feet. The mountains of southeastern Arizona often more resemble tropical Mexican ranges than they do the spruce-, fir-, pine- and aspen-covered Rockies that lie to the north in parts of Colorado, New Mexico and Utah. All four of North America's deserts—the Chihuahuan, Sonoran, Mojave and Great Basin—can be found in the Southwest, as can the western extent—in eastern New Mexico and Colorado—of prairie land. Extremes are common here; it is possible to find wintering shorebirds in the warm desert in January and white-tailed ptarmigans on mountain snowfields in July. There is always something new to discover in the Southwest; few regions on earth can boast such a wealth and variety of both wildlife and habitats.

GENERAL TIPS, CAUTIONS AND SUGGESTIONS

Virtually every spot recommended in this book is on public land. Common sense and good doses of courtesy are your best guides when pulling onto the sides of roads or venturing into areas on or adjacent to private land to view wildlife. Many of the public lands described offer brochures and interpretive displays, or may have visitor centers and even personnel to help visitors better appreciate the area. Most of these places also require entrance fees, and the best way to hold this expense down, particularly if you plan to visit a number of these sites, is by buying a Golden Eagle Pass. This $25 annual pass allows the holder's vehicle and/or family into almost all federal lands, including national parks, national monuments and national wildlife refuges. It pays for itself after half a dozen trips and can be purchased at most of the places at which it can be used.

Given the extremes of temperature one can encounter in the Southwest, it is always a good idea to be prepared for desert heat as well as mountain blizzards. Sun lotion, brimmed hats and extra water are essentials in summer, as are warm clothes and snow tires and chains in winter. Binoculars arc always a must. In many parts of the Southwest a full tank of gas is absolutely essential as filling stations may be few and far between. Good maps are also a must. Beyond the standard atlases or road maps, the DeLorme Mapping Company (P.O. Box 298, Freeport, ME 04032; 207-865-4171) makes outstanding state atlases for Colorado and Utah. These topographic maps of each state, invaluable for travelers, show public lands and back roads as well as more common map features. *Arizona Highways* magazine puts out a fine map of Arizona known as, simply, the Arizona Travel Map (call 1-800-543-5432 for ordering information); and AAA of southern California puts out one of the finest maps of the Southwest, a large, detailed foldout known as the "Guide to Indian Country," which covers the northern half of Arizona, the southern third of Utah, southwestern Colorado and northwestern New Mexico (Southwest Parks and Monuments Association, 221 North Court, Tucson, AZ 85701; 602-622-1999). Forest Service maps, both topographic and planimetric, are available at many ranger stations or through the Forest Service offices in each state (see the appendix).

Two final concerns. Hunting is extremely popular in the Southwest, and many of the species listed here (e.g., deer, elk, turkey, pronghorn and waterfowl) provide sport for hunters in many areas of the region. Hunting is allowed only during specific seasons and at certain times of day, so it is wise to check ahead before venturing out. Big game hunting is common, particularly in national forests, from late summer through early winter, and many national wildlife refuges allow waterfowl hunting at various times throughout the year, usually on weekends and usually before noon. Finally, always remember that animals in the wild are both dangerous and vulnerable: a buffalo may charge you if it senses danger; some birds often permanently abandon their nests if humans approach too closely. Treat animals respectfully by being as unobtrusive as possible.

A REQUEST FOR HELP

One of the more problematic aspects of writing a guide-book is that the physical geography one describes can often be altered between research date and publication date: roads get paved or renumbered; signs change and landmarks become obscured. While every effort has been made to ensure that the directions in this book are as accurate as possible, it is an unfortunate and inevitable fact that new roads, new bridges and many other changes will render some of the descriptions herein useless. In order that future editions of this book may keep pace with these changes, readers are encouraged to send corrections to the author c/o Fulcrum Publishing, 350 Indiana Street, Suite 350, Golden, CO 80401-5093.

If readers have any suggestions for wildlife spectacles that may have been overlooked in this volume, please send them, including directions and as much specific information as possible, to the address above for consideration in future editions. The criteria for natural events included in the *Seasonal Guide* series are as follows: they should be consistent from year to year in time and place, be of unusual interest or exceptional quality and occur on public land or on private land that is open to the public.

JANUARY

1

Shorebirds and Marsh Birds

The Colorado River, the West's most storied waterway, begins in Colorado's Rocky Mountain National Park, a land of towering peaks and alpine meadows that is, in January, as cold and snowbound as it will get all year. But if you follow the river south and west, down out of the mountains and into mesa land, through the mighty Grand Canyon and past the gigantic plug of Hoover Dam, you will come to the lower Colorado River valley, a region where freezing temperatures are rare and birds by the thousands find a wet, temperate habitat for the winter. In fact, from Bullhead City south to Yuma, the Colorado River, the boundary between Arizona and California, offers several outstanding sites to the birder looking for wetland species.

This 200-mile-plus stretch of the Colorado has changed dramatically over the last century. Once covered with thick forests of mesquite, willow and cottonwood, the region is now a relatively barren valley of farms and resort towns. Desert land, fiercely hot in summer, still prevails in much of the region, of course, and the lush greenery that formerly shaded the river has retreated or disappeared in most places. The floods once endured by the valley have been tamed by a series of dams; roads line portions of either side of the river. The character of the valley has changed forever.

The river, though, has not been wholly denuded. Prominent is the human-introduced and often-cursed "weed tree" known as salt cedar or tamarisk. Whereas the lush forests of one hundred years ago teemed with birds such as the vermilion flycatcher, summer tanager and willow flycatcher, newer species, better suited to salt cedar, now call the valley home. Blue grosbeaks and mourning doves inhabit salt cedar stands in warmer months; in winter the habitat is quiet and virtually empty. So at the coldest time of year, the shores and marshes of the great Colorado—usually subject to only brief winter storms and enjoying low humidity—are the places to find birds.

Canada geese winter here by the tens of thousands, and spotted sandpipers, marsh wrens and American pipits occur in larger numbers in winter than anywhere else in North America. Gadwalls, American wigeons, common goldeneyes, common mergansers and buffleheads are among the more common ducks one may see. Stilts, avocets, grebes, herons, terns, sandpipers and cormorants can be found in many areas, and with some luck, one may see an American white pelican. Perhaps best of all, the weather is good and the river, despite its many changes, is still impressive.

HOTSPOTS

For a trip from north to south, it is easiest to head west from Kingman on State Road 68 for 30 miles to Bullhead City, then turn south on State Road 95 for about 20 miles until just outside of Needles. Here State Road 95, also called Bullhead–Topock Road, turns east for a 15-mile jog through **Havasu National Wildlife Refuge**. This is classic Colorado River marshland—Topock Marsh, specifically—where cattail and bulrush stands, tree snags and nearby rocky desert land make the area a prime wintering haven for many waterfowl. Travel about 5 miles on Bullhead–Topock Road and come to the Pintail Slough/North Dike area. A dirt road leads to these two areas, 0.3 mile and 1.1 miles off the highway, respectively. North Dike has more accessible open water areas, while Pintail Slough has cultivated fields for wintering geese and plenty of salt cedar and mesquite. Look for pintails, teals, mallards, grebes, double-crested cormorants, sandpipers, blue herons, Canada geese, egrets and coots. Also present in high numbers are

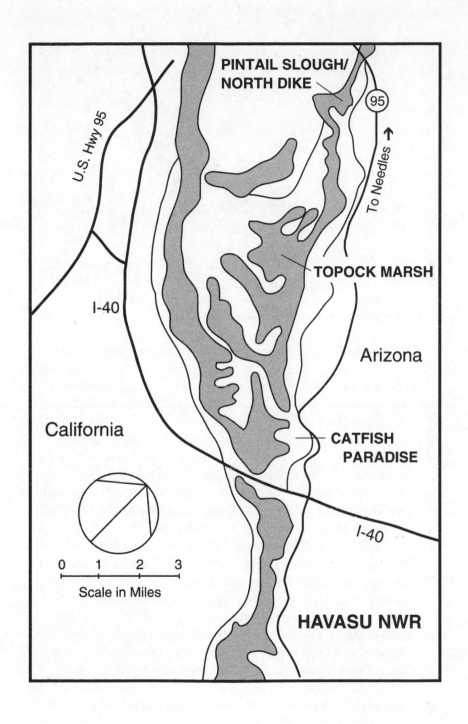

PINTAIL SLOUGH/
NORTH DIKE

95

To Needles ↑

U.S. Hwy 95

TOPOCK MARSH

I-40

Arizona

California

CATFISH
PARADISE

I-40

0   1   2   3

Scale in Miles

HAVASU NWR

A northern harrier, also called marsh hawk, in flight.

Gambel's quail, northern harriers, red-tailed hawks and the mistletoe-eating phainopepla. There are three other viewing areas as the road continues south; the best is Catfish Paradise about 8 miles beyond Pintail Slough/North Dike. A parking area here is directly adjacent to open water. Continue south for 3 more miles to where State Road 95 connects to I-40, but watch for collections of water on this last section of Bullhead–Topock Road as the area is subject to flooding if a rain comes.

Head east on I-40 for 9 miles, then take the first exit south and follow State Road 95 roughly 40 miles to the vicinity of the **Bill Williams Delta National Wildlife Refuge**, formerly a part of Havasu National Wildlife Refuge. The road crosses an arm of Lake Havasu just about at the point where the Bill Williams River empties into the lake, and a parking area immediately north of this bridge provides a fine view of the delta area's vast marshland. Enormous cattails rise from the water in the shadow of saguaro-dotted, jagged hills, as ring-billed gulls circle overhead. Look for western and Clark's grebes in particular here, as well as coots, cormorants, Canada geese and a variety of ducks.

An impressive and relatively pristine riparian area, one of the last in the valley, can be found by taking a turnoff onto a graded

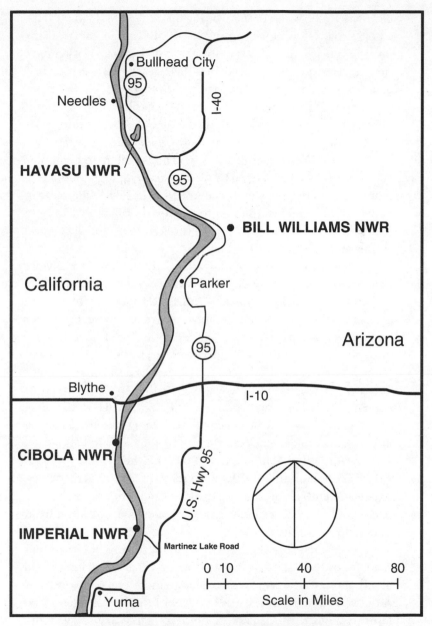

Bullhead City

95

Needles •

I-40

HAVASU NWR

95

• **BILL WILLIAMS NWR**

California

Parker

Arizona

95

Blythe

I-10

CIBOLA NWR

U.S. Hwy 95

IMPERIAL NWR

Martinez Lake Road

0 10   40   80

Scale in Miles

Yuma

GENERAL OVERVIEW OF
THE LOWER COLORADO RIVER VALLEY

dirt road 1 mile south of the parking area on State Road 95. This 10-mile road—look for it on the left—follows the Bill Williams River. While it is not a hotspot for waterfowl, it is an outstanding side trip. Here one finds the greatest diversity of bird species in the entire valley, though a summertime trip would be far more rewarding. Still, a January drive past the brilliant red cliffs and through the stands of willow along the quiet river can bring views of white-throated swifts and hawks and kestrels.

Returning to State Road 95, you'll find the road continues south and climbs high above Lake Havasu. Several pullouts allow more views of the many gulls that sail over the lake. After passing Parker Dam, continue 15 miles to the town of Parker. The road parallels the river for much of the stretch. Look for ducks and grebes and egrets along the way.

For an intriguing detour after Parker, head for Blythe, California. Take the Neighbors Boulevard exit and head south for 19.5 miles to **Cibola National Wildlife Refuge**, which is worth the trip if only to see the great number of Canada geese that winter here. The "Canada Goose Drive," a 3.5-mile, self-guided loop through salt cedar, farmland and marshland, features thousands of Canada geese, as well as ducks and perhaps a great blue heron or an American white pelican. The geese are the stars here, as Cibola contains the largest population of wintering Canadas in the state.

Cibola is a fine but somewhat remote refuge, and it may be just as worthwhile to stay on State Road 95 out of Parker and travel a long 89 miles to Martinez Lake Road and head west to get to **Imperial National Wildlife Refuge**. This 26,000-acre refuge, which stretches along nearly 30 miles of the Colorado River, is a major wintering site for many types of waterfowl and is within an hour's drive of Yuma.

Ten miles up Martinez Lake Road, turn right onto a dirt road, follow it for 2 miles, then stay to the left at a fork in the road a mile ahead to reach the refuge headquarters 1 mile beyond this. An observation tower provides a view of the refuge-maintained farm areas and the marshland beyond. Look for Canada geese and perhaps a few snow geese.

Return to the fork in the road and take the right turn this time to reach four outstanding overlooks. Palo Verde is 0.6 mile up the

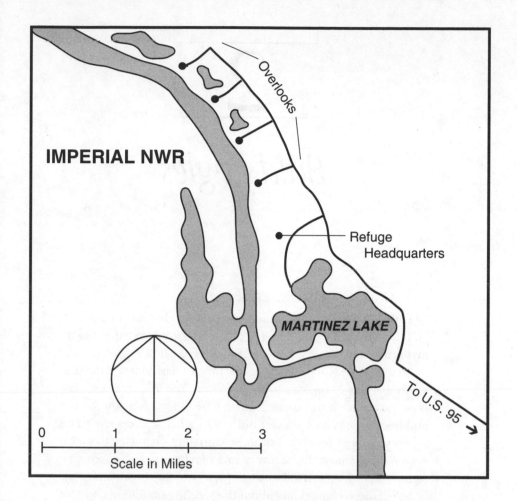

IMPERIAL NWR

Overlooks

Refuge
Headquarters

MARTINEZ LAKE

To U.S. 95 →

0   1   2   3
Scale in Miles

road, Mesquite Point 0.9 mile farther, Ironwood Point a mile beyond
that and the last, Smoke Tree Point, 1 mile farther. The road can be
rough and sandy in spots, but the views of the small lakes and
marshes make the trip worthwhile. Look especially for great
numbers of double-crested cormorants roosting in the snags of
trees that dot the waters. Coots, mallards, cinnamon teals, northern
shovelers and western and pied-billed grebes are common, and
rails, herons, sandpipers and pelicans are also fairly easy to see.
Yuma lies just 25 miles down the road back on State Road 95, a
total of about 225 miles from Bullhead City: a day's drive and a
river's worth of birds patiently waiting out the mild Arizona winter.

2

Bald Eagles

Like the Southwest, the American bald eagle has an aura so clouded with mystique that it is difficult to know what is purely mythical about the great bird and what is factual. We often project upon the bald eagle our most heroic images, fashioning it into the symbol of all we consider nobly American. The true creature, alas, is not nearly as ideal as we might like: it steals food from the osprey and flees from certain smaller birds with what would seem to be an unwarranted timidity. But these apparent character flaws do nothing to diminish the beauty of one of nature's most impressive sights—a bald eagle in full soar against a sparkling blue winter sky.

If there is any doubt about the wealth of tradition and lore that clusters about the bald eagle, one need only look at the back of the dollar bill to see the bird surrounded by symbolic paraphernalia. It is a well-known fact that Benjamin Franklin strongly objected to the selection of the bald eagle as our national bird and promoted the wild turkey instead. The eagle, he contended, was a cowardly, lice-infested scavenger. But back when the bird was relatively plentiful, its impressive and powerful beauty made it an obvious choice for the emblem of our young nation.

Perhaps as many as fifty thousand balds once thrived in the lower forty-eight states, living near lakes and rivers, primarily, just as they do today. During this century, however, the bald eagle population diminished rapidly. The bird's habitat was destroyed, it was the victim of illegal shooting and pesticides poisoned it to the brink of extinction. Before 1940, when federal law made it illegal to harm bald eagles, many were shot indiscriminately; in Alaska, as a means of protecting the interests of the salmon and fur industries, bounties were offered on paired eagle feet. Even after this time, DDT, the main chemical culprit, destroyed bald eagles by poisoning their food supply and causing them to lay eggs with shells too thin to allow adequate hatching. Our national bird seemed to have become a symbol of everything that was wrong with our country.

With the restriction of DDT use in 1972 and the passing of the Endangered Species Act a year after that, the effort to preserve the bald eagle gained full steam. The number of breeding pairs in the contiguous United States, about eight hundred just twenty years ago, has risen to over three thousand at present, and well over a thousand eagles have been released to natural habitats in recovery projects across the nation. In some northern states bald eagles have returned in encouraging numbers, and Alaska sees large congregations of the birds, particularly during summer breeding.

All the facts and anecdotes about the bald eagle do little, though, to communicate the experience of actually seeing one in the wild. With their immense wingspan and white head and tail, the bald eagle is one of the most immediately recognizable of all birds. It seems somewhat heavy and deliberate in flight, but with its startlingly keen eyesight it can spot a fish or rabbit or faltering duck from miles away and descend on it at speeds of well over 100 miles per hour. To see one of these birds pull up from a dive with or without its prey and zoom back up into the air is to witness an awesome blend of speed and power. One sign of a nearby eagle that the wildlife viewer should remain alert to is a nervous gathering of ducks on a winter lake. A flock of them skittering anxiously across the water may mean an eagle is soaring nearby, looking for any weak members.

But the bald eagle can be a patient sort also, commonly sitting on tree branches for hours surveying the surrounding fields or waters until some sign of food moves it. To the critic, this is a sign of the bird's laziness; to the bird-watcher, it is an excellent opportunity to view the bird for long stretches of time.

It is notoriously difficult to discern the immature bald eagle from the similarly feathered golden eagle. Bald eagles go through a series of annual molts during their first four or five years, and until that time they lack the characteristic white head and tail. If you can see it, the patch of gold on the back of the golden eagle's head readily distinguishes it from the immature bald eagle. In flight, look for a general white on the underside of the wings in the immature bald, markings that are not as prominent on the golden eagle. To distinguish both eagles from virtually all other soaring birds, look for a dark breast and body; hawks are generally light in breast and body. Turkey vultures, another bird mistaken for bald eagles at a distance, fly with their wings slightly raised in a V shape, whereas eagles and hawks soar on flat wings. "V for vulture" is a handy mnemonic.

In the end, though, only bald eagles occupy such an important niche in the American psyche. It is good for them—and us—that they have not disappeared.

HOTSPOTS

In the Southwest, bald eagles are almost entirely migratory; they spend the winter near waterways before their spring return north. Fish—alive and dead—are their principal food, though as the continent's largest bird of prey after the California condor, bald eagles are efficient hunters of small mammals and waterfowl. In midwinter there may be as many as eight hundred bald eagles in Colorado, and two places you are virtually certain to see them are right in the Denver area. One is the **Rocky Mountain Arsenal**, a 27-square-mile wildlife oasis where, beginning in 1942, the U.S. Army initiated chemical and weapons production. The various production plants in the arsenal were separated by mile-wide strips of preexisting natural habitat, and even as Denver grew, the 17,000 acres within the arsenal remained a thriving natural environment. Today the work done at the site is limited to cleaning up waste left over from the past, with no new production of weapons or chemicals. The only way to visit the arsenal is on a free tour bus (call 303-289-0132 for information). It's well worth the time, for the multitude of wildlife that thrives in this unexpectedly pristine habitat within easy view of downtown Denver is remark-able. Even if you don't take the guided tour, it is possible to see some of the estimated one hundred bald eagles that visit the arsenal in winter by trekking to the Bald Eagle Observatory Area on the arsenal's east side. To get there, take Exit 280, Havana Street, on I-70 and head north on Havana Street for 1.4 miles to East 56th Avenue. Turn east on 56th for just under 4 miles, and then turn north on Buckley Road and travel for 1.5 miles to the signed observation area. The gate and parking area are open from 3:00 P.M. to sunset daily and Saturday from 8:00 to 10:00 A.M. Outside of these times there is no access to the observation area. A short trail leads to a blind where at dusk it is possible to see several bald eagles in the cottonwoods less than a mile distant. Free spotting scopes and a video screen—a camera is mounted in the trees used for roosting—highlight this unique viewing area.

The other spot near Denver, **Barr Lake State Park**, offers near-guaranteed viewing of bald eagles, this time a nesting pair that has made the south end of the lake their home. There are only about a dozen known bald eagle nesting sites in Colorado, and Barr Lake is the only known nesting site in this part of the state. This is one of Colorado's best and best-known birding areas, with its 1,900-acre prairie lake, wooden boardwalks, abundant wild-life—including a recorded 330 bird species since the early 1900s—and a fine Wildlife Center. The eagles, who have been at the lake every year since 1986, can be seen by taking a 3-mile round-trip hike from the Wildlife Center. The walk near the lake's edge is easy, and a gazebo near the nest offers good viewing. Morning and evening, when they are more likely to be near their nest, are the best times to see the eagles. To reach Barr Lake, take I-76 north out of Denver for about 20 miles to Exit 22. Drive 1 mile east to Picadilly Road, go south on it for 3 miles, then look for the park entrance sign on the right. A dirt road leads to a pay station and park office area just ahead. Stay to the left to reach the Wildlife Center parking area.

Fewer bald eagles, perhaps four hundred, winter in New Mexico, but there are some good places to see them. The spillway at **Cochiti Lake Dam** finds a number of bald eagles wintering virtually in its shadow. They roost in the cottonwoods directly south of the dam and fly up the canyon north of the lake during the day, making sunrise the best time to see them. The dam itself is an enormous earth-filled plug that sits just 4 miles from Cochiti Indian Pueblo. A visitor center is at the west end of the dam, but you needn't go that far to reach the spillway area, which is 11.2 miles off I-25 on State Road 22. The turnoff to State Road 22 is approximately 35 miles north of Albuquerque, and the route to the base of the dam is well signed. Park at the spillway, cross the road and follow—quietly—the Rio Grande a short way south to see the eagles.

Maxwell National Wildlife Refuge, in northeastern New Mexico, also has a large population of wintering bald eagles, as many as sixty-plus in some years. With three sizable lakes, abundant grassland and cottonwoods and a large population of waterfowl, Maxwell is an ideal site for eagles. Lake 13 especially, the largest of Maxwell's lakes, and Lake 14 are very good for dawn and dusk viewing. The eagles generally come to the refuge in autumn along with large numbers of Canada geese, then depart with them in the spring. To get to Maxwell, get off I-25 at the town of Maxwell and at 3d Street turn north onto State Road 445 for 1 mile. Turn left onto State Road 505 and proceed 2.8 miles to the refuge entrance to the right. A dirt road leads to a parking area by Lake 12, then just beyond this to the refuge headquarters and the other two lakes. Also in New Mexico, check **Bosque del Apache National Wildlife Refuge** (see chapter 62) for many wintering bald eagles.

The potential for seeing eagles in Utah and Arizona is generally pretty good. Well over five hundred winter in Utah, with roughly half that number in Arizona. **Mormon Lake** or the nearby **Upper** and **Lower Lake Mary** may be the best bets in northern Arizona, though the roads to these lakes may be snow covered at times in winter. Lake Mary Road out of Flagstaff reaches Lower Lake Mary at the 13-mile mark, or continue for another 7 miles to Mormon Lake, a high, forest and grassland area tucked beside high cliffs. Stay on the east side of the lake for a signed overlook. If the eagles aren't there, try Upper and Lower Lake Mary on the return to Flagstaff.

JANUARY

Utah holds a "Bald Eagle Day" at the very end of January, or lately, the first Saturday in February. Call the Utah Division of Wildlife Resources (see the appendix) for details about the locations of telescopes and displays in several viewing areas. The **Ogden Bay Waterfowl Management Area** (see chapter 56) is also outstanding for bald eagles in winter.

3

Winter Constellations

It may seem odd in a book about the Southwest's more distinctive seasonal and natural attractions to include a chapter on constellations. The night sky, after all, can hardly be claimed by only one corner of the world. And yet the Southwest's sky, its clarity and brilliance, its quality of light and, in the daytime, the intensity of its color, is perhaps the most pervasive feature of the region. Few visitors to the deserts and arid highlands and snowy mountains of this region remain unmoved by it.

Painters and poets have long been drawn to the Southwest to imbibe some of its divine light. "Never is the light more pure and overweening than there," wrote D. H. Lawrence of the Taos Valley, where a shrine containing his ashes can be found today. "[It] arches with a royalty almost cruel over the hollow, uptilted world." Many other writers have commented on the pure and ethereal nature of the Southwest's skies, how the turquoise blue of a summer's day or the thick scatter of stars against a pulsing black winter sky seems to make one more aware of the motion of our planet through the heavens. In the Southwest, the earth seems to wheel gently beneath the endless bulk of the sky. Sun, moon and stars seem less like points of light that rise and set than like luminous creatures beneath which we revolve. And no time is more powerful and mysterious than the night, when stars seem so big and bright that one feels, as a Pueblo Indian leader once said, that this is "the roof of the world."

The brilliance of the Southwest's skies is more than an illusion. The region's generally high altitudes mean that there are fewer oxygen molecules or particles of dust than at lower elevations. Low humidity in parts of the Southwest also decreases the amount of water vapor in the air. Thus, relatively purged of interfering bits of dust and water, light descends on the Southwest virtually undistorted, revealing rich hues throughout the day. The effect is most noticeable at dawn and dusk, as pastel pinks and volcanic reds contrast with an already rich purple-blue sky. Distances become obscured in the seemingly limitless visibility granted the Southwesterner who keeps his or her eyes open.

And so it is that wherever one wanders throughout Arizona, Colorado, New Mexico or Utah, the sky will always be there too, a point not nearly as obvious as it might seem. Sky is more immediate, more dominant here than elsewhere. "To comprehend the arid and beautifully strange land of desert, mesa, and mountain, one begins by studying its sky," wrote Ross Calvin in his classic survey of the Southwest entitled, appropriately enough, *Sky Determines*. "As source of the intense heat and frugal moisture, sky determines climate, and climate determines flora, fauna, and the general aspect of the country." In fact, with all the marvels the Southwest holds as its seasons unfold, its subtlest and perhaps most beautiful surprise is the one always directly above, the one we contemplate from the roof of the world.

HOTSPOTS

The Southwest has some of the clearest skies and most unobstructed vistas in North America. We look through an atmosphere here that is anywhere from one-tenth to one-fourth less dense than it is in many other parts of the United States. And while there is no doubt that January can be a bitterly cold month in most years and in most parts of the Southwest, there is also little doubt that the winter constellations are about the finest of the year, with bright stars and enchanting configurations in abundance. If you are lucky enough to encounter a windless and relatively warm January night, your stargazing can be pure magic. The English playwright J. B. Priestley once wrote, after seeing the night sky in Arizona, "If Shakespeare had ever seen such nights of stars, he would have gone mad trying to improve upon his 'Look how the floor of heaven is thick inlaid with patines of bright gold!'"

Look to the east as brilliant Orion ascends, then just below it to find Canis Major with the brightest of all stars, Sirius. The glittering Pleiades will be nearly overhead, as will the bright star Capella. Castor and Pollux, the twins in Gemini, will be to the left of Orion, and beneath them will be Procyon, the bright star in Canis Minor. Always a treat to find is the hazy cloud of the Andromeda galaxy, just above Pegasus high to the west.

There is a well-documented mythology—Greek, primarily—of the constellations as we know them. But the Southwest's native peoples, of course, had their own conceptions of the stars, a fact obscured in the myriad star charts and books available to the amateur astronomer. The Navajo believe that the stars were placed in the sky by First Woman in order to inscribe the laws of the universe on the slate of heaven. The Big Dipper and Cassiopeia— man and wife—were formed first, with the North Star between them to serve as their home fire. The twins in Gemini were accidentally misplaced, leading to dissension among human beings. And coyote, the trickster, swung First Woman's blanket of stardust up into the sky, creating the Milky Way.

Aside from having at your disposal a knowledgeable star enthusiast, the best way to learn the constellations is from a chart or book. *Star Maps for Beginners,* by I. M. Levitt and Roy Marshall, is one of the best available, its easy-to-read diagrams far superior to the confusing and common disk-charts that often fail to clearly indicate the relative distances between horizon and zenith. And incidentally, if a particularly bright object seems to be at a point in the night sky where it seems it should not, odds are it is a planet. Consult any reputable annual almanac for information on planet locations.

A drive on many of the interstates in the wide-open Southwest can bring you to areas with distant horizons and skies fairly unobscured by city lights. Try east and west of Denver on I-70, west of Phoenix on I-10 or I-8 and almost anywhere along I-40 from California to Texas. The Four Corners area, or US 50/6 or State Road 21 in western Utah, can take you many distant miles from the nearest congregation of electric illumination.

But if you desire elemental and stirring surroundings, travel to **Arches National Park** just outside of Moab in southeastern Utah and gaze at the night sky through nature's gigantic sandstone windows. You can drive into the park well before sundown, making sure to be at the Windows Section, 13 miles from the park entrance, as dusk arrives. The arches known as North Window and South Window provide particularly good access and viewing and are just a few hundred easy yards from the parking area. Snow or mud may cover the ground at this time of year (though at night, muddy ground will be hard and solid), whereas in summer the park's red rock seems nearly afire. Come a week or so before the full moon and the glow of its light to the southwest may be just enough to illuminate your path without blotting out the brilliant stars to the south and east. The night undoubtedly will be cold, so dress appropriately.

If warm weather stargazing is more to your liking, try southern Arizona. **Organ Pipe Cactus National Monument** and **Picacho Peak State Park** (for both, see chapter 9) are both outstanding.

4

The Cisco Spawn

On a spring day in 1864, Brigham Young, the Mormon leader, visited Bear Lake on what is now the Utah–Idaho border and found it full of large, lively trout. He was greatly impressed, though if he had come a few months earlier, he might have witnessed an event so unique it occurs in no other lake in the world: the Bonneville cisco spawn, a short, intense run of hundreds of thousands of fish that occurs over about a twelve-day period.

Bear Lake is unique among freshwater bodies in North America in that it features four endemic fish, including the Bear Lake whitefish, the Bear Lake sculpin and the Bonneville whitefish. But it is the small, herringlike cisco that captures most of the attention with its spectacular midwinter run, drawing the curious—and the hungry—to Bear Lake's rocky east shore in late January.

The cisco is tiny, about 6 or 7 inches at most, but the sheer number that move inshore usually sometime around January 15 can be staggering. Dip netters show up by the hundreds on some days during the run, scooping loads of fish from out of the lake and carving holes in the ice if the spawning area has frozen over.

Because the cisco is a popular sportfish and because trout fatten themselves on it, there have been attempts to transplant the cisco to other spots in the West, Lake Tahoe and Flaming Gorge

Reservoir in particular. These efforts have been unsuccessful, indicating a fragile connection between species and habitat that began, according to wildlife biologists, when the cisco originated perhaps thirty-five thousand years ago. Apparently the cisco, a member of the whitefish family, is suited only to Bear Lake's particular combination of plankton, the cisco's primary food source, temperature and depth.

Transplant efforts may have ceased, but the cisco's seasonal run persists. For both the netter and the wildlife viewer, it is fortuitous that the cisco spawns primarily in shallow waters, 2 to 5 feet in depth, and that they do so almost entirely within a 2-mile stretch of the lake between North and South Eden creeks. Few of nature's spectacles are so accommodating.

HOTSPOTS

Records have been kept on the cisco run for several decades. From 1960, when dip netting was first allowed, through about 1990, the earliest date on which the ran began was January 10; the latest was January 19, with the run itself lasting anywhere from nine to sixteen days. It is a somewhat inexact science for biologists to predict the dates of the cisco run. A call to Bear Lake (see the appendix) sometime in early to mid-January will give specifics for any particular year's run. Dress warmly to view the cisco spawn, and if possible visit the lake on a weekday to avoid weekend crowds. Mobs can descend on the lake when a strong run is under way.

To get to Bear Lake, an enormous body of water nestled between mountains to the east and west, follow the signs north out of Laketown (10 miles south of Garden City on State Road 30; Garden City is 37 miles northeast of Logan on US 89) to the **Bear Lake Eastside** area. This part of the lake, known as Cisco Bay South or Cisco Beach ($3 daily fee), lies 9.5 miles north of Laketown and has a boat ramp and extensive camping areas. This is probably the best and certainly the most popular area for cisco dip netting.

5

January Shorttakes

Desert Bighorns

Desert bighorn sheep, smaller than their Rocky Mountain cousins, are difficult to see at most times of the year, but January is outstanding for spotting them in the Arizona desert. **Kofa National Wildlife Refuge** (see chapter 9), where approximately one thousand bighorns roam the dry mountains, is the best place to find them. Check at the refuge headquarters in Yuma before setting out, and heed the same travel precautions mentioned in chapter 9. Try Palm Canyon or Horse Tank on a January morning, and bring your binoculars.

Javelinas

Collared peccaries, commonly known as javelinas, are most active in the morning and late afternoon and in the dead of winter. These desert dwellers bear a resemblance to pigs, to which they are related. You'll rarely see one alone; groups of ten or more are commonly found in the rocky scrublands of southern Arizona. The **Castle Hot Springs Road** through the Hieroglyphic Mountains northwest of Phoenix is ideal for seeing javelinas. This gravel road passes through the Sonoran Desert land in which the animal resides. Take Exit 223 off I-17 and head west on State Road

74 for 12 miles. The Castle Hot Springs Road begins here, meandering north, then looping back south for a total distance of 37 miles, coming out a mile east of where State Road 74 and US 89 intersect.

6

Breakout: The Threat of Pollution in the Skies

At one of the overlooks on the South Rim of the Grand Canyon there is a series of photographs that show how air pollution from as far away as Los Angeles is fouling the skies of northern Arizona. One photograph shows a clear northern view from the South Rim, the way it must have looked on cloudless days until just a few decades ago. The others show the same view marred by varying amounts of smog, some of it so thick it smudges the view of the North Rim less than 15 miles across the canyon. It is sobering to think that here, the one place Theodore Roosevelt believed every American should see at least once, sulfates from over 300 miles away muddy the air.

It is not merely a matter of pollutants from distant locales infiltrating our southwestern skies. The Navajo Generating Station near Glen Canyon Dam just north of the Grand Canyon has long been blamed for the sulfur dioxide smog that descends on the canyon each winter. A recent Park Service study indicates that even with the passage of the Clean Air Act in 1990, visibility at the Grand Canyon may decline as much as 300 percent by 2030. Many other rural areas in the Southwest are equally at risk. For proof, one need only drive north toward Farmington or Shiprock in northwestern New Mexico and see the San Juan Mountains—pure white on clear days—drearily discolored behind a band of brownish-pink smog from the nearby Four Corners Power Plant.

Of course, metropolitan areas are worse off. South of Salt Lake City, the Provo–Orem region has been cited as one of the five worst in the nation for particulate pollution. The descent to Albuquerque from the hills to the west reveals an entire valley clouded by smog. Phoenix ranks among the top ten metropolitan areas nationally with the most days per year with unhealthy air. And Denver, despite progressive programs to combat air pollution, still suffers from an unsightly and unhealthy brown cloud of smog that lies trapped beneath heavy, cold air during winter months. Few sights are more dismal than a polluted Denver at dusk in winter, the foothills of the Rockies shrouded in smog, the sun a melancholy gold.

But these are relatively well-known facts, and it would seem that a corner has been turned in both public awareness of the problem and public policy to combat it. Less well known is the battle against what is known as light pollution, the term for any excessive and wasteful artificial lighting that dulls our view of the night sky. The effect is most pronounced in large cities, where the glow of thousands of lights allows only the brightest stars to be seen even on moonless nights. In fact, a nighttime satellite picture of the United States reveals a nation flecked with glowing points of light: the larger the city, the larger the point. And from within these glowing cities and towns, even some of the brighter objects in the heavens can no more be seen than the dark side of the moon. It is a peculiar and disheartening fact of our century that there are many, many people alive who have never seen the Milky Way.

Just as with air pollution, light pollution is not restricted to big cities. Electric lights can be found in even the remotest areas of the country, and even those who live 100 miles north, say, of a large metropolitan area find the stars on the southern horizon obscured. Lights mean security, and in those places where more people congregate, there will be more lights.

Some cities, however, have changed their ways. Tucson, where just a few decades ago light pollution was growing by some 20 percent per year, has placed restrictions on lighting fixtures; it is now possible to see the Milky Way from parts of the city. Of course, some of the urgency behind the so-called dark sky effort in Tucson derives from the proximity of the famous Kitt Peak Observatory, which, fortunately, is still a productive site for astronomical research.

The general opinion lingers, though, that light pollution simply is not pollution as such. Carbon monoxide in the air clearly damages the lungs, but light in the air seems to have no ill effects on our health. The continued clouding of our senses—the distancing of them from the experiences that have informed humankind for all times—is surely damaging, however. If a decrease in visibility at the Grand Canyon is cause for alarm, how much more so the progressive washing-out of the most deeply mysterious sight of all—the night sky. In this context, light pollution joins ranks with virtually every other form of technology or technological by-product that insulates us within man-made experience while removing us from genuine experience. It is, finally, debilitating, and one of the more unfortunate legacies our generation will leave to future ones. "[Our] children," laments Leslie Peltier in his book, *Starlight Nights,* "will never know the blessed dark of night."

FEBRUARY

7

Desert Reptiles

February is when spring truly returns to the desert. Temperatures that would make for a respectable early summer day in most northern states become common, trees and flowers begin to blossom and reptiles begin emerging from their winter burrows. That said, and before the desert's reptilian residents can be examined, a less than obvious question must be addressed: What, exactly, is a desert? The popular conception—or misconception, rather—is that a desert is a dry, nearly lifeless region dominated by sand dunes, where rain almost never falls and humans tread at risk of dehydration and snakebite. Deserts of the American Southwest go a long way toward confuting this impression.

There are actually four distinct deserts in the United States, each with its own characteristic life-forms. These are the Great Basin Desert, which covers most of Nevada and parts of eastern Oregon, southern Idaho and western and southern Utah; the Mojave Desert, centered in the region where Nevada, California and Arizona meet; the Chihuahuan Desert, a Mexican desert primarily, with fingers stretching into New Mexico and Texas; and the Sonoran Desert, also more of a Mexican desert, with large areas in southern Arizona and parts extending into southern California. These distinct regions hold in common the elements that characterize most deserts: they not only have generally high temperatures and relatively low moisture but the precipitation they do get tends to evaporate quickly. In the desert, even if plenty of rain falls, it may not be available to plants because of evaporation or runoff in dry, quickly saturated soil or rocky ground. Sand dunes, a staple of Hollywood deserts, account for a slight fraction, perhaps 5 percent, of American deserts. And far from being lifeless, deserts, despite their often sparse vegetation, support an astonishing variety of curiously adapted life-forms.

Reptiles, though hardly restricted to the desert or as vicious as popular imagination would hold, are nonetheless among the desert's most representative animals. As with all living things in the desert, reptiles have well-developed methods of dealing with heat and drought, including scaled bodies that reduce water loss. Most of them also withdraw during the colder periods of winter to underground burrows, avoiding the low temperatures that prevail even in the southern parts of Arizona and New Mexico. But when warmer weather returns in February, the desert's reptiles begin returning to the world aboveground.

Whereas the heat of summer restricts many reptiles to nocturnal activity, the relative warmth of a late winter/early spring day brings many creatures out of their burrows which might never be seen during the day in midsummer. Those reptiles that remain active during winter also respond to warm February days the way northern vacationers respond to Hawaiian beaches: check the desert rocks for lazy, sun-soaking lizards. The more common species to see in February include the ever-present side-blotched lizard, a small, brown critter sure to be about on warm days; the zebratail, a swift, agile lizard with black and gray stripes on its tail; the desert iguana, its long, roundish body covered with a fine lattice of red and brown dots; the chuckwalla, a chunky, skittish lizard that has the amusing habit of wedging its body into rocky crevices and puffing itself up when frightened; and even the desert tortoise, an amiable vegetarian who might stir a short distance from its winter burrow. The Gila monster, the only venomous lizard found in the United States, may also be about, as well as a variety of rattle-snakes: the western diamondback, blacktail and tiger rattlesnake in particular. It need hardly be mentioned that these snakes are venomous and should not be handled or approached.

In February in the Sonoran Desert, look for any of these species on the southern and southwestern slopes of hills and mountainsides, where the warm sun attracts basking reptiles. If it is not too windy and there hasn't been much wet weather, it is possible to uncover a nice variety of emerging desert creatures, particularly near rock crevices that can serve as windbreaks. Saguaro and palo verde areas—vegetation typical of the Sonoran Desert—are a good place to start, and creosote valleys are good on particularly warm days.

Aside from the smaller and more active lizards, some reptiles will not stir far from their burrows this early in the year. Since reptiles maintain their body temperature by outside sources, soaking up heat from the air, ground and sun (and giving off heat when temperatures become excessive), it is crucial that they remain close to a warm burrow. Reptiles need very little food and water to maintain their minimal metabolic levels, which can be as little as one-seventh that of mammals, when at rest. February is the time to see their first stirrings; a sunny day is as welcome to the strange creatures of the desert as it is to any of us who visit their land.

HOTSPOTS

A word of caution is always in order when discussing desert reptiles. While the overwhelming majority of the reptiles of the western United States are harmless, others—the rattlesnakes, the Gila monster and the Arizona coral snake—should definitely be approached with extreme caution. The best way to learn how to identify them is by consulting a good desert field guide, many of which are available (see the bibliography). A few general tips: never reach where you cannot see, always pick up objects carefully, move slowly away if a venomous snake is close by, and get to a doctor quickly if bitten. None of this should make you overly fearful. With proper caution, deserts are immensely enjoyable and safe places, and very, very few people in the United States are killed by desert reptiles. Bring a first-aid kit and a field guide with you, take plenty of water and a good map, and enjoy.

It should be noted that the Hopi people have respectfully handled rattlesnakes in their sacred snake dance ceremonies for centuries. Snake Society priests hold the snakes in their teeth as they dance about the plaza atop the high mesas of their land in northeastern Arizona. Bites are very rare, and at the ceremony's conclusion the snakes are released back to the desert. It is said that the desired rains frequently follow the dances.

Look for early-stirring reptiles in the more reliably warmer parts of the Southwest, the Sonoran Desert especially. The same areas that are good for early-blooming wildflowers will also be good for snakes and lizards. **Kofa National Wildlife Refuge** (see chapter 9), **Organ Pipe Cactus National Monument** (see chapter 9) and **Lost Dutchman State Park** (see chapter 15) are all good choices. For surprisingly good viewing opportunities, also visit some of the city parks in Phoenix. At just over 1,000 feet above sea level, Phoenix is already warm in February; and with several accessible, rugged and well-maintained desert parks within the city limits, there are ample opportunities for productive wildlife day trips.

Start with **South Mountain Park**, the largest municipal park in the world. This enormous desert preserve, just 7 miles south of Phoenix's downtown, offers pristine terrain: ocotillo, saguaro, towering rock outcroppings and miles and miles of hiking trails. Look for basking lizards on the rocks rimming any of several trails throughout the park. The Mormon Trail to Hidden Valley has an abundance of weird rock formations; look for chuckwalla and side-blotched lizards. A good map of the park can be obtained at the gatehouse just inside the park boundary. To reach South Mountain Park, follow Central Avenue south out of the downtown Phoenix area. After going under I-17, continue straight ahead for 5.5 miles, following the road as it goes uphill and veers to the right over the last half-mile. Central Avenue crosses the Salt River on the way to the park.

On the other side of town is **North Mountain Park**, far smaller than its southern brother but just as interesting. North Mountain Park and **Squaw Peak City Park**, another great nearby spot, are at the heart of the Phoenix Mountains Preserve area, untouched wilderness regions in the middle of the city. Squaw Peak offers several trails, including one—among the most popular hiking trails in the entire nation—to the top of Squaw Peak. North Mountain Park has two good hiking trails. Both spots are right off

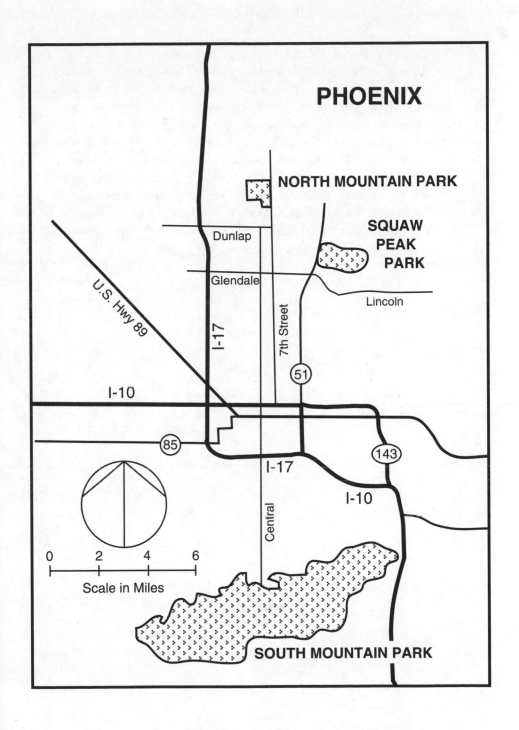

PHOENIX

NORTH MOUNTAIN PARK

SQUAW
PEAK
PARK

Dunlap

Glendale

Lincoln

U.S. Hwy 89

I-17

7th Street

I-10

51

85

143

I-17

I-10

Central

0   2   4   6

Scale in Miles

SOUTH MOUNTAIN PARK

main city arterials, offer great views and are home to abundant wildlife, including wildflowers. It is an odd feeling to ascend one of the higher trails in either of these two parks and watch lizards dart across the warm rocks while city traffic races by in the distance below. To reach Squaw Peak, take State Road 51 to the Glendale exit, and go east on Glendale as it almost immediately veers south and turns into Lincoln Drive. Between 16th Street and 24th Street, turn north off of Lincoln onto Squaw Peak Drive. The park entrance is immediately ahead. To reach North Mountain Park, take I-17 north to the Dunlap exit, go east for approximately 3 miles to 7th Street, then head north. Take a left at the stoplight just ahead at Peoria, and enter the park.

8

Winter Tracking

A natural human curiosity is aroused at the sight of an animal's tracks on the ground. The desire to know what creature left a particular mark is almost irresistible, a part of the sense of wonder, certainly, that fires the interest of so many naturalists. But at a deeper level, that spontaneous curiosity is a vestige of skills once central to human survival. The ability to read not only tracks but all of nature's signs, while now practiced almost exclusively as a hobby, was once the most valued of skills. To re-create these efforts on a cold February day is thus pleasurable as a means of gaining a deeper understanding of the world around us and of senses long dormant within ourselves.

One of the nicest and most obvious aspects of winter tracking is that it can be done practically anywhere. A new snowfall, even in a big city, creates a clean pad on which local wildlife writes its story. And while elk and mountain lion tracks probably won't be found on most front lawns, the principles of tracking and wildlife observation apply in urban areas as well as in a deep winter forest.

Tracks made in the snow are especially delightful to study and are generally easier to follow than those made in mud and dirt. But tracking goes beyond mere identification and can reveal to the knowledgeable observer specific information about an animal that made a given mark, even what was occurring in the surrounding area as the animal passed through. Although the subject of tracking can hardly be covered in a short chapter, some general tips for tracking wildlife in winter will help.

After gaining a general understanding of the differences between the marks of various groups—knowing, for example, that the tracks of members of the cat family are generally more rounded than those of members of the dog family—identification usually becomes a matter of matching a given track to a drawing in a good field guide. But just as it is impossible to understand a book's story simply by identifying letters and words, so it is impossible to comprehend an animal's story simply by identifying an individual track. Distance between tracks can reveal the rate at which the animal was traveling, informing speculation about whether it might have been chasing something or was being chased; a noticeably deep track or disturbance of snow around it might indicate that the animal became spooked and began moving rapidly; and because many male mammals are broader at the shoulders than are females, their rear prints generally leave an impression to the inside of their front prints. Many more elements, such as gnawed vegetation, scratched trees and the condition and contents of scat, can reveal much about an animal, everything from sex and weight to what its intentions were at a given moment.

There is always the possibility, of course, that a set of tracks will lead to the animal that made them. That's why it is best to wear inconspicuous clothing, avoiding bright and solid colors that would stand out against the snow. A plaid wool, best for cold weather anyway, is a good choice. And if your desire is to see wildlife, early mornings or late afternoons are usually when creatures are out and about. Not so incidentally, these are also the better times to view tracks since, without a high sun to obscure them, the shadows they cast make reading easier.

It probably goes without saying that bad weather for humans is bad weather for animals; a snowstorm is hardly the time to hunt for tracks or animals. Immediately following a snowfall, however, an area may be buzzing with wildlife seeking food and leaving abundant tracks. There are some problems with snow tracking, however, that can make it more of a challenge than tracking in summer. One is that unless the snow is fresh, it can be almost impossible to tell how long a track might have been there. Tracks made in mud and dirt often show distinctive marks of their age, but snow easily distorts tracks. It is also difficult to tell much about the pressure of a track in snow, since deep tracks usually depend more on the quality of the snow than on the condition of the animal. For instance, a deer's dewclaws might only show on a muddy summer trail if it was galloping, while they will appear almost always in a moderately deep snow.

Some essential items to take along are a good map, crucial when wandering in a snowy forest; a notebook for sketching tracks; a tape measure for calculating both track size and the distance between tracks; and a good field guide, Olaus Murie's *A Field Guide to Animal Tracks* in the Peterson series being among the best. Tom Brown, a noted tracker and wildlife expert, also has a tracking guide that provides excellent insight into how to observe nature, not just what animal made a given mark. For that is the whole point of looking more carefully at the world around us. Surrounded as we are by man-made sights and sounds, it is important to remember that nature's stories and nature's pace will not reveal themselves if we force our accustomed ways of seeing on the natural world. Tracking transcends mere identification; it opens us up to a way of looking at the world that, for many, has been long forgotten.

HOTSPOTS

While it is true that winter tracking can be done virtually anywhere, most of the more intriguing species are wary of humans and will avoid houses and urban areas. It can be difficult in winter, though, to get to some of the places where a variety of tracks might be found. A good spot to investigate in Colorado is **Golden Gate Canyon State Park,** as it is close to Denver and quite easily accessible in winter. The park is wonderful year-round, but in winter human visitors are few and deer and elk are numerous. Check at the visitor center for the best areas of this nearly 11,000-acre park to investigate, as weather conditions will determine which of the park's fourteen trails can be hiked. Or bring your snowshoes or cross-country skis and go where you like. To reach Golden Gate Canyon State Park, head north out of the town of Golden on State Road 93 for 1.4 miles, turn left onto the signed Golden Gate Canyon Road, and follow it as it winds up and down through pine and aspen to the visitor center 15 miles ahead. There is a $3 fee, and maps and winter information brochures are available.

One of the best winter wildlife spots of all is in Utah at **Hardware Ranch**, once a livestock ranch and now a wildlife feeding area where elk, deer and moose roam throughout the winter. Open fields and sage flats are home to over seven hundred elk and also moose, surprisingly abundant in Utah. Their huge tracks, clearly larger than elk tracks, are almost unknown in any other state this far south, making the sight of them or a moose a rare treat. A fine visitor center has telescopes for easy wildlife viewing, and sleigh rides ($3 fee) are offered for great elk viewing. Get out and walk around, though, and study the numerous tracks in the area. To get to Hardware Ranch, head east on State Road 101 out of Hyrum—on State Road 165 just south of Logan—for 16.3 miles until you reach the visitor center. Hardware Ranch is open from December 15 through March 15, daily from 10:00 A.M. to 5:00 P.M.

9

Early-blooming Desert Wildflowers

Spring comes early to the low deserts of the Southwest. While most of the rest of the country is still shivering through the heart of winter, wildflowers begin sprinkling the Sonoran and Mojave deserts with exotic colors as early as late January. Arizona's deserts are never without wildflowers of some sort—fairy duster or brittlebush may be in bloom at Christmas—but the showy, spectacular wildflowers, the ones flower lovers will drive hundreds of miles to see, generally don't begin blooming until mid- to late winter, making February the month to begin casting an eye toward the warmest regions of the Southwest.

One of the most frustrating aspects of desert wildflower viewing is its unpredictability. Flower watchers sometimes expect to see the same magnificent spread of poppies in the same place and on the same weekend as they did the previous year. But wildflowers, like all life in the desert, must be able to respond to the demands of heat and drought, and a variety of conditions can delay or diminish any given year's wildflower bloom. One February may bring a dense spread of lupines and goldpoppies along the interstate west out of Tucson, while the next February may bring only spotty blooms and dry grass. The wildflower viewer must be as flexible as the flowers themselves, ready to travel on short notice to find the delicate and fleeting fields of evening primrose or globemallow.

Whether spectacular or humdrum, the blooming of annuals—the showier wildflowers—can only be predicted about two weeks in advance and will only last about two weeks. Rain is the triggering element, but the rains that have the greatest effect on spring annuals are the ones that descend on the desert in early autumn. Seedlings are actually germinated by the rains of September and October, with heavier rains having the most beneficial effect. Throughout autumn and early winter, annuals need fairly consistent rain—an inch a month—and mild temperatures. Insufficient rain and too many cold days will bring a relatively colorless late winter or early spring, regardless of how warm or wet January or February is.

Still, even if all the factors seem favorable, there may be great variations in wildflower blooms even within small areas. A frost in a low valley may stunt the flowers there, while the ridges just above may be thick with poppies. And several partially understood factors may play large roles in foiling the best guesses of experts and amateurs alike, for example, soil conditions or the intensity of sunlight and the seed-stifling cover of last year's dead vegetation. The ability of spring wildflowers—and remember that in the desert regions of Arizona, "spring" can begin in January— to be flexible in maturation time, size and number is their distinguishing survival mechanism, though it can drive the flower lover crazy.

It is one of the loveliest of all sights, though, to encounter a field of yellow goldpoppies and purple lupines in the lushest center of their bloom, gauzy and aglow in a late afternoon desert sun or brightly radiant at noon. The mass flowerings, the carpets of blues and reds and yellows that seem to have shaken loose from the rarest bands of the spectrum, can be breathtaking. Mexican goldpoppy is the acknowledged star of the spring wildflowers; fields of it burst forth from the desert floor like an eruption of cool, petaled lava. It is sure to be in bloom in March, particularly in the higher elevations around Tucson; in the lower areas near Phoenix or out west near Yuma, there is a high probability of its being in bloom the last two weeks of February.

Lupine is another popular early bloomer, its violet blooms and gentle fragrance a soothing counterbalance to the blazing goldpoppy, with which it is often found. Other flowers common as early as February include bladderpod mustard, whose yellow flowers are wildly abundant in wet years; the delicate, light blue Papago lily or bluedick; and in lower, sandier areas, the startlingly beautiful ajo lily, whose white flower emits a gentle perfume.

There is something almost bittersweet in all flower watching: the knowledge that such beauty is so transient. Thus it is a deep pleasure to be fortunate enough to witness a spectacular bloom, the finest of which may occur only once a decade. "Ephemerals," as the briefly blooming annuals are called, are gone almost as soon as they appear, resplendent, passing spirits that cast their light on the desert like the briefest flash of sun at dawn before the day begins and the magic fades.

HOTSPOTS

Since the warmest spots in Arizona are in the south and west, it makes sense to look for the earliest wildflowers in these areas. Poppies and lupines may not peak until the spring equinox, but under ideal conditions, the last half of February is not too soon—and may be the best time—to search them out. Before embarking on a long trip to Yuma or Phoenix, however, it would be a good idea to contact one of the several fine botanical gardens, museums, state or national parks or national monuments in the area. (See the appendix: in particular, the Desert Botanical Garden in Phoenix; the Boyce Thompson Arboretum near Superior; Tohono Chul Park in Tucson; Organ Pipe Cactus National Monument or the Arizona–Sonora Desert Museum near Tucson, or call the Wildflower Hotline: 602-481-8134.) Any of these places should have good, up-to-date information on wildflowers for their area and, perhaps, much of the rest of the state. Many of the parks or monuments, being federal or state lands, are also among the best areas to view wildflowers. Relatively untrammeled by humans and off-limits to livestock, national monuments and state and national parks offer pleasant wildflower viewing opportunities and are certainly much safer than pulling off on the side of the highway in heavy traffic. Be thoughtful, also, in remoter areas; flower picking on private property is illegal (as it is on most public lands, too) and discourteous. Flowers should be "captured" with eyes or cameras only. Bring allergy medication on your flower-hunting excursion if pollen bothers you, and remember sun lotion and a good wildflower field guide. A word of caution about guidebooks: some flowers go through many color changes, and some have several different names, including English and Spanish designations and Indian names. Try to get to know the flowers for what they are and worry less about what they are called.

Picacho Peak State Park is one of the most dramatic and reliable spots for finding goldpoppies. Just off I-10 between Tucson and Phoenix, the oddly blunted mountain known as Picacho Peak was the site of a minor Civil War battle. In some years the blanket of poppies on Picacho is so brilliant that interstate traffic actually slows to a crawl. Numerous campsites, picnic areas and well-maintained trails make this a popular stop between Arizona's two largest cities. To reach Picacho Peak State Park, simply head north out of Tucson on I-10 for about 40 miles to Exit 219. The park, impossible to miss, is just west of the interstate. The Hunter Trail, just south of the park office, leads to the top of Picacho Peak and can put you in the middle of poppy fields. Bring water and sunscreen, even in February. There is a $3 fee to enter the park.

One of the loveliest and most historic of all southwestern spots likely to have early-blooming wildflowers is **Organ Pipe Cactus National Monument**, named for the many-branched, clustering cactus that grows only in this region. The monument contains areas of lush vegetation and is classic Sonoran Desert— creosote, mesquite, palo verde, cactus and ironwood—with low peaks, rolling desert hills and the charming oasis of Quitobaquito Spring, a watering hole used by Indians and explorers for centuries. This area is scorching hot in summer, making late winter/early spring one of the best times to visit, particularly to see the acres of owl clover, brittlebush, lupine and poppies that can be abundant here. As at all national monuments, there is an entrance fee, $3 per car. Call ahead (see the appendix) for wildflower and camping information. A large campground, surprisingly popular even in winter, lies just 1.5 miles south of the visitor center. Organ Pipe Cactus National Monument can be reached from Tucson by taking State Road 86 119 miles to the small town of Why, then heading south on State Road 85 for just over 27 miles to the visitor center. From here you have a choice of two gravel roads, both well graded. The Ajo Mountain Loop, a 21-mile drive east of the visitor center, and the Puerto Blanco Drive, a 35-mile road that terminates at the town of Lukeville—about 4 miles south of the visitor center on State Road 85—are both outstanding for flowers and birds. The Estes Canyon–Bull Pasture Trail on the Ajo Mountain Drive is rewarding, if demanding; Quitobaquito Spring, with its cottonwood and mesquite trees, is a bird magnet. Flowers, of course, will be nearly everywhere in a good year.

One other warm weather spot to investigate in February is the **Kofa National Wildlife Refuge**. Unlike many wildlife refuges where water and wildlife are abundant, this site in the southwestern corner of Arizona is dry and desolate. In a good year, though, wildflowers can be abundant, and a variety of desert vegetation is always present. Desert bighorn sheep are the most famous residents of this refuge, and a pocket of rare palm trees adds to its mystique. Military war games are conducted in areas adjacent to the refuge, and the sights and sounds of jets and flares provide a startling contrast to the silent bleakness of the dry desert mountains. Kofa is not for the timid flower hunter. It is remote and accessible only by rugged dirt roads. But the poppies, globemallow and brittlebush are often spectacular. Get information and a map from the refuge headquarters in Yuma (see the appendix) before you visit; take sun lotion and plenty of water; and drive more than a few miles up any road only if you have a four-wheel-drive vehicle and a full tank of gas and have notified someone of where you are going. Several roads lead into Kofa; the main ones are at signed turnoffs 17.5 miles south of the town of Quartzsite and at the Stone Cabin turnoff 27 miles south of Quartzsite. Both roads get rough after 5 or 6 miles, which is also where much of the colorful plants will begin.

A reminder: desert wildflowers are highly variable in time and location. Always call ahead before visiting a site.

10

Wintering Ducks

Ducks possess an air of determined patience in winter. While other animals hole up or quietly tread through snowy forests and chilled lowlands, wintering ducks pass the cold days on open water, splashing about for food and enlivening the air with their quacks and whistles. Come February, migration is still at least a month away for most, and any reasonably sizable and unfrozen body of water in the Southwest may be home to a diverse collection of these colorful creatures. In fact, since spring and summer deplete parts of the Southwest—its more southerly regions, in particular—of much of its waterfowl, winter is the best time to admire ducks as they wait out the cold season.

Ducks are among the most studied, most loved and most colorful group of birds on earth. Their near-worldwide distribution and lengthy migrations make them common almost anywhere there are people, and their habits and coloration make them endlessly fascinating. What other bird is featured on an annual conservation stamp or has its own magazine? Ducks, simply, are appealing.

Most North American ducks spend their breeding season in northern regions, even the far reaches of northern Canada. Most can be found in summer across large sections of the United States. But in the Southwest, many of the more interesting species are found in winter only. Furthermore, since the region is the

A flock of mallards congregates near a lakeshore. Male mallards are easily identified by their bright emerald green heads.

northernmost extension of wintering grounds that stretch south to Mexico and beyond, some ducks will only be found in the Southwest at this time of year.

Some of the dabbling or "puddle" ducks can be found in the Southwest throughout the year. These include the mallard and pintail, which are widely distributed throughout North America. Generally, dabblers can be found in smaller lakes and shallow marsh or river areas feeding on the surface of the water or just below. Diving ducks, which can descend far beneath the water to feed on fish and bottom vegetation, tend to winter in the Southwest and then depart to the north by March. Thus, in a typical year, winter offers the greatest diversity of waterfowl in the Southwest. Sure to be seen in most any suitable region of Utah, Colorado, New Mexico and Arizona are the gadwall, green-winged teal, ring-necked duck, common goldeneye, bufflehead, common merganser and, of course, mallard. Other regular winter visitors include the northern shoveler, ruddy duck and redhead, while certain ducks, red-breasted and hooded mergansers, are coastal species that occasionally show up in this area.

One seemingly obvious point about wintering ducks that bears mentioning is that they must have open water to survive. It is not uncommon to see a flock of ducks huddled about one open patch of water on an otherwise frozen lake, seemingly fending off the ice through group willpower rather than body heat. But if the water freezes and no food is available, the birds will go elsewhere. Most ducks also prefer areas with many small water surfaces to one single large lake: the former provides more shoreline for food and protection.

Once the ducks are found, identifying them becomes the next challenge. There are dozens of different species, and their varied plumages and behaviors can make them difficult to distinguish. Everything from wing beat to habitat, voice and flocking arrangement can reveal the identity of a duck if it is not apparent simply by its color and plumage pattern. February is out of range of the eclipse plumage period—those times when breeding behavior alters a duck's plumage so much that a drake resembles a hen—so most ducks will look much like their depiction in a good field guide. Other clues help reveal a duck's identity: dabblers can spring into the air directly, while divers flutter across the water before taking off; certain ducks such as wigeons and pintails flock loosely, while shovelers and teals form tight bunches; and most dabblers have a bright, iridescent patch on their wings known as the speculum, a marking divers lack. These and many other traits can tip off an expert duck-watcher in an instant, even if he or she sees only a silhouette against the sky— a feat that can seem remarkable to those who think all ducks have green heads and go "quack." The U.S. Fish and Wildlife Service puts out an outstanding booklet called "Ducks at a Distance" that shows how to go about identifying ducks on the water or in the air.

Unfortunately, despite their beauty and renown, ducks are in decline, primarily because wetlands are in decline. Drought, pollution, drainage, development—all these and more have contributed to an alarmingly severe reduction in waterfowl habitat and hence waterfowl over the last decade. Several governmental efforts, the North American Waterfowl Management Plan, in particular, seem to have begun to improve the situation, but it is nonetheless troubling to consider how much damage humans can inflict on delicate ecosystems. The drive for progress, a peculiarly human impatience, appears all the more improper when contrasted with the simple calm of a group of ducks on a cold, blue winter pond.

HOTSPOTS

For a view of some of the less frequently seen species, such as the red-breasted merganser, head for the national wildlife refuges on the lower Colorado River. From north to south, **Havasu**, **Bill Williams Delta**, **Cibola** and **Imperial National Wildlife Refuges** (see chapter 1 for all four) are all great spots in western Arizona for ducks and will not disappoint.

A consistently good winter waterfowl site in northeastern Arizona is **Lyman Lake State Park**, a broad, open lake created by a dam on the Little Colorado River. Representative wintering ducks—mallards, common mergansers, pintails—are sure to be present, and look also for more exotic non-native birds such as snow geese and bald eagles. The large dam, which you can walk across, commands a good view of the lake; the road and state park grounds skirt the shoreline. A fee is required, though in winter this park may be fairly deserted except for the ducks. Another attraction here is the small herd of eight or ten bison kept in an area near the park entrance as a tourist draw by the small nearby town of Springerville. Lyman Lake State Park is 13.5 miles north of the intersection of US 666 and US 60 (4 miles north of Springerville) on US 666, or 12.5 miles south of St. Johns on US 666. The park is well signed on the east side of the road.

The two best spots—hands down—in New Mexico for ducks in winter are **Bosque del Apache National Wildlife Refuge** and **Bitter Lake National Wildlife Refuge** (for both, see chapter 62). Both refuges provide habitat for tens of thousands of ducks and other waterfowl from November through March. Just as with the refuges in western Arizona, these two spots are guaranteed outstanding viewing. One unique site to view ducks in winter in New Mexico is actually right in the city of Albuquerque at the **Rio Grande Nature Center**. This 270-acre preserve adjacent to the Rio Grande offers hiking trails amid cottonwood and willow trees and access to the river itself. Right next to the visitor center lies a small pond that harbors, among others, ring-necked ducks, cinnamon teals, gadwalls and the beautiful wood duck, worthy of special attention since it is widely acknowledged as one of the most beautiful birds in the world. An observation room, with large plate glass windows and speakers that relay the sounds of the ducks, overlooks the pond, so that even a chilly day can still offer great viewing. The center is open daily from 10:00 A.M. to 5:00 P.M. A nominal fee is charged. Be sure to take the walk to the river, where ducks can also be found. The Rio Grande Nature Center is easily reached by taking the Rio Grande Boulevard exit (157-A) off I-40, heading north for 1.4 miles, then turning west on Candelaria Boulevard. The parking area lies 0.5 mile ahead.

In Utah, the **Bear River Migratory Bird Refuge** (see chapter 56) is a great site, particularly for diving ducks. The other sites on the Great Salt Lake that are outstanding for wintering ducks are the **Ogden Bay Waterfowl Management Area** and the **Harold S. Crane Waterfowl Management Area** (for both, see chapter 56). These are can't-miss sites.

Colorado offers a range of good spots, though none is as clearly outstanding as in the other three southwestern states since many of the state's waters are frozen during February. For an impressive gathering of ducks, though, travel to **Jackson Lake State Park** on the high plains of the northeastern portion of the state. Although ice forms on the lake in winter, flocks of ducks—mallard, primarily—numbering well over ten thousand gather around open water holes. The sight of such a dense gathering of birds is well worth the visit to this irrigation reservoir rimmed with dry mudflats and stands of cottonwood. Bald eagles are also drawn to the lake in February, as are gulls and other waterfowl, including many Canada geese. To reach Jackson Lake State Park, take Exit 66 off I-76, head north on State Road 39 for 7.2 miles through Goodrich, then look for a sign for road Y.5 to your left. Follow it for just over 2.5 miles to the park office. An entrance fee is required. The campground on the west side of the lake, 0.5 mile from the entrance, offers good viewing.

A great spot for ducks and other waterfowl in the Denver area is **Prospect Park** along the Wheat Ridge Greenbelt, one of the finest urban wildlife viewing spots in the Southwest. A paved trail follows Clear Creek as it winds its way past cottonwood and willow trees, marshes, meadows and, incongruously, the interstate. The best area for ducks is the lake at Prospect Park, which in winter attracts ring-necked ducks, mallards, wigeons, gadwalls, buffleheads and even a few wood ducks. To reach Prospect Park, take I-70 west to the Kipling Street exit (267), head south 0.3 mile to West 44th Avenue, then turn west on West 44th. Prospect Park lies 0.7 mile ahead, with the entrance on the left side of the road. If you have time, take an hour or so to examine **Sloan Lake** at Sloan Lake Park in Denver. It can be reached from Prospect Park by taking West 44th Avenue east to Sheridan Boulevard, turning south, and proceeding to 20th Avenue, where the park is on the left side of the street. Total distance is about 6 miles, and the trip is well worth it to see Denver's best waterfowl lake.

11

February
Shorttakes

Merlins

Merlins are spectacularly beautiful but infrequently seen falcons, smaller than peregrines or prairie falcons. Males have the same attractive bluish color that kestrels have but lack the rusty back and the bold facial stripes. Much admired but rarely found, they winter in the southern United States and are best seen in winter perched on utility poles looking for prey. Check the fences and poles that line the road into **Hamilton Reservoir**, north of Fort Collins on County Road 82 off Exit 288 on I-25. Also in Colorado, try **Tower Road** on the east side of the Rocky Mountain Arsenal (see chapter 2).

12

Breakout: The Grand Canyon in Winter

First the facts. Arizona's Grand Canyon measures roughly 280 miles along the Colorado River, at a width that varies from 4 to 18 miles and a depth that averages just about 1 mile. The area known as Grand Canyon National Park was established in 1919, includes just over 1,900 square miles and welcomes about four million visitors a year, the bulk of whom stop only at the South Rim. The North Rim is harder to get to, is closed from mid-October to late May and is, at 8,500 feet, more than a thousand feet higher than the South Rim. Piñon and juniper dominate the terrain on the South Rim, which lies 4,500 feet above the Colorado River and has an average daytime temperature of about 75°F in summer and nearly 40°F in winter. One guidebook sums up the canyon in a single sentence: "The forces of erosion have exposed an immense variety of formations that illustrate vast periods of geological history." A pocket dictionary calls the canyon, simply, "an immense gorge in Northern Arizona."

Armed with these bits and pieces of information, let us state the matter unequivocally: the Grand Canyon is the most spectacular sight on earth. And decades of travelers, sightseers and writers would agree. John Wesley Powell, the one-armed adventurer who first explored the river (in a dory) in 1869, believed it to be the most beautiful and inspiring spot imaginable. The geologist Clarence

Dutton proclaimed that "those who have long and carefully studied the Grand Canyon of the Colorado do not hesitate for a moment to pronounce it by far the most sublime of all earthly spectacles." Edward Abbey once rolled a tire into the canyon, then spent five weeks at the bottom and called it Eden. The countless photographs snapped at the canyon's edge, as well as the untold number of words writers have spent while groping to describe a sight, which is, in fact, beyond words, attest to the canyon's unparalleled magnificence. It is, truly, the Grand Canyon.

Yet most people come at the wrong time of year: summer. Actually, spring and fall can also be the wrong times of year. More and more, the South Rim has become something like everyone's favorite beach. It's too crowded, and if you are there, you will wish for the days when no one knew about the place. And that brings us to winter, when the crowds are at their lowest ebb and the canyon is at its most beautiful. The canyon most people come to, the summer canyon, has been described at length: the colors, the shadows, the size, the space, the *drama*. Winter is different. The snow blanketing the rim and then gradually disappearing from the cliffs as the eye travels downward alternately mutes and highlights the rock, sometimes conjuring more red out of the cliffs than it seems should be there, sometimes imparting to them a softness and tranquility usually seen only during summer's dusk and dawn. While the canyon in warm weather exhibits a quiet and powerful beauty, when snow lies upon it, it seems more serene and mysterious, deeper even. Cliff ledges, and the piñon and juniper trees on them, may be heavy with snow, but the sheer rock faces above and below them will be dry, creating stark patterns of red and white.

Often the clouds will hang low over the snow-dusted buttes that reach up from within the canyon. In fact, inclement weather usually creates the most pleasing displays of light and color as shadows, clouds, snow and rock all mix together. Or fog will fill the gorge with a thick bank of white, making the canyon seem like some enormous lake of clouds.

The wildlife is fairly typical for winter in piñon–juniper lands. Jays—piñon, scrub and Stellar's—will be about, as will robins, juncos, nuthatches, mountain chickadees, bluebirds, white-crowned sparrows and, of course, ravens. An eagle might soar over the canyon. Mule deer search for food. Life on the South Rim is difficult in winter, though. It is cold and wet, with rapid changes in weather.

Drive there on a nice day, when snow doesn't make the roads dangerous, and find a place to sit and watch. If you have only been to the Grand Canyon in summer, it will seem a different place now. If you have never been at all, it will seem a place wholly different from any other—and may spoil your future summer visits. This is Eden in winter, perhaps.

> *Note: The North Rim is closed in February. The South Rim, though open year-round, receives 4 to 5 feet of snow in winter and may be difficult to reach after a storm. Call ahead (see the appendix) for weather and travel conditions, fees and camping and hiking information.*

MARCH

13

Sage Grouse and Prairie Chicken Leks

The noise, a sort of drawn-out burbling that sounds uncannily like someone gulping underwater, is the first thing one notices in the predawn darkness. Morning light is still at least half an hour away, but sage grouse cocks, as many as fifty of them, have left their night roosts to begin their loud and beautiful mating ritual. And if you know where to locate their lek, or strutting ground, before sunup, if the wind isn't too fierce and if cold weather and the prospect of sitting still for hours don't dissuade you, it is possible to witness what is surely one of nature's oddest procreative efforts.

By any measure, the sage grouse is an impressive bird. About the size of a small turkey, North America's largest grouse has a very noticeable black belly and long, pointy tail feathers. The male also has a ruffed, almost flabby-looking white breast, which, when he is "lekking," puffs up enormously to reveal two yellowish sacs. It is the quick inflating and deflating of these air sacs that produces the distinctive bubbly popping that fills the air as cocks gather to strut.

As the name suggests, sage grouse are found in sage land, the vast, rolling plains that dominate huge areas of the West. They feed almost exclusively on the buds and leaves of various species of the abundant sage, moving downslope in winter if need be to find stands of brush free of snow. Thus, in contrast to most other animals, when spring arrives, the birds are fairly healthy and well-fed, ready to begin the mating ritual that has been called everything from Druidic to comedic. It is, without a doubt, fascinating.

By about the middle of March in most locations, male grouse begin establishing their territories on strutting grounds, generally low, open clearings in the surrounding sagebrush, often on a ridge or knoll. It is believed that many of these courtship grounds have been used for centuries, hence the appropriateness of the strange but often-used term "ancestral lek" to describe these sites. The battles that ensue are, like most such contests in the wild, a means of establishing rank, the dominant male or males earning breeding rights. The wing fights the grouse engage in, however, can be fierce and, particularly during the earlier parts of the season, common. The dominant cocks generally take their places at the center of the lek, with weaker ones farther from the center—a means, it is thought, of ensuring that the most precious genes will not be snared by an opportunistic coyote. Morning after morning the males will return to the same site where, with territory staked out, they can go about the more pressing business of attracting hens. In groups ranging from a half-dozen to well over fifty, males will raise their tail feathers into spiky fans, ruffle their wings, strut and bob and then, with chest puffed up beyond what would seem to be the bursting point, begin a quick series of pops. Hens, clearly impressed, descend on the lek, allowing the male into whose territory they enter to breed them; they almost invariably move to the most dominant male. It is estimated, in fact, that this central male will mate with about three-fourths of the hens that enter the lek.

While establishing territory and on into the peak of the mating season, cocks will strut well past sunup. Snow and cold seem to do little to keep them from their dawn dancing, though hens, with perhaps a more practical outlook, may not respond until the weather turns warmer and their nesting prospects appear less chilly. Nests are hidden in thick stands of sage, leaving a hen's clutch of eight or so eggs vulnerable to predators. Thus cocks gather and strut for several weeks in spring, hoping some hen who was bred in late March but lost her eggs will return again in early May. As the odds of attracting females drop with the passing of weeks, fewer males show up at the lek and their time there shortens to little more than an hour. Elevation also plays a role in the timing of breeding season, the numerous leks of northern Colorado's North Park area seeing courting activity a few weeks earlier than some leks at higher elevations.

As abundant—and boring—as sagebrush land seems to the traveler in, say, western Colorado, it is in decline. Of little use to ranchers and their livestock, much sage range has been "rehabilitated," with native sage species cut, burned or poisoned, then replaced with grasses that livestock find more palatable. While such practices have both advocates and critics, there is little question that the decrease in sage habitat has led to a decrease in wildlife species dependent on it. While sage grouse remain common locally, like most birds, their numbers were far, far greater just a few decades ago. To see dozens of sage grouse stomping about at dawn on the same open fields their ancestors have danced on for generations is to witness what is persistent and timeless about the natural world, not what has been altered.

Two related species, the greater prairie chicken and the lesser prairie chicken, have also seen their habitat, plains grassland, diminish. Both species, though smaller than the sage grouse, perform mating rituals similar to it. The greater prairie chicken has golden neck sacs, the lesser prairie chicken has reddish sacs and both make a "booming" sound while displaying. Both are also in serious decline, the former's range extending into northeastern Colorado, the latter's into southeastern Colorado and eastern New Mexico.

HOTSPOTS

Sage grouse viewers must respect the habits of the birds they are watching. When visiting a lek, arrive before dawn, stay until the birds have departed and remain in your vehicle while they are on display. Grouse, skittish and wary, will flush if you either drive up or leave while they are on their leks. Your vehicle acts as a blind; as long as you are in place before the sun comes up, and as long as you stay in your vehicle and don't leave while the birds are out, your presence will not disturb them. In sum, stay in your car! It is a bit of advice that all wildlife personnel will echo. Also, scout out the lek before making your morning visit. It is nearly impossible to locate a lek in the dark if you haven't been to it before. The directions below will get you to good sites, but it is always advisable to check with the appropriate local office, for example, the Forest Service or the Bureau of Land Management, to get specific details. Furthermore, some leks are on private land. View from the shoulder of roads and respect landowners' rights.

Colorado is the best of the four southwestern states for finding sage grouse and prairie chickens. Utah has some small leks in the eastern part of the state and even a rare sharp-tailed grouse lek near the Golden Spike National Historic Site; and New Mexico has sage grouse in remote areas of the Santa Fe ski basin and lesser prairie chickens on Bureau of Land Management lands near Roswell. Colorado, though, has the most abundant and most accessible leks for all of the listed birds. The best area of all is known as **North Park** in the north central part of the state. A high, open basin region, source of the North Platte River, North Park is an outstanding and untrammeled wildlife paradise, with everything from abundant waterfowl and raptors to moose and elk. Forests, meadows, streams and lakes are plentiful here, as are the sage flats that attract grouse. While there are many leks in the vast North Park area, the best is known as the Coalmont Sage Grouse Viewing Area. Classic sagebrush flats here see gatherings of several dozen birds at peak season. To reach it, follow State Road 14 just south of Walden for 14.7 miles southwest, then turn west on County Road 26, travel 1.6 miles and take the road to the right. A sign indicating the viewing area lies 0.2 mile ahead. Be in place well before sunup and watch the best of all the accessible sage grouse shows the Southwest has to offer. Also nearby is a site north of Lake John, about 12 miles north of the Coalmont area. To reach it, take County Road 12W west out of Walden for 5.2 miles, turn north at the sign for Lake John and at a fork in the road 2.7 miles ahead, stay right on County Road 7. Stay on this road, bypassing the turnoff to Lake John 5.4 miles ahead. Keep going straight here, and 2.2 miles ahead look for a low hill immediately to the east of the road. This can be a very active lek throughout the spring. For more information about these spots and North Park in general, call the Walden Chamber of Commerce at 303-

723-4600, or the Arapaho National Wildlife Refuge (see the appendix).

In southwestern Colorado, an isolated but fine sage grouse lek lies just south of the tiny community of **Parlin**. To reach it, drive 10 miles east of Gunnison on US 50 to Parlin, which is basically one store and a gas pump. Turn south on County Road 43, and at 0.3 mile cross a cattle guard (with a gate that, if closed, may be opened and reclosed) and another gate 0.2 mile past it and continue on. Go under the power lines, and at a fork in the road 2 miles from Parlin, go left. Sage grouse gather immediately to both the right and left of this road and at a spot 0.2 mile down the road on the left, directly in front of a horseshoe-shaped parking area. As in most sage areas, look for pronghorn that may be out and about. For more information, call the local Bureau of Land Management office at 303-641-0471.

Greater prairie chickens are best found in the northeastern part of Colorado. These birds prefer the prairie grasslands for their leks, seeking food and shelter in the tall, clumpy grass of this dry region. The best leks are along County Road 45 near the small town of **Wray**. Drive north from Wray on US 385 11.5 miles to County Road 45, turn right and travel for 4 or 5 miles, listening and driving slowly. Stop immediately on hearing sounds and stay in your vehicle. There are at least seven leks on either side of the road, and while they are all fairly reliable, prairie chickens, just like grouse, tend to favor certain grounds in their area over others in any given year. The popping or boom sound that the prairie chickens make is very strange. Call the Colorado Division of Wildlife at 303-484-2836 for more details. This office offers guided trips to the leks during peak season and is well worth contacting.

Finally, the only place in Colorado to find lesser prairie chickens is in the southeastern short-grass prairie land of **Comanche National Grassland**. This is dry, lonely country, where sage and grasses dominate; the land is barren; and Kansas and Oklahoma lie not far off to the east and south. The prairie chickens are found by taking County Road J out of the small town of Campo on US 287 and following it due east for 8 miles. Here take Road 36 south for 2 miles to Road G, then head east for 4 miles. Just before crossing a culvert, turn south and go through a fence-gate and proceed 1.3 miles on a poor road to a parking area. You will know you're there when you see the old railroad ties facing the lek. Call the U.S. Forest Service at 719-523-6591 for more information.

It is difficult, though rewarding, to see these birds. Keep in mind that you need to be settled before the birds arrive. Also, leks are invariably along remote dirt roads in uninhabited regions. *Always* call the responsible office or facility in the area and get specific, up-to-date information concerning leks. If you're lucky, some knowledgeable researcher or area manager might be happy to accompany you to a lek before dawn.

14

White-winged Doves

One of the surest signs of the arrival of spring is the return of thousands of white-winged doves to the saguaro and mesquite desert lands of the Southwest. Though not rare and exotic like the elegant trogon, or possessed of intriguing habits like the burrowing owl or sage grouse, the white-winged dove has a certain alien grace that sets it apart. The fact that it is so common in parts of the desert makes it easy to take for granted, but with its delicate and considerable beauty, the white-winged dove is a charming symbol of spring.

Massive numbers of white-wings begin arriving in southern Arizona and southwestern New Mexico by the end of March through about the end of April, their nesting season lasting until the end of August. Very few winter in the areas they dominate throughout the summer, though it's possible to find a few in the Tucson area in midwinter. Once they begin returning from their wintering grounds in Mexico, however, they can be found in abundance in a variety of habitats, including cities and towns. Though they may nest singly, it is more common to find huge groups of the birds nesting in characteristic desert habitats: mesquite and tamarisk thickets along rivers and streams, cottonwood and willow riparian zones, palo verde and saguaro desert areas and desert oases. Like the robin elsewhere, the white-winged dove seems suddenly to be everywhere and, also like the robin, its presence means spring.

Several doves are common in the Southwest, the mourning dove in particular. But the white-wing, with its seasonal return and distinctive coloration, stands out. When the bird is sitting, the white patches on the wings—so noticeable in flight against the otherwise grayish wings—appear as delicate white lines rimming each wing's underside. The tail feathers are also tipped in white, though the white-wing's tail is shorter and rounder than its mourning dove cousin's. With a brownish body and a purple sheen to the shoulder and head, the white-winged dove has a coloration somewhat similar to most doves and pigeons, though the black spot on its neck and the striking ring of blue around each eye are distinctive.

White-wings subsist on seeds and fruit, including cactus fruits and berries; but unlike some birds that get enough moisture from the foods they eat, white-wings must find water to drink. Their gatherings at water holes, perhaps their most distinctive group trait, are well-known desert spectacles. In the early morning or late evening, large groups of white-wings will congregate in the trees or bushes or cacti around a pond or spring, furtively examining the area before attempting to drop down for a drink. In fact, the rocks and vegetation surrounding an open body of water may become so thick with white-winged doves before even a single one dares to slake its thirst, that it might seem the birds are there for some reason other than to drink. One finally will descend to water's edge, setting off a frenzy of drinking as the rest of the birds drop to the water, dip in their bills and swallow once or twice. Quickly they depart, their caution and speed an indication of their wariness of the predators—hawks, in particular—that also frequent water holes. Gale Monson, the noted Arizona birder, once recommended sitting from dawn to dusk at a desert water hole just to watch white-winged doves come in for a drink.

It is not necessary, though it would be pleasant, to wait long hours to see the doves, since they can generally be found on a Tucson telephone line almost as easily as they can on a remote springside ocotillo. They can only be found in the Southwest's lower deserts, though, and only when spring arrives.

HOTSPOTS

Catalina State Park, about 15 miles north of downtown Tucson on the north side of the Santa Catalina Mountains, offers an impressive spread of mesquite trees, foothills dotted with saguaro and palo verde and a riparian area along occasionally flowing Sutherland Wash. White-winged doves are very common here as the weather gets warmer. Long trails lead up into the mountains through typical desert scrub, while shorter trails wind through the mesquite and cottonwood areas near the picnic and camping grounds. Catalina State Park is one of the most accessible and diverse natural areas near Tucson, good for a range of familiar desert birds such as the Gila woodpecker, northern cardinal, Gambel's quail, cactus wren, brown towhee and even the vermilion flycatcher. To reach the park, head north out of Tucson on US 89 (Oracle Road). After crossing Ina Road, continue for 5.5 more miles and, after crossing a bridge over Canada del Oro Wash, look for the park entrance sign to the east 0.3 mile ahead. The park contact station, with maps and information, lies 0.5 mile up the road into the park. There is an entrance fee of $3.

Tohono Chul Park, a small, private park in northwestern Tucson, is a nice spot to see desert birds. Trails wind through common Sonoran vegetation mixed with more exotic (non-native) desert species. Birds, plants and desert reptiles abound here, and it is one of the few places in all the Southwest where a few white-winged doves actually linger through winter. In spring they are plentiful. To reach Tohono Chul Park, head north on Oracle Road just as if you were going to Catalina State Park, but head west on Ina Road instead of continuing through. Go 0.3 mile to Paseo del Norte, turn right and look for the entrance 0.3 mile ahead. A $2 donation is requested.

In Arizona, also try **Organ Pipe Cactus National Monument**, particularly around any of the spring areas, and **Kofa National Wildlife Refuge** in the western part of the state (for both, see chapter 9).

In New Mexico, try **Percha Dam State Park** (see chapter 19) for plenty of white-winged doves in the trees alongside the river. A unique spot south of here near Las Cruces is **Dripping Springs Natural Area**. Nestled in the Organ Mountains just east of Las Cruces, the Dripping Springs area has a history of human occupation stretching back nearly seven thousand years. Earlier in this century, a resort and sanitarium were built here. Creosote and mesquite dominate the lower elevations leading up to Dripping Springs, while the visitor center area is juniper and scrub oak with pines at the higher elevations. The best place for white-winged doves is around La Cueva Rock, a jut of red cliff with an archaeologically significant cave just west of the visitor center. Many white-wings can also be seen on the trees on any of the trails in the area; also check the telephone lines around the visitor center. To reach Dripping Springs, get off I-25 in Las Cruces at the University Avenue exit, and go east on University Avenue. After winding for 2.6 miles, the pavement ends for 1 mile, then resumes again for 1 mile. Where it ends again, look for a sign indicating "Dripping Springs Natural Area." Continue for 3.9 miles, following the signs, and reach a self-paying fee box ($3). From here the road climbs 1 mile to the A. B. Cox Visitor Center, where information is available. Dripping Springs, managed by both the Bureau of Land Management and the Nature Conservancy, is open year-round from 8:00 A.M. to 6:00 P.M.; hours are extended in the evenings in spring and summer.

If you don't see any white-wings, listen for their distinctive call, an owllike "who cooks for you." It is beautiful and strange, just like the bird itself.

15

The Desert
in Bloom

If February is the month to see wildflowers tentatively beginning to dab their color on the desert floor, March is the month to watch them streak the earth like splashes of paint on a canvas. Indeed, from March into mid-April is the time of the greatest and most colorful diversity among the desert's annual wildflowers, though the same factors that affect these wildflowers in February—early autumn rains and fairly steady winter rains—also apply in March. The only difference is that March sees the appearance of more of the perennial wildflowers and thus can bring a multitude of flowers of all shapes, sizes, and colors to the spring desert.

The temperature, obviously, increases by the time of the spring equinox, allowing annuals that have been steadily growing during the cold months to bloom. Some of the ephemerals are indifferent to the amount of daylight available and will flower simply because of favorable weather conditions. Winter's frosts are gone by mid-March, and any ephemerals intent on showing off their flowers will probably start doing so at this time if they didn't already begin in February. In most years, March brings the most spectacular show of ephemerals the desert will see all year.

Perennials, which, unlike their single-season annual cousins, live and bloom for years in a row, are less sensitive to the rains of the previous autumn. Good winter rains will trigger the flowering of perennials, and in March such species as penstemon and blackfoot daisy may peak at the same time as the showier poppies and lupines.

These differences in response to rainfall are among the more interesting aspects of desert flora, ones that will have a decisive and predictable effect on wildflower blooms as the year progresses. The classic categorization of desert plants separates them into three groups: the drought escapers, the drought evaders and the drought resisters. Examined as a group, they provide insight into how plants deal with extremes of temperature and drought. The drought escapers, such as poppies and lupines, grow quickly, bloom even faster, then produce seeds that will lie dormant for most of the rest of the year. These ephemerals effectively escape the desert's heat and dryness.

As do deciduous trees and bushes of northern forests, drought evaders shed leaves and enter a period of dormancy until rain and relatively mild temperatures return. Good spring and summer rains see desert standards such as palo verde and ocotillo burst into flower, only to go dry and dormant again when the rains pass. Their most spectacular season is usually late spring and on into summer, so that with the advent of monsoon season, ironwood, palo verde and other trees and large shrubs are fairly reliable and colorful bloomers.

The same season is usually good for the drought resisters, the toughest residents of the desert. Cacti, with their efficiency in soaking up any available water and storing it in their spongy flesh, are the best-known members of this group. Mesquite, another drought resister, sends roots as far down as 100 feet in its effort to suck water from the generally dry ground.

To appreciate March's wildflower show, it is not necessary, of course, to be aware of these distinctions, but understanding them does shed light on plant adaptation. Look for poppies and lupines again, as well as the lovely desert mariposa, rich stands of owl clover, blazing star, desert sunflower and many others. It's hard to go wrong in March in the desert. The days aren't too hot yet, the air is fresh and the flowers are bound to be wonderful.

HOTSPOTS

One of the nice things about desert wildflower viewing is that because so many people enjoy it, there is plenty of help and advice available. The best place to start is by calling the Arizona Wildflower Network hotline at 602-481-8134 or 602-941-2867. Surely one of the most unusual telephone information services in the nation, the hotline provides weekly updates of where to go and which flowers to see in Arizona. Hoping to see owl clover? Just call the hotline and then be willing to drive to the recommended locations. The service is available beginning the first Friday in March and is updated every Friday thereafter through the end of April. The telephone number and locations listed in chapter 9 are also good places to start for locating March blooms.

While the hotline is one of the more reliable ways of getting information on current wildlife conditions, some areas are worth a visit because they almost always produce good spring shows. The **Pinal Pioneer Parkway**, the "back road" between Tucson and Phoenix, is a beautiful drive any time of year, but especially when its spring wildflowers are in bloom. Although it is a paved road—US Route 89, specifically—the 42-mile parkway amounts to nothing less than a vast, pristine desert preserve. Aside from a few mileage and information signs, virtually nothing man-made distracts the eye. From Tucson, take US 89, or Oracle Road, north about 30 miles to Oracle Junction. Take the left fork, US 89, and you will see the sign for the Pinal Pioneer Parkway. Although it may not seem like it, the elevation at the beginning of the parkway—just over 3,300 feet—is fairly high for the Sonoran Desert, and the entire trip northwest to the town of Florence, at just under 1,500 feet, is ever so slightly downslope. Signs, some of them more confusing than helpful, point out some of the more familiar types of vegetation along the route—mesquite, creosote, yucca, palo verde, prickly pear, saguaro and cholla—though the wildflowers will draw your eye. Look for lupine, goldpoppy, globemallow and desert verbena all along the road, and get out to investigate at one of several roadside stops. The Tom Mix Memorial, 23.5 miles north of Oracle Junction, is a well-known stop, with winding trails leading through the abundant brush. The town of Florence lies 17 miles farther on, though the drive north to Florence Junction is well worth it. It is only 16 miles, and the area around Florence Junction can also be a wildflower hotspot.

Another place, not far from Florence Junction, is **Lost Dutchman State Park**. The sharply rising Superstition Mountains, where a hidden treasure of gold is supposedly still lost, loom over this 300-acre spread of saguaro, mesquite, ocotillo, palo verde and, in spring, dazzling wildflowers. Filaree, lupine, brittlebush, fleabane daisy, chuparosa and more can be found here, and a fine native plant trail sits at the park entrance to show off more common vegetation. Trails also wind up into the mountains, but be sure to take water and sun lotion if you plan to take a long hike. Lost Dutchman State Park is northeast of Apache Junction on State Road 88. Follow this road 5.1 miles from where it leaves US 60/US 89 in Apache Junction, look for the park sign on the right and enter the park immediately off the road. The visitor center is directly ahead. There is a fee of $3.

One other recommended spot, noted for its broad views of poppies, globemallows, owl clover and more, is the road to **Kitt Peak National Optical Astronomy Observatory**, home to several of the world's largest and most famous telescopes. While the observatory is a great attraction in itself, nature lovers will be more drawn to the broad views of wildflowers that the high road to the peak offers. The skies around Kitt Peak are remarkably clear, the result of concerted efforts in Tucson to keep astronomical viewing as pristine as possible. The dramatic 360-degree view from the many public observatory areas at the top of the mountain (elevation 6,875 feet) is spectacular. When the flowers are in bloom, color seems to leap off the lower hills. There are also many turnouts with views along the 12-mile road to the visitor center/observatory area, including a popular picnic area 1.5 miles from the top. To reach Kitt Peak, follow State Road 86, also known as Ajo Way, west out of Tucson approximately 36 miles to the signed turnoff on State Road 386. From here it is 12 miles to the top.

16

The Joshua Tree

Of all the trees in the West—indeed, in all of North America—the strangest may be the evocatively named Joshua tree. The largest of all the yuccas and a symbol of the Mojave Desert as surely as the saguaro cactus represents the Sonoran, the Joshua tree elicits the most polarized of reactions. Captain John C. Frémont, an early explorer and naturalist of the West, said that the Joshua tree's "stiff and ungraceful forms [made it] the most repulsive tree in the vegetable kingdom." And while it is undoubtedly dry and barren-looking, almost skeletal, there is also a gentleness and simplicity that strikes some Southwesterners as almost spiritual. Against a backdrop of dusk's reds and yellows, the silhouettes of scores of Joshua trees can make the desert appear like some spare and vast garden, gently arranged and open to the sky.

Early Mormon travelers certainly invested a spiritual quality in the giant yuccas. In fact, it was they who gave the tree its common name. Invited to Salt Lake City by Brigham Young in 1857, a group of Mormons set out from San Bernardino and soon encountered several small forests of a tree that seemed to be standing with arms uplifted, indicating the way to the Promised Land. Indeed, an imaginative mind can discern a biblical prophet in the tree's form: its many thick, forking branches bend at the "elbows," and a shaggy "beard" of dead leaves coats its branches and trunk. Found only in the Mojave Desert, impressive stands exist in areas of southern California, southern Nevada, extreme southwestern Utah and northwestern and north central Arizona. Although the Joshua tree is rightly thought of as an indicator of the Mojave, it is more of a transition species and marks its desert's limits or boundaries. Creosote and bursage actually are far more abundant in the Mojave, while the 15- to 30-foot Joshua trees, needing about 12 inches of rain a year to thrive, can be located on the desert's higher edges. Now found roughly from 2,000 to 6,000 feet above sea level and generally in definite pockets, the Joshua tree probably once had a much greater range. In fact, a curious archaeological find indicates as much: the fossilized dung of the extinct giant round sloth found far north of the present-day Joshua tree range reveals that the creature's diet consisted almost entirely of Joshua tree leaves.

The tree's flowers, a March delight, grow in bunches from out of a crown of rigid leaves, which in turn encircle the end of each branch. Daggerlike, with sharp points and saw-toothed edges, the pale green leaves form the "head" atop each stout branch and, on dying, cover their branch with a dry, wispy fur. The flowers are fairly unspectacular—2-inch-long bells with a leathery texture and a creamy green color. They even smell bad, at least to most noses: "mushroomlike" is one of the kinder descriptions of their aroma. But the Joshua tree's flower gains luster in multiplication. Bunched with its brothers, it appears thick and fresh. A tree fully loaded with flowers looks downright luscious. And a grove of Joshua trees all in thick bloom—an occasional treat—ranks with the most spectacular desert wildflower shows. Some years, Joshua trees in a given area do not bloom at all, though neighboring trees, blessed with better rainfall and temperatures, may bloom profusely. While the flowers open for only one night—and not nearly as broadly as most yucca flowers do—they persist for about three weeks, usually from early to mid-March. The Joshua tree, in fact, is one of the earliest-blooming yuccas, tending to flower well before the 100-degree days of the Arizona spring.

While the Joshua tree has intrigued travelers for well over a century, it has served as a magnet for wildlife for countless ages. And though there are many interesting species that nest or live in the Joshua tree—the desert night lizard, for example, and the ladder-backed woodpecker—one animal in particular has such a startling relationship with the Joshua tree that it confounds human understanding. The female yucca moth gathers balls of pollen from the Joshua tree's flowers, lays her eggs in another flower's ovaries, then climbs to the top of the now egg-laden pistil and rubs the collected pollen into the stigma. It is the only known instance of an insect seemingly deliberately pollinating a flower. As the fruit develops from the ovules, the moth larvae grow within and feed on the fruit's seeds. Thus the flower is assured of pollination while the female moth provides her developing young with plenty of food. How she can know what the result of her pollen gathering and stigma rubbing will be is a mystery. It is an instinct that is seamlessly perfect—scientifically explainable, no doubt, though so nearly resembling an intentional act it approaches the miraculous.

HOTSPOTS

While the most famous Joshua tree region in the country is in California at Joshua Tree National Monument, there are equally outstanding Joshua tree forests in parts of western Arizona and, for the really adventurous, in extreme southwestern Utah. The Mojave and Sonoran deserts overlap in western Arizona, and it is here that Arizona's best-known Joshua tree forest lies. The section of US 93 designated the **Joshua Forest Parkway**, roughly 25 miles northwest of the town of Wickenburg, connects Phoenix to Las Vegas. Heavily used by eager vacationers, bleary-eyed gamblers and, unfortunately, the intoxicated, US 93 is a notoriously dangerous route after dark. Numerous signs along the road advise drivers to stay awake, sober and within the speed limit. As if these official notifications weren't enough, dozens of family-erected crosses stand sentinel along the roadside at points where some loved one met his or her end. These cautions—hardly what one expects in a wildlife guidebook—need not deter you. Daytime driving is generally safe and is, certainly, the only time to see the road's spectacular Joshua trees. Take US 60 out of Phoenix to Wickenburg, a distance of approximately 60 miles. From here, continue northwest on US 93, entering the Joshua tree

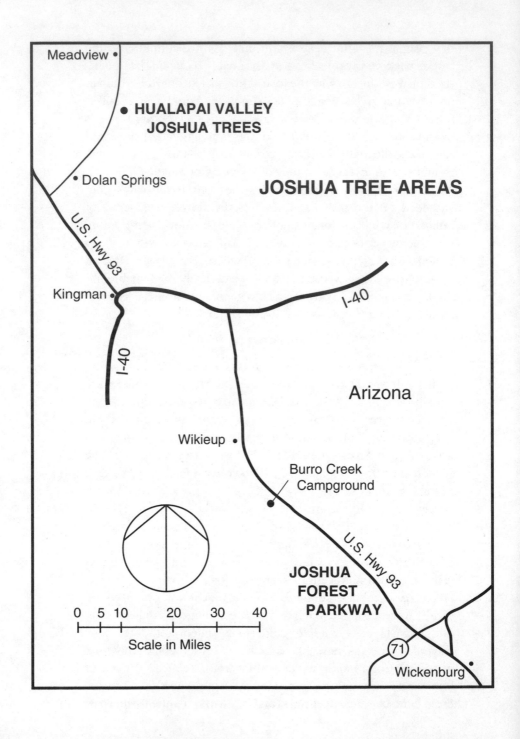

Meadview •

● **HUALAPAI VALLEY**
JOSHUA TREES

JOSHUA TREE AREAS

• Dolan Springs

U.S. Hwy 93

Kingman •

I-40

I-40

Arizona

Wikieup •

Burro Creek
Campground

●

JOSHUA
FOREST
PARKWAY

U.S. Hwy 93

0   5 10   20   30   40
Scale in Miles

⑦①

Wickenburg •

forest 22 miles past Wickenburg. Look for the sign indicating the beginning of the parkway. For the next 16 miles the landscape is dominated by countless Joshua trees, stretching to the horizon in a dry, dense and oddly spaced arrangement. Cholla, creosote, ocotillo, brittlebush, palo verde—all seem to give way to the strange and vast Joshua tree forest. There is a good roadside table 27 miles after leaving Wickenburg, with a few trees on the highway side of the fence. There are a few other turnouts here and there, though the area as a whole is designed for passing through, not for getting out and walking. Be sure to pull far off the road if you want to get a better look at the trees; traffic can be brisk here. The parkway and the trees end 38 miles beyond Wickenburg, though if you continue on US 93 all the way up to I-40, there are a few Joshua trees scattered around the town of Wikieup, 76 miles from Wickenburg. The interstate lies 30 miles north of Wikieup. Another nice spot along the way, though with only one Joshua tree in its fine little desert garden, is the Burro Creek Campground, 19 miles south of Wikieup. Stop here for a break if the day is getting too hot.

Far north of here in the **Hualapai Valley** lies another huge Joshua tree forest, one less well known and less visited. Centered roughly 40 miles north of the town of Kingman, the Joshua tree forest of the Hualapai Valley is reputedly the largest in the world. The trees are abundant along a nearly 30-mile stretch and much more accessible than the ones on US 93. You can get out and walk around here. To reach the area, head northwest on US 93 out of Kingman for 27 miles, and at milepost 42 look for the sign for Dolan Springs along Pierce Ferry Road. Take the road 6 miles northeast to Dolan Springs and continue as far as you like before turning around. The Joshua trees begin in abundance roughly 3 miles north of Dolan Springs and continue on up to Meadview. You almost certainly will never see more Joshua trees along one drive ever again. Mount Tipton is just east of Dolan Springs, and the views of low ranges in nearly every direction are an added scenic bonus. If you continue all the way to Meadview, the view to the southeast of the other side of the Grand Canyon is spectacular.

The best—and almost the only—place to see the Joshua tree in Utah is at **Joshua Tree National Landmark** in the

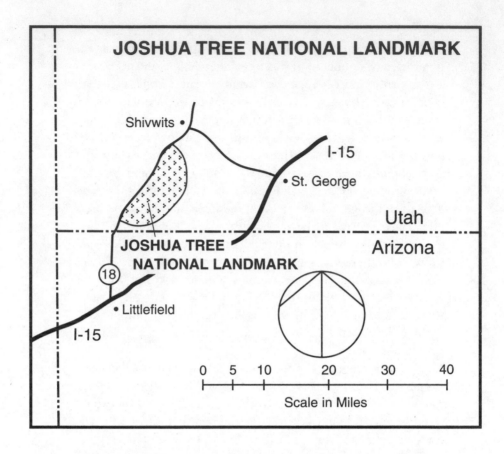

JOSHUA TREE NATIONAL LANDMARK

Shivwits •

I-15

• St. George

Utah

Arizona

**JOSHUA TREE
NATIONAL LANDMARK**

(18)

• Littlefield

I-15

```
0    5   10        20        30        40
|----+----+---------+---------+---------|
```

Scale in Miles

southwesternmost part of the state. This is one of those places you have to seek out intentionally, since it is fairly well out of the main flow of traffic unless you are traveling between Salt Lake City and Las Vegas. This Mojave Desert/Great Basin Desert transition area is the northernmost range of the Joshua tree, as well as desert tortoises, barrel cactus and cottontop cactus. Joshua trees grow here as low as 2,000 feet on the southern foothills of the Beaver Dam Mountains before giving way to piñon and juniper a bit farther up the slopes. The easiest way to reach the landmark area is to take I-15 into Arizona to the Littlefield exit, 28 miles southwest of St. George, Utah. From Littlefield, head north for 9.5 miles on a paved road—old US 91/SR 56—and turn east onto a gravel road. Look for the "Woodbury–Hardy Desert Study Area" sign. Joshua trees abound on this route, which winds east for about 9 miles, then turns north for another 10 miles to put you back out on US 91/SR 56 1.8 miles south of Shivwits. This is dry, remote country, the road is well-maintained dirt and gravel and an occasional mining truck may come lumbering down the road. If you don't plan to take the entire 19-mile drive, the landmark area lies just 2.1 miles east of US 91/SR 56 after first getting on the gravel road.

17

March Shorttakes

White-tailed Ptarmigan

The snowy, high Rockies are home to the beautiful white-tailed ptarmigan, a much admired cotton fluff of a bird found in its spotless plumage only in winter. During the rest of the year, it is blotched to varying degrees with brownish color. A permanent tundra dweller, it resides on many of the higher mountains in the Colorado and New Mexico Rockies, though its camouflage makes it hard to spot. **Guanella Pass** in Colorado is the very best place of all to see the white-tailed ptarmigan. Most birders find it among the willows just up from the parking lot at the pass. This willow area is on the side of the hill that lies to the east of the road. Guanella Pass, at 11,669 feet, is 9.7 miles south of Georgetown (see chapter 64) on the Guanella Pass Road.

18

Breakout: Flyways—Migratory Highways

People have always known that birds migrate. "The stork in the air knows its seasons; turtledove, swallow and thrush observe their time of return," reads a passage from Jeremiah, echoing what is universal knowledge: when spring arrives, so do the birds; when summer leaves, the birds depart with it. Birds assuredly can navigate by means of sun and stars and landmarks on the earth. Some manner of magnetic or electrical detection is also at work. And it seems apparent that when northerly latitudes begin to warm up, the abundant food and elbow room make breeding conditions ideal. But just how this process began is in doubt.

A look at a map of our nation's wildlife refuges reveals a pattern: birds are more likely to be found within certain fairly well-defined boundaries. Migratory species do not travel pell-mell in their intended general direction along any given route. Instead, they travel along corridors, referred to as flyways, where water and food can sustain them on their lengthy flights.

Occasionally denigrated as mere academic boundaries defined so broadly as to be of no practical use, flyways are nonetheless a handy means of defining, at least generally, the pathways birds follow in spring and fall. There are four flyways recognized in the United States: the Pacific, Central, Mississippi and Atlantic. Most of our national wildlife refuges are established along these natural routes. The Atlantic and Pacific flyways take in the coastal regions; the Mississippi Flyway follows the length of the Mississippi River from the Gulf of Mexico, then diverges at St. Louis and travels up both the Mississippi and Missouri rivers; the Central Flyway, hundreds of miles wide at some points, is the least definite of all the flyways, beginning in southern Texas and sweeping across the plains and the Rockies into Canada and Alaska. It is the flyway most birds in the Southwest, waterfowl, in particular, use to travel to and from their breeding grounds. A glance at the map reveals that many of the Southwest's wildlife refuges are clustered about the region's more important water sources: the Rio Grande, the Green, Colorado and Pecos rivers and the Great Salt Lake. And since our country's more northerly refuges are primarily breeding areas, the southerly ones wintering grounds and the middle ones used for either of the two or as migratory stops, many of the Southwest's refuges are best from early autumn through about midspring.

Spring migrations are a bit more predictable than autumn ones. Though the West's migrations aren't as concentrated as those in the East, there are still more definite beginnings and endings to migratory movement in spring than in fall, when birds tend to arrive or depart less predictably. An orderly progression— first cranes and other waterfowl; then sparrows, raptors and shorebirds; and finally groups of warblers, thrushes, flycatchers, tanagers and orioles—departs from, arrives at or passes through the Southwest in spring. Most waterfowl head far north for the summer; raptors pass through or come to breed; and swarms of insectivorous passerines enter from the south. It is an exciting time, with migrating species seeking food and shelter and mates in a suddenly warm, green world. The seasonal recurrence of birds in migration is nature's most admired blend of color and activity, a bustling reminder both of our world's diversity and the passing of time.

APRIL

19

Roadrunners

The roadrunner is the one bird most visitors to the Southwest hope to see. Some simply want firm evidence that the critter really exists in the wild and not just on the Saturday morning cartoons, while others are intrigued by stories of its comical and daring ways. In an assertion that would seem unnecessary to Southwesterners, who encounter the bird daily, the roadrunner *does* exist; and it is an unusual character, inquisitive and lively and very often quite comfortable around humans. In Mexico it's called *paisano*—"countryman"—a fitting name for the Southwest's most endearing bird.

The roadrunner is markedly different from most other desert-dwelling birds, who tend to be small, avoid the heat of day and fly off quickly at any hint of danger. In contrast, roadrunners are large birds, almost 2 feet long (half of that is tail), remain active throughout the broiling desert day and almost always run—rapidly—rather than fly, which is a ground-hugging, brief undertaking for them anyway. They are odd-looking but only vaguely resemble their cartoon representative. In real life, roadrunners have a scruffy and streaked, black-and-white appearance, with long legs, tail and bill, a crest on the back of the head and a curious dash of blue and red by the eye. Because two of its toes point forward and the other two point backward, the roadrunner leaves

Gary Zahm

El Paisano—the famous roadrunner of the Southwest. Fledgling roadrunners are able to catch their own food when three weeks old.

a sort of mirror-image track in the shape of a cross, making it difficult to tell if the bird was coming or going. No matter which direction it's headed, the roadrunner can run quickly—15 miles per hour or more—and its dashes into shrubs to nab lizards are quick and deft.

Legends about the roadrunner abound. Some Mexican Indians believed that eating roadrunner meat would help them to become swift runners, while one of the New Mexico Pueblo groups felt that tracing the roadrunner's inscrutable tracks around a deceased person would confuse nearby evil spirits. The most widely circulated, and believed, of all stories, though, is one claiming that roadrunners pen sleeping rattlesnakes within a cactus fence, peck the snake sharply to roust it, then watch as it starts up quickly and impales itself on the surrounding cactus spines. Interesting, but untrue. The way a roadrunner really kills a rattlesnake may be just as remarkable, however. When it spots an appetizing-looking snake, the roadrunner circles it warily, occasionally dropping its wings to give the appearance of docility. If and when the rattler strikes, the roadrunner quickly leaps back, then jumps forward to grab the snake in its bill and quickly fling it into the air. After it lands, the roadrunner bites the unfortunate creature on the head and proceeds to beat it to death against a nearby rock. Lizards are usually captured with less danger, and insects, rodents and small birds—virtually anything the desert has to offer—are all acceptable fare for the roadrunner.

Spring is the time to hear the male roadrunner's mating song, a gentle cooing that he uses to attract females. Perched on a rock or fence post, the male lowers his head, then begins to raise it up as he sings. It is an unexpectedly tender sound—loud, but dovelike. A willing female may come forward, and if she does, the male offers her a bit of food as a gift before mating. Nests are usually made in cholla cactus, a place few predators care to enter.

Roadrunners are best seen from early morning to early afternoon. One curious habit they have is their morning "sunbathing" ritual. Able to lower their body temperatures by more than 5°F during the night to conserve energy, roadrunners warm up in the morning by turning their backs to the sun and ruffling their feathers. This exposes the black skin near their backbones which quickly soaks up heat. Warmed and ready, the desert speedster, the killer of snakes, the paisano is ready for another day.

HOTSPOTS

Roadrunners are found throughout much of New Mexico and Arizona in lower elevations, the mesquite and scrubland regions especially. Remember that roadrunners are most frequently seen dashing across the less-traveled back roads. New Mexico has several outstanding spots where the roadrunner will be found. It is, after all, the state bird. The road into **Oliver Lee Memorial State Park**, 4 paved miles passing through creosote flats, is ideal roadrunner habitat. This state park, at the foot of the Sacramento Mountains just outside of Alamogordo, has a perennial stream and plenty of cottonwoods and ash trees. Known as "Dog Canyon," this is one of the few oasis areas for miles around, though trails leading up into the canyon can be scorching hot by midday. You needn't go as far as the state park and trail areas if all you hope to see are roadrunners and a few other desert species such as cactus wrens, pyrrhuloxia, crissal thrashers and verdin. Take US 54 south out of Alamogordo 8.5 miles from where it branches off from US 70/82. Look for a sign indicating Oliver Lee State Park on your left, and turn east. This road, 3.9 miles long, is flat, perfect for roadrunners. You may see several, and the towering Sacramento Mountains just ahead are an equally attractive sight.

Due west of here about 80 miles lies **Percha Dam State Park**, the premier birding spot in the 75-mile region between the towns of Truth or Consequences and Las Cruces. Roadrunners are frequently seen along the road just before the entrance to the park, though the park grounds are equally productive for a variety of birds, including black phoebes, northern orioles, western kingbirds and black-headed grosbeaks. A low dam helps divert some of the Rio Grande's swiftly flowing water for irrigation here, and lining the river are stands of cottonwood, mesquite and salt cedar. A stroll through the park and along the river may reveal twenty or thirty species fairly easily, though again, just as at Oliver Lee State Park, you may avoid the $3 entrance fee if all you care to see are the roadrunners on the drive leading into the park. More so than Oliver Lee, however, this state park is well worth investigating for birds. To reach Percha Dam State Park, take I-25 south from Truth or Consequences for about 18 miles and get off at Exit 59 (look for the sign that reads "Caballo and Percha Dam State Parks"). Once you get off the interstate, a sign directs you to the right—west— to Percha Dam. A sign 0.8 mile ahead will put you on a dirt road to the left. Follow this road, staying to the right at a fork 0.4 mile ahead, for a total of 1.2 miles. Look for roadrunners along this road, particularly as you get closer to the little bridge right before the park entrance.

At **Dripping Springs** (see chapter 14), look for roadrunners all along the gravel road from Las Cruces leading up to the visitor center. At **Bosque del Apache National Wildlife Refuge** (see chapter 62), roadrunners are always about, particularly on the west side of the North Tour Loop. And at **El Malpais National Monument** (see chapter 32), look for roadrunners anywhere along State Road 117 in the region of the Sandstone Bluffs Overlook past La Ventana Arch.

In Arizona, the **Arizona–Sonora Desert Museum** (see chapter 31) has plenty of roadrunners that will, at times, walk

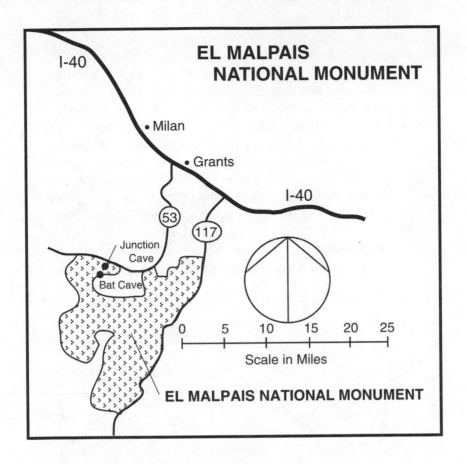

EL MALPAIS
NATIONAL MONUMENT

I-40

• Milan

• Grants

I-40

53

117

Junction
Cave

Bat Cave

0   5   10   15   20   25

Scale in Miles

EL MALPAIS NATIONAL MONUMENT

boldly in the parking areas and on the museum grounds. The same is true at **Sabino Canyon Recreation Area**, one of the most popular places in the Tucson area. Packed on weekends and busy during the rest of the week by midday, Sabino Canyon is Tucson's nearest riparian area. A perennial stream, thick with cottonwoods, plunges through an idyllic canyon in the Santa Catalina Mountains, with saguaro-sprinkled slopes above and steep cliff walls higher still. Although roads lead 4 miles up the canyon and down into the lower canyon areas, you may not drive them in your own vehicle. Instead you can either take a shuttle bus (departure 9:00 A.M. to 4:30 P.M. daily; fee of $3 or $5 depending on where you go) or walk. Next to the large parking lot there is a visitor and information center to help orient you, and booths to buy tickets for the shuttle.

Here is the best place to see roadrunners, as several enjoy scampering through the crowds preparing to board the buses. Take a walk up the canyon, too. The first accessible streamside spot lies about a mile up the road in Upper Sabino Canyon. Be sure to visit the dam at Lower Sabino also, early in the morning if possible. The cottonwood area behind the dam is considered the best birding spot in Sabino. To reach Sabino Canyon Recreation Area, take Speedway Boulevard east from Stone Avenue in Tucson. Travel 6.5 miles to Wilmot Road, turn north and watch for the Tanque Verde Road that veers to the right just ahead. Take Tanque Verde 1.1 miles, then turn left onto Sabino Canyon Road. This winds for 4.5 miles to the parking area.

Catalina State Park (see chapter 14) is another area near Tucson where roadrunners are easily seen.

20

Wild Turkey

Say the word *turkey* to the average American and two general images come to mind: the steaming centerpiece of a holiday meal, or a fidgety, curiously decorated bird who barks out a comical gobble and is noted for a distinct lack of intelligence. These popular notions of the turkey, however, are only half-correct. With regard to the domesticated turkey, debeaked and fattened en masse for our Thanksgiving tables, these notions hit the mark. But with reference to the wild turkey, North America's largest game bird, they miss entirely. To the surprise of people more accustomed to thawing out a plastic-sheathed tom than encountering one in the forest, the wild turkey is considered to be among the sharpest of all animals, possessing not only near-unmatched powers of sight and hearing but an intelligence said to be foremost among fowl of its type.

The domesticated turkey we buy at grocery stores has been bred so exclusively for its meat that it lacks virtually all survival skills. Notoriously stupid, some have to be taught how to eat and drink. The smaller, slenderer wild turkey shares none of its domesticated cousin's ineptitude. On leaving the branches of the tall forest trees where it roosts at night, the wild turkey spends its days foraging on the ground for acorns and other nuts, seeds and insects, all the while maintaining strict vigilance. At the slightest

An adult wild turkey and two juveniles go for a stroll. Turkeys forage mostly on the ground for seeds, nuts and acorns, which are their staple foods, and also eat some insects, reptiles and amphibians.

disturbance or suspicious sound, a turkey breaks into a quick run and hop before lifting into the air and rising over the trees, reaching speeds, briefly, of more than 50 miles per hour. At a mild trot, a turkey can move faster than 15 miles per hour. With their many predators, including eagles, coyotes and mountain lions, their wariness serves them well.

Despite its prominent place in both colonial legend and holiday feasts, turkey meat was disdained by many Indian tribes, and the wild turkey was in serious decline just a few decades ago. Some native peoples, for instance, the Aztecs, farmed and raised turkeys, though perhaps more for their feathers than their meat. The wing feathers were often used for arrows and ceremonial paraphernalia, and the spurs, the sharp claws on the rear of the toms' feet, were used for arrow points. The turkey the Aztecs domesticated was taken back to Spain by Cortez in the 1520s, proving so tasty it became common throughout Europe by 1600. When English colonists brought the turkey with them to the New World, they found it already plentiful here, though evidence indicates most of the native peoples they encountered avoided eating the meat. In the Southwest, too, the Apaches, among others, did not like to eat turkey. And in Anasazi ruins throughout the area, turkey bones are often found in the rubble, but the birds may have been used for ceremonial purposes.

The days of abundant turkey flocks began to pass as early settlers, frontier explorers and hunters killed the bird in ever-increasing numbers. Deforestation also took its toll. By the 1920s, nearly twenty states that had once been home to the wild turkey had not a single one left. The bird became warier, more alert and precariously less numerous. "Trap-and-transfer" efforts undertaken in the 1950s, in which turkeys in one area were relocated to regions lacking the birds, increased their numbers to over 300,000, a tenfold increase over the early 1940s. By the early 1990s, wild turkeys in North America were estimated to number over three million, with large patches of mountain forests in New Mexico, Arizona, Colorado and, in more limited areas, Utah supporting sizable populations.

In April you are far more likely to hear a turkey than see one. The familiar gobble (one trait the wild and domesticated turkeys still share) can be heard echoing through the pines of the southwestern forests throughout early spring. It is at this time of year that the flocks of adult males begin to break up, territorial squabbles ensue and the calling and strutting meant to attract hens begin. Toms gather small harems together, the hens visiting their chosen male almost daily during breeding season. The displaying toms, with their chests thrust out, tail feathers fanned and faces undergoing chameleonlike color changes because of a fluctuating blood flow, are an impressive, though rare, sight. Listen for the gobbling. It is possible to hear an amorous tom from well over a mile away.

HOTSPOTS

Turkeys are hard to find. Count on hearing them if you're in the right place at the right time, but these wary birds often stay out of sight. Wild turkeys also frequent more remote areas, generally the deeper parts of forests and the less-visited mountain slopes. Throughout much of the Southwest, the turkey has been reintroduced and, while abundant in some areas, is fairly well scattered about in patches. In Colorado, it would be rare to find many in much of the northern half of the state, but visit the **U.S. Air Force Academy** (see chapter 70) for a great chance to see some strutting about on the grounds in early morning. Just as this area is unexpectedly fine for seeing deer, it is equally good and accessible for turkey.

Farther south, try the **Apishapa State Wildlife Area**, a high, upland region with prairie grass, deep canyons, juniper and cottonwood and plenty of solitude. This is a remote area, best avoided in wet weather but otherwise accessible, particularly in a four-wheel-drive vehicle. The Apishapa River, which joins the Arkansas River about 40 miles east of Pueblo, has cut a deep canyon here that serves as a retreat for bighorn sheep, mule deer, pronghorns, bobcats and turkey. As in most turkey areas, it is impossible to recommend one definite spot where the birds will be. Rather, drive the many dirt roads in this 8,000-acre wildlife area, listen for gobbling and keep an eye out for a tom. One might be just about anywhere here. To reach Apishapa State Wildlife Area, take State Road 10 northeast out of Walsenburg for 17.5 miles to a sign on the right indicating the wildlife area. Follow this dirt road south. It becomes County Road 220 after 2.5 miles, then forks left—east—after 5.2 miles to become County Road 90. Follow this road to reach the wildlife area after 10 miles.

In New Mexico, the best place to find turkeys is at **Bosque del Apache National Wildlife Refuge** (see chapter 62), where an introduced flock of Rio Grande turkeys is frequently seen on the east side of the North Tour Loop, particularly on the levee. Get there early in the morning for the best view of strutting toms the state has to offer.

Another outstanding spot to hear turkeys, if not see them, is on the road to the **Pajarito Mountain Ski Area**, a pleasant, paved road that, within just a few miles, ascends from ponderosa pine to oak, aspen and spruce. This is near Bandelier National Monument, and the road to Pajarito passes through the many building-complex areas of the Los Alamos National Laboratories. To reach the road, continue past the main entrance to Bandelier National Monument on State Road 4 west for 6 miles, then turn north onto State Road 501. Follow 501 for 2.8 miles, then take the signed road to the left. Stay to the left at the first fork in the road to reach the ski area, which is very popular in winter, in just 3.9 miles. Stop along the way at any of the numerous dirt roads that lead downslope and listen for gobbling. Drive one of the roads—

almost all are maintained by the Forest Service—if you feel adventurous. A strutting tom just might appear.

Arizona actually has more turkeys than might be expected, though again, many flocks are in inaccessible areas. The best spot in northern Arizona is at **Coleman Lake** near the town of Williams. An oak and ponderosa pine, marshlike area specifically improved to draw waterfowl, this 180-acre green basin attracts plenty of ducks, elk and turkeys. The lake covers roughly 90 acres, while the forested areas rimming it attract strutting toms in spring. Look for them throughout the area and on the road leading in. Coleman Lake is easily reached by taking the paved Perkinsville Road (Forest Road 173) south out of Williams for 7.7 miles, then turning west on Forest Road 108. This is a well-maintained dirt road that leads, in 2.1 miles, to Coleman Lake.

21

Ocotillo in Blossom

Like some spindly-limbed monster reaching its score of greenish arms skyward, the ocotillo is one of the most abundant and spectacular of all southwestern plants. Common below 5,000 feet in southern Arizona and areas of southern New Mexico, ocotillo can be found on rocky hillsides in the most desolate reaches of the desert or on the landscaped medians of busy city streets. And it is, of course, instantly recognizable, even startling. The red flowers that sprout from the tips of its stems every April are among the sweetest and most welcome signs of a desert spring.

Because of its brown and greenish color and the thorns that sprout along each stem, the ocotillo is frequently thought to be a type of cactus. It is closer botanically to the olive or primrose and is definitely *not* a cactus. Unlike the succulents, too, ocotillo does not store water but, rather, responds dramatically to a good, hard rain, each stem sprouting green leaves along its length and a head of flowers on its top. The long, unbranching stems, which generally reach heights of 10 to 15 feet, remain fairly dormant during dry periods. But when moisture arrives, they become coated with small green leaves. The bright red flowers, dense clusters of fleshy, tubular blossoms, may appear when the leaves are not present, though a fully adorned ocotillo presents a particularly lush and vital figure. When dry weather reclaims the desert, the leaves and flowers turn brown and are shed. But ocotillo can respond to any period of rainfall, repeating its cycle of flowering and shedding several times during spring and summer. Its omnipresence notwithstanding, the sight of a stand of ocotillo arrayed with leaves and flowers is one of the finest the Chihuahuan and Sonoran deserts have to offer.

Birds also find pleasure—more precisely, food—in the ocotillo in spring. In fact, there is a close synchrony between ocotillo blooming and the migrations of some hummingbirds. During a three- to six-week period in April and May when the five-lobed corolla flowers produce their nectar, broad-billed, black-chinned, rufous and several other types of hummingbirds are common visitors to ocotillo plants. The blazing red flowers of a single ocotillo can be literally buzzing with several hummingbirds and scores of carpenter bees on an April day.

Humans have also found practical uses for the plant. Local Indians once used the tough stems to build thatch huts. And fences made from ocotillo are attractive additions to some homes in the Southwest. Stems from a thriving ocotillo are cut (by landscapers only; it is illegal to cut roadside plants), then replanted in a row where, taking root, they will grow and produce leaves. In time they create a distinctively southwestern living fence.

HOTSPOTS

Although ocotillo can be found throughout the southern deserts—along highways, in towns, on desert slopes—the dense stands or "forests" of ocotillo are the most impressive sights. One such stand can be found in the **Santa Rita Experimental Range**, a desert grassland region south of Tucson. The range area is on the way to Madera Canyon in the Santa Rita Mountains and is a fairly representative slice of palo verde, cholla and mesquite desert. A fine ocotillo stand lies in the open grassland just before the road begins climbing up to the oak woodlands above. To reach the ocotillo, head south out of Tucson on I-19 for 40 miles to Exit 63 and look for the Madera Canyon Recreation Area sign. Follow it left under the interstate and head east for 1.1 miles. Turn right onto White House Canyon Road. Seven miles ahead, be sure to stay to the right; a mile beyond this fork puts you in the midst of plentiful ocotillo. This road continues up to **Madera Canyon,** 4 miles ahead.

Another good forest of ocotillo occurs on the famous **Apache Trail**, a mostly gravel, partly paved byway that is the most direct, and most adventurous, route northeast out of the Phoenix area. State Route 88, its official name, winds through deep canyons, past three desert lakes and ends up at Roosevelt Dam, a masonry arch dam that, not so incidentally, was built to stop up the Salt River, thus granting Phoenix the stored water it needed to become a thriving desert city. While the route has a reputation for ruggedness, it is easily drivable in any type of vehicle. The area of ocotillo comes before the pavement ends and the gravel begins. To reach it, continue past Lost Dutchman State Park (see chapter 15) on State Road 88 to the small town of Tortilla Flat, 18 miles from Apache Junction. The road is full of twists and turns, but the views of Canyon Lake and the desert landscapes are well worth the slow going. Three miles beyond Tortilla Flat lies a thick stand of ocotillo. Two miles beyond this, the pavement ends, with 25 miles of gravel road and scenic desert ahead until Roosevelt Dam pops into view.

To see an ocotillo fence, visit the **Desert Botanical Garden** in Phoenix (see the appendix).

22

Burrowing Owls

Few birds have fascinated humans more than the owl. Well represented in myth and legend, owls have come to symbolize everything from wisdom and victory to disaster and bad luck. Perhaps their appearance—the oddly simian or catlike face, the penetrating eyes—is responsible for their association with the supernatural; or maybe their soundless flight and stealthy proficiency at hunting have made them seem removed from the realm of ordinary creatures. Whatever it is, owls undoubtedly are regarded as mysterious creatures, agents of good or ill, yet always retaining a sort of quiet dignity. Most of them, that is. Track down the burrowing owl, the so-called comic of the plains, on the Southwest's open prairie land in spring and prepare to have your notions of owl decorum shattered.

All owls, of course, share certain general characteristics: the large heads that, for some species, can rotate through nearly three-fourths of a complete circle; the striking face masks, created by a pattern of feathers about the eyes; the hooked bill and long, sharp toes; the forward-oriented, staring eyes. Burrowers, midsized owls about 10 inches long, have all these traits and some differences. For starters, they are one of a very few species of land birds that opt to nest underground. Although they can dig their own burrows with their thick claws, it is far more typical for them to take over a hole vacated by a prairie dog or ground squirrel, enlarging the tunnel, then lining it and the nesting chamber with horse manure, a sort of wallpaper and carpeting all in one. The quantities of dung found in these abandoned lairs have done little to dispel the image of burrowing owls as anything but the odd cousin of the owl family. In their defense, it's believed that the odor of the manure acts as a protection by masking the smell of the owls.

Burrowing owls occasionally take over entire colonies vacated by smaller prairie rodents, creating, in turn, their own owl colonies, though they may also nest in pairs, very loving ones at that. Aside from one small area in Florida, they are found only in the West, and only in open, generally treeless land. Prairie country, particularly uncultivated land, is their preferred habitat, though desert scrub and sagebrush flats suit them almost as well.

Unlike the more regal owls, like the great horned, who sit patiently on branches and hunt like silent, graceful ghosts, the burrowing owl moves about near its den frenetically and spends almost all its time on or under the ground. It even hunts on foot, though it also flies low and jerkily when it needs to, or hovers above prey. Its long legs are another distinctive trait of the burrowing owl, as is the flamingolike habit of standing on a single leg as it surveys the plains. But it is their impatience, their inability to stand still for long, that can make them seem so downright comical. A burrowing owl will chatter and bob and lean forward, stand motionless at the rim of its burrow, pop down its hole, lift into the air, twitch its face or wings, scan the area with its pale yellow eyes and then stand still again—for a moment. It takes good luck to photograph one, though periods of patience can strike a burrower.

Burrowing owls are readily identified by their habits and habitat. A brownish bird with a striped or barred breast, it also has a stubby tail and lacks ear tufts. It clucks and chatters if upset, though the male makes a particularly lovely cooing sound at night. Burrowing owls seem also to be able to approximate the sound of an agitated rattlesnake—for defensive purposes, no doubt. And speaking of rattlesnakes, because burrowing owls take over prairie dog holes, and because rattlesnakes are common in these areas and will try to enter owl nests to find prey, legends used to circulate on the plains about how well the three animals coexisted underground. While wholly untrue, these rumors of diverse companionship must have added greatly to the burrowing owl's oddball image. Without question, few birds have so much character.

HOTSPOTS

Southeast Arizona is home to thirteen species of owls, including the smallest in North America, the aptly named elf owl. And while it may be possible to find burrowing owls in southern Arizona and New Mexico year-round, some of the better spots lie farther north where, in the short-grass prairies, they begin arriving on their migration by mid-April.

Colorado has abundant burrowing owl colonies. Near Denver, try the **Rocky Mountain Arsenal** (see chapter 2), or a few areas near it. Just north of the Bald Eagle Observatory Area (again, see chapter 2) on Buckley Road, it is possible to see burrowing owls near 72d Avenue. Look through the wire fence of the arsenal and you can see the birds, or check the area on the east side of Buckley Road around 72d Avenue for their mounds. Keep driving slowly north if you don't see them here; they may be farther up the road. In fact, for a good chance to see another sizable burrowing owl colony, continue north to 88th Avenue, turn east for 1 mile, then turn north onto Tower Road. Continue north for 3 miles just past 112th Avenue and then look for mounds to the west. In recent years, large numbers of burrowing owls have been found here.

Southeastern Colorado and northeastern New Mexico are prime burrowing owl regions. An enormous prairie dog town, fairly well deserted by prairie dogs now but with numerous burrowing owls, lies in Colorado on the north side of the **John Martin Reservoir** in the state wildlife area of the same name. This huge reservoir, with a dam built by the U.S. Army Corps of Engineers, is heavily used by waterfowl in winter and during migration. Prairie land and low bluffs comprise the reservoir's northern shore, while other parts of it are marshy, cottonwood flats. Drive on the county road on the north side of the lake and look for burrowing owl mounds everywhere. To reach John Martin

Reservoir State Wildlife Area, head northeast from Las Animas on US 50 for 11 miles to County Road 19—clearly signed—on the right. Go south on 19 for 0.9 mile, then turn east onto County Road JJ (19 ends at JJ). This road skirts along the reservoir's northern shore area through short-grass prairie. After 5 miles—this stretch is the best for burrowing owls—the road meets County Road 24. One mile to the left lies the town of Hasty on US 50, and 1.5 miles to the right lies the reservoir's dam. Also in Colorado, try **Pawnee National Grassland** (see chapter 33).

In northeastern New Mexico, travel to **Maxwell National Wildlife Refuge** (see chapter 2) for reliable burrowing owl viewing. Just off the southeast corner of the refuge along State Road 505 is a prairie dog town that the owls frequent. This massive field lies just before the 2-mile marker on State Road 505 and to the north of the road. Maxwell National Wildlife Refuge is well known for the burrowing owls that return to it each year.

23

April Shorttakes

Mississippi Kites

The Mississippi kite is a grayish, steely-eyed ghost of a bird that winters in South America and returns to the United States by midspring. It is uncommon in the Southwest, though an isolated population returns by April or May to the area near Dudleyville north of Oracle in southeastern Arizona on State Road 77. The birds are also found in the city of Roswell, New Mexico, by late April. The surest bet, though, is **Willow Creek Park** in the small town of Lamar in southeastern Colorado. Located on the south side of town off US 385/287 between Memorial Drive East and Parkway Drive, the birds come here to nest by mid- to late April. Mississippi kites were only discovered nesting in Colorado within the last thirty years, indicating that they are pushing their range westward. It is believed the Arizona population first started nesting in that state in 1970.

24

Breakout: The Southwest's Sand Dunes

As you drive down the western slope of New Mexico's Sacramento Mountains, from a point roughly 10 miles above the city of Alamogordo, you can see a line of white far on the horizon shimmering like some distant, ghostly lake. It isn't water, of course, but sand. And as you draw closer to it, to White Sands National Monument, it becomes apparent that this is a vast, looming blanket of sand that stretches far across the basin in which it lies. For 275 square miles, the pure white gypsum of White Sands swells, ripples and falls in continually altering patterns of dunes, some entirely barren, some lightly covered with tough vegetation. Life is difficult here, and what does survive must be hardy and adaptable. But it is not so much the wildlife that is the attraction here as it is the stuff that ends up in your shoes and in your hair— the sand.

About 400 miles to the north, in the broad San Luis Valley of southern Colorado, lies another dune field, smaller than the one at White Sands and with a generally plain, brownish sand. But what it lacks in size and brilliance, it makes up in height. The dunes here at Great Sand Dunes National Monument are the tallest in North America—some are nearly 700 feet high—and their sheer enormity makes them as impressive as the otherworldly white dunes of White Sands. Life is tenuous here also, though in ways different from New Mexico's desert land. Different, too, are the forces that created these strange sand fields.

The region around White Sands was once a vast, shallow sea with gypsum on its floor. When the waters dried up, the gypsum turned to stone and was eventually caught in the upheaval that formed the Rocky Mountains. An enormous dome of gypsum formed, then collapsed, leaving the San Andres Mountains to the west, the Sacramento Mountains to the east and the Tularosa Basin at the middle. A dry lake bed here offers up a constant supply of gypsum particles that the winds from the Southwest carry onto the dune fields.

At Great Sand Dunes, the Rio Grande, after ages of flowing through the high, flat San Luis Valley, has left vast deposits of dry sand. Here too, a southwestern wind sweeps off the San Juan Mountains to the west and across the valley, casting the sand in high mounds at the base of the Sangre de Cristo Mountains to the east.

Certain key elements are necessary for the creation of sand dunes, these being the sand, a prevailing wind to disperse it and some natural barrier to allow the sand to collect. What may not be so apparent is that animals and plants can prosper here in a limited fashion. In fact, at White Sands, two types of lizard, one type of mouse and several insects have acquired a white coloration to protect them from predators. The bleached earless lizard, like a bit of darting vanilla, is one of the strangest sights on these dunes.

One of the most interesting things to do on a dune field in spring, when many animals are becoming more active, is to search for their tracks in the sand. These delicate marks are instantly wiped out when the wind picks up, but while they last, they provide clues to what transpires on these dunes during the night. At White Sands and at Great Sand Dunes, roadrunners, raccoons, pocket mice, kangaroo rats and a variety of lizards may leave their tracks in the soft sand. Tracks may intersect where a lizard has fallen prey to a hungry roadrunner; most trails seem to wander aimlessly.

For all their apparent dryness, dunes hold plenty of water, acting as huge sponges for any rain that falls. Little of this moisture evaporates or runs off. If you dig down a few inches you can discover this for yourself. Even when the surface of a dune is scorching, it is cool and damp less than a foot below. Although dunes have water available that could be used to nourish plants, the shifting sand makes this a difficult proposition. Some plants manage it, however. Soaptree yuccas, saltbush, even some cotton-woods grow at White Sands. Scrubbier plants—low grasses and scurfpea—are found at Great Sand Dunes. Stable dunes, the ones that shift very little, are fairly well anchored by the vegetation that grows on them. Shifting dunes are almost always barren.

Summer is too hot for a visit to these dry fields, and winter finds less animal activity than any other time. Come in spring, visit in the morning and look for the tracks that, like the shifting dunes themselves, are soon covered with the endless waves of sand.

MAY

25

Ladybugs, Cicadas and Forests Full of Insects

Spring brings a complete transformation to the forests of the Southwest. Drab stands of naked oak, cottonwood, willow and aspen suddenly press deep shades of green from out of their limbs, and the forests are full and alive again. On some mountain ranges, there is a second and equally dramatic change of color when millions upon millions of ladybugs descend on rocks, bushes, trees, even the ground, overwhelming the other hues with enormous living masses of reddish-orange. More than one hundred million ladybugs per acre gather in certain mountain areas—generally the same sites year after year—to create one of the least-known but most colorful of all spring events.

Because ladybugs are so common and familiar, most people hardly give them a second thought beyond admiring the shiny shell and polka-dotted back of a stray bug. Take the name, for instance, which in full is actually the "convergent lady beetle"—ladybugs are really beetles, not bugs—or the "ladybird beetle." The term "ladybug" is, at least to the fussy, less than proper. "Lady beetle" actually comes from the insect's name in Europe where, honored for the aid it provides to crop growers, it was dedicated to the Virgin Mary as "our Lady's beetle."

What assistance can a fingernail-sized beetle give to farmers? Singly, little; in bunches, plenty. In fact, the annual cycle

of the ladybug, including its mass gatherings on spring mountainsides, is defined by a series of remarkable group efforts. It begins
in about February when, awakening from their winter hibernation
in the mountains, ladybugs mate, then descend to the valleys below
by about mid-March. Farm fields are their preferred destinations,
and here they find the white aphids they feed on almost exclusively. Farmers and gardeners welcome the swarms of ladybugs
that, by gorging on the aphids and other pests, curtail what would
otherwise be enormous populations of crop-destroying insects.

The aphid-feeding frenzy—each ladybug eats its own
weight in aphids daily—serves to stimulate the ladybugs to lay
hundreds of eggs on surrounding weeds, bushes and trees—
anywhere their young will be able to continue feeding on aphids.
This done, the adults die, the larvae hatch in just a few days and
then, in their wingless, wormlike state, they strive to outdo their
parents as aphid eaters. After a few weeks of feeding, they affix
themselves to leaves and transform into chrysalides, only to
emerge a week or two later as familiar ladybugs: reddish-orange
shell, twelve black dots on the wing cover and an appetite for
aphids. Now that it is late spring, however, and most of the pest
insects are on the decline, masses of ladybugs fly, literally straight
up into the air, seeking cooler temperatures. When they reach an
altitude with temperatures in the low 50s, they make directly for
the nearest mountain range, join up with several million of their
cousins and cover everything in sight.

Mid- to late spring, when they are busy congregating on
any open spot or filling the air so thickly it seems as if an electric
red mist has descended, is the best time to see them. Some
mountain forests have isolated clumps of ladybugs that gather on
certain bushes or trees, while others have whole acres coated in
red. Ladybugs are more active in the afternoon, flitting about,
seeking the pollen that has taken the place of insects in their diet.
The changes of food and habitat, however, induce a sort of torpor
known as estivation, or summer hibernation. Heat or rain may
rouse them, but they become generally less active as the summer
progresses, eventually finding shelter for winter under tree bark or
any other dry area, waiting for February to arrive so that the cycle
can begin again.

Spring also sees the reemergence of the cicada throughout the Southwest. Several species of this loudly buzzing insect inhabit the area, and the symphony the males create to attract mates is perhaps the single most ubiquitous sound in the entire region. About 1 to 2 inches long, cicadas live in the soil as immatures, then emerge and fly up into nearby trees or plants—cottonwood in some areas, yucca and ocotillo in others. They call, mate and die in waves throughout spring and summer, bringing the forests alive with sound just as the ladybugs do with color.

HOTSPOTS

There is a remarkable consistency from year to year in locations preferred by ladybugs for summer visitation. The reasons for such specificity are unknown, though such factors as humidity, amount of sunlight, temperature and even the lingering odor of previous years' ladybugs probably have something to do with it.

One such spot is **Signal Peak** in the Pinal Mountains east of Phoenix. It can be a rough ride to the top of the mountain: the gravel and dirt road is winding and narrow and can be muddy after a rain, when it should be avoided. Fir and pine abound on Signal Peak, while lower elevations have riparian areas with fine birding. But it is the ladybugs, millions of which coat the communication towers and the area around the lookout tower atop the peak, that are most spectacular. The whole area, in fact, may be covered with the red beetles if you happen to arrive at peak time. To reach Signal Peak, turn south on the signed road to Pinal Mountain Recreation Area 2 miles west of the town of Globe and follow the signs 16.5 miles to the peak. Drive to the parking area at the end of the road, take the trail to the fire tower, and look for the red ladybugs everywhere.

Another spectacular ladybug area in Arizona is in the **Pinaleno Mountains** about 80 miles due northeast of Tucson. Mount Graham, at 10,713 feet, is the highest point in southern Arizona, and the Pinalenos are the highest of Arizona's "sky islands" (see chapter 54). There are a number of good ladybug ridges that can be reached on the drive up into the Pinalenos, the best being Heliograph Peak. To reach it, head south from the town of Safford on US 666 for 7.5 miles to the turnoff to State Road 366.

Go west on 366, climbing the winding, paved road for 22 miles. Look for the sign for Heliograph Peak to the right and follow the bumpy, unpaved road 2 miles to the top. This road has been closed recently and may have a locked gate across it. It is okay to park your vehicle here and walk to the area at the top. This 10,300-foot peak with a lookout tower and electrical towers is coated with bugs in late spring.

A great spot in New Mexico, and a place that offers one of the finest views in the entire Southwest, is atop **Sandia Crest** just east of Albuquerque. The Sandia Mountains dominate the sky east of the city, and a tramway, the world's longest, carries visitors to the top of the 10,000-foot-plus crest in about 15 minutes. You can also drive to the top by approaching from the east, or "back" side, of the mountains, a route that takes you from desert plains to fir and spruce forests in less than an hour. To reach the 10,680-foot top of the Sandias, take I-40 east out of Albuquerque for about 10 miles and get off at Exit 175 ("Cedar Crest North 14 Exit"). From here, travel north on State Road 14 for 5.5 miles to State Road 536. Turn west on 536 and follow the twisting, turning road 13 miles through ponderosa pines to the top. The trail south from the parking area to the top of the tramway passes through meadows where ladybugs can be seen on bushes and boulders.

Aside from the opportunity to see ladybugs at these three spots, the scenery is uniformly spectacular. Broad vistas, cool pines and early wildflowers are great at each spot. Look for the ladybugs, and enjoy the rest of the sights, too.

26

The Elegant Trogon

Heard but not seen—to invert a phrase—is often the lament of bird-watchers seeking the elegant trogon, the most spectacular bird in the Southwest's most spectacular birding region. Indeed, there are a handful of locations in southeastern Arizona where from late spring to midsummer it is fairly certain the trogon will be heard calling. And while seeing it isn't quite as difficult as some birders would hold—assuming one searches in the right places—the trogon's solitary ways make a glimpse of it one of the rarest and most desirable prizes for an American birder.

That the trogon is surpassingly beautiful probably goes without saying. It is, after all, a relative of the quetzal, the bird revered by Mayan emperors. The only way to appreciate the trogon's singular allure, though, is to seek one out in one of the desert mountain canyons it returns to annually for nesting. When first seen, generally perched stiff and upright on a sycamore, perhaps, or on some other streamside tree, the trogon seems to be a misplaced visitor from some exotic equatorial jungle, so striking is its coloration. It has a habit of keeping its back to an approaching viewer, revealing only its delicate sheen and the square-tipped, greenish-blue tail. "Coppery-tailed trogon," a fair description of the long tail that points straight downward as the bird warily turns its head to one side, is what it was once called. Gray shows on the wing, the head is deep emerald with a red eye ring and a broad, bright yellow bill. Its silence and stillness as it sits alone on its branch can be unnerving, particularly when most birders are accustomed to watching some rarity flit off at the first approach of a human. The trogon sits motionless, as if willing itself not to be noticed.

When and if the bird turns around, its colors become even more dramatic. The deep green of its head halts abruptly with a white line across its breast, beneath which lies a bright red lower breast and belly. If a large part of the attraction of birding lies in witnessing the extraordinary colors nature can paint her creatures, the trogon will never disappoint.

While it is common to virtually stumble upon a silent trogon perched midway up a tree, it may be more common to locate it by its call. Actually, *call* is too kind a word for the trogon's barking croak, a sound that seems to fit the lovely bird about as well as glasses would fit the Mona Lisa. Think of combining the call of a hen turkey with both a pig's grunt and a dog's bark, and you have a fairly good idea of the trogon's decidedly undignified, unmistakable and unforgettable call.

The trogon was almost wiped out by collectors half a century ago, though its numbers seem to be on the rise. As one of the few truly exotic birds that breed north of Mexico, it has always drawn an interest that vastly exceeds its very slight numbers. "Where is the trogon?" becomes one of spring's most frequently asked questions in those two or three canyons it most often inhabits. And with a lot of patience and only a bit of luck, it is very likely that an hour or two of tramping though the forest will bring the industrious birder face-to-face with the Southwest's most fabulous bird.

HOTSPOTS

One of the greatest pleasures of searching for the trogon is that it inhabits such beautiful areas—the sky islands. While the deserts below are starting to swelter, the forested mountains above are shady and moderately cool and may have running streams. It is this combination of terrain and temperature that also draws the trogon, making it a very exact science to calculate where the bird returns to year after year.

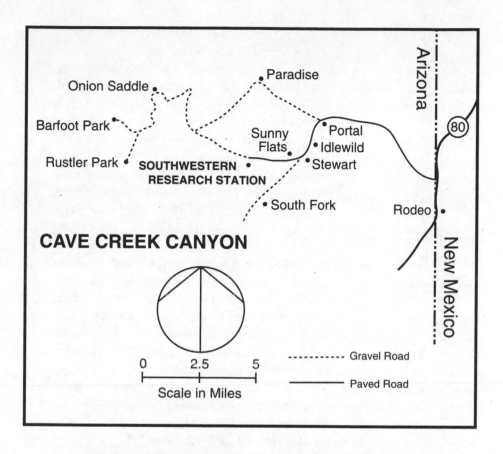

CAVE CREEK CANYON

Onion Saddle

Paradise

Barfoot Park

Rustler Park

Sunny Flats

Portal

Idlewild

Stewart

SOUTHWESTERN RESEARCH STATION

South Fork

Rodeo

Arizona

New Mexico

80

0   2.5   5

Scale in Miles

- - - - - - - - Gravel Road

———————— Paved Road

Undoubtedly the single best spot to find the elegant trogon is **Cave Creek Canyon**. Variously referred to as the loveliest area in southeastern Arizona, the single best birding spot in the Southwest (and perhaps the whole country) and the region with the most richly diverse wildlife in the entire United States, Cave Creek Canyon is one of the few places that lives up to its reputation. Certainly few entrances are as dramatic as the one into the canyon. Set in the heart of the Chiricahua Mountains, the approach to the canyon from the east is unforgettable. Towering, jagged cliffs, seemingly able to capture every hue of gold and red on their sheer faces, are pocked with shadowy caves and cracks. Beneath them, lush green sycamores and oak fill the canyon. No other place in America can match Cave Creek's mix of wildlife, beauty and exotica; and few spots have such a unique blend of

habitats: desert grasslands, tropicallike highlands, pine–oak woodlands and high forests of fir and spruce. No wonder the Southwestern Research Station, located on the road that leads up into the
high mountains from the canyon, draws researchers from around
the world to study the region's wildlife.

To reach Cave Creek Canyon, head south on State Road 80
from the small community of Road Forks, New Mexico (Exit 5 on
I-10, just before the interstate crosses into Arizona). Drive on State
Road 80 for 26.5 miles through rocky foothills, creosote and yucca,
and (2.5 miles before the town of Rodeo) look for the sign for State
Road 533, also known as Portal Road. Take this road west—a "Cave
Creek Canyon" sign is clearly visible—and follow it for 7 miles to the
town of Portal. The store at Portal, incidentally, is a good source of
information about recent sightings in the canyon (they also have
plenty of fine books, brochures and fliers), and the feeders in back
attract hummingbirds. Continue on State Road 533, and at 0.6 mile
beyond the store, stay on the paved road to the left of a fork. There
is a sign here, and the rest of the area is equally well signed; you won't
get lost. The spectacular view—dazzling cliffs with the dark green
canyon nestled below—is at its best here. A visitor center/ranger
station lies 0.8 mile beyond the fork in the road; stop for good
information here. Continuing, you will pass Idlewild and Stewart
campgrounds, then come to another fork in the road 1.4 miles
beyond the ranger station. The left road—the gravel one—is known
as South Fork; the right, paved for 2 miles, leads up into the
mountains to Rustler Park. Most sightings of the elegant trogon are
made by walking along the South Fork Road, listening for the bird's
call and peeking into the trees for a glimpse of it. If this is
unproductive, drive the 1.3-mile gravel road to where it ends at the
South Fork Forest Camp Picnic Area. A signed trail leads up the creek
from this picnic area, and the first mile or so is also good for finding
the trogon. A trail between Stewart Campground and Sunnyflat
Campground (which is 0.2 mile up the fork on the paved road toward
Rustler Park) is the third good area to find the trogon. Listen for its
weird, croaking call, and don't forget that there are scores of other
spectacular birds also to be seen. Look for painted redstarts, Scott's
and hooded orioles, Lucy's and Virginia's warblers, Cassin's kingbirds, tanagers, hummingbirds, white-breasted nuthatches, white-

winged doves, western wood-peewees, dusky-capped and ash-throated flycatchers and bridled titmouses, with acorn woodpeckers and gray-breasted jays everywhere.

The other good spot for finding the elegant trogon is at **Madera Canyon** (see chapter 21). Though not as accessible or reliable as Cave Creek, Madera Canyon offers a good chance to see a trogon for those willing to hike a bit. Drive to the upper parking area—Roundup—at the end of the road and take the upper trail—the blocked road—leading to the Vault Mine Trail. Trogons have nested along the stream about a mile or so from the trailhead. The other trail leading out of the Roundup Trailhead Area is known as the Super Trail; the trogon has nested in this oak and sycamore area about a mile up the trail. Give both a try, and keep your fingers crossed.

27

The Vermilion Flycatcher

When a bird has a catchy or interesting name, it's usually because it has a trait so distinctive that it can't be ignored. The elf owl, for instance, fits its name to a T, and the American dipper is noted for taking extended plunges into the waters of swiftly flowing streams. An even better example is the vermilion flycatcher, a bird so brightly red that the word *vermilion* only begins to suggest its brilliance. The bird's Spanish name may better capture this flycatcher's beauty: *brasita del fuego,* "little coal of fire." In Mexico it's called *sangre de toro,* "bull's blood." Even the scientists, who usually affix drably clinical names to even the most spectacular species, got it right this time, christening the bird *Pyrocephalus,* "the firehead." Of all the more common birds found in the desert lands of southern New Mexico and Arizona, the vermilion flycatcher is the most colorful and beloved of all. And it's not hard to see why. With its striking red and brown coloration and alternately bold and tender ways, the vermilion is easy to like.

That the vermilion flycatcher is dazzling is well known, but that such coloration should be found in a member of the flycatcher family is quite surprising. It is almost as if the vermilion were trying to make up for the general drabness of its cousins, so gaudy does it appear. Flaming red on its crown and underparts, with a bold brown across the face, upper parts and tail, the vermilion flycatcher contrasts emphatically with the pale brown and gray kingbirds, phoebes and flycatchers to whom it is related. So uniform and unremarkable in plumage are the thirty or so members of the flycatcher family found in the United States, that one group, those known as the *Empidonax* flycatchers, are among the most frustratingly difficult of all birds to distinguish by appearance alone. The vermilion is definitely the showoff of its family.

Like all flycatchers, the vermilion perches stiffly upright on branches or shrubs, frequently darting about to snap up flies, beetles, bees or grasshoppers—any insect it can capture with its long, flattish bill. It is also a fairly bold fellow, perching in plain sight on tree limbs or bushes, a rare conspicuousness in such a noticeable bird, as if to announce that modesty and beauty have not converged in its tiny body.

Found in mesquite woodlands and streamside areas, the male vermilion flycatcher can be fierce in protecting the area around the nest it shares with its female mate, which is very plain-looking in comparison. The courtship between the two, which occurs in midspring, is lovely. The radiantly red male alternately shoots up into the air and then stops and hovers, the slight crest on his head ruffled and his tail flickering. He sings a cheerful, liquid tune as he ascends, a song that reaches its climax as the bird reaches a height of 50 or 60 feet. Then suddenly, spotting his mate hidden in the brush below, he flutters to the ground to join her. Dramatic, surely, but then style and flair are what the vermilion flycatcher is all about.

HOTSPOTS

The Tucson Audubon Society calls its monthly newsletter the *Vermilion Flycatcher,* at least partly because, as with so many other intriguing birds of the Southwest, southeastern Arizona is the best place to find the publication's namesake. Sonoita Creek in the **Patagonia–Sonoita Creek Preserve** (see chapter 67) is the best place in the United States to find the vermilion flycatcher. If you take the trail along the stream, you are sure to see a number of them if you walk slowly and look carefully. **Catalina State Park** (see chapter 14) is another spot where vermilions can be found with a little effort, particularly in the mesquite thickets in the day use area.

Far south of Catalina and to the southwest of Sonoita Creek lies **Peña Blanca Lake**, a popular recreation spot set amid the desert scrub of the extreme southern reaches of the state. A mile long and very narrow, Peña Blanca attracts cardinals, pyrrhuloxia, phainopeplas, Say's phoebes, white-winged doves, Cassin's kingbirds, black-headed grosbeaks, Scott's orioles and more, including quite a few vermilion flycatchers. Fishermen and campers frequent the lake, though even a short hike on the trail along the west shore will bring relative solitude and plenty of birds. To reach the lake, take State Road 289, also known as Ruby Road (Exit 12) off I-19, 8 miles north of Nogales, Arizona. Go west for 9.3 miles to the sign for Peña Blanca Recreation Area, then turn right to go downhill to the parking area 0.3 mile ahead. Take the path along the west side of the lake. The dam lies at the north end of the lake, roughly half a mile up the trail. Scan the trees nearest the lake for vermilions.

Despite its small size, **Rattlesnake Springs**, just south of Carlsbad Caverns in New Mexico, is one of the finest and most unexpectedly pleasant of all birding areas in southern New Mexico—and a true hotspot for vermilion flycatchers. In the midst of hot, shadeless scrubland, Rattlesnake Springs is an oasis of green grass, towering cottonwoods, willow trees and a sweetly trickling spring whose waters are held, unobtrusively, in a sizable concrete pool. Over three hundred species of birds have been recorded at Rattlesnake Springs, including four types of oriole—Scott's, orchard, northern and hooded. Vermilion flycatchers may be seen along the right side of the gravel road leading past the picnic area and up to the spring. To reach Rattlesnake Springs, head south from Whites City on US 180/62 for 5.1 miles, turn right at the sign and travel 1.5 miles to a fork in the road. Follow the sign to the left, and after 0.3 mile, look for a sign that reads "Carlsbad Caverns National Park/Rattlesnake Springs Picnic Area." The picnic area lies 0.3 mile ahead, the spring 0.3 mile beyond that. Spend some time here while searching for the vermilion to also find painted and indigo buntings, cave swallows, summer tanagers, Bell's vireos, Cassin's sparrows and other colorful birds.

28

Spring Torrents and Raging Rivers

It is said that Will Rogers, on first seeing the Rio Grande, pronounced it the only river he had ever seen in need of irrigation. Obviously, he didn't visit the great river in spring. In fact, during May and June, when the rivers of the Southwest are swollen with runoff and racing through the mountains and deserts like frenzied, liquid demons, they are every bit as dramatic and vibrant as those waterways in parts of the country blessed with more moisture. And while it is true that for months out of the year most of the Southwest's rivers are somewhat less than mighty, take a look at them in late spring, when the driest region of America is suddenly brimming with the most precious gift of all—water.

When snow begins to melt in the Rockies and groundwater begins to resurface, the mountain slopes become awash in trickling rivulets. These upland waters gather into streams and join at lower elevations, growing into the wider, slower rivers that flow through the foothills and lowlands. In the southern Rockies of Colorado and New Mexico, snowpack is at its maximum in April and then, after melting steadily for two months, is almost totally gone from the middle and lower regions by mid-June. The two primary river systems of the Southwest, the Colorado and the Rio Grande, are known as "exotics" in the deserts they pass through, since the water they bear is, primarily, derived from elsewhere. And because the Continental Divide snakes through Colorado and New Mexico, the Rockies' waters are carried both east and west: the Rio Grande empties into the Gulf of Mexico, the Colorado into the Gulf of California.

But these are all fairly mundane facts. Water, after all, is as familiar as any substance can be. Why go on about something so universally well known? Perhaps it is because water holds a different aspect in the Southwest, parts of which measure annual rainfall in single digits or receive the bulk of their rainfall in flashes of instant summer monsoons. No wonder the Colorado has been called the most used, most fought over and most politicized river in the nation, if not the world. And no wonder native prayers and accompanying ceremonies for rain, a sort of Hollywood caricature, are taken seriously here. It's safe to say that the sight of a river overflowing its usually narrow bed, tearing rocks, vegetation and soil from its banks, is more welcome in the Southwest, particularly its desert regions, than in almost any other part of the country.

As any visitor to the West discovers, cottonwood and willow are the dominant trees along rivers of the lowlands; their ability to tolerate days or even weeks of flooded roots accounts for their preeminence. This is because rivers have two beds—a narrow one for normal water levels, and a wide one for storms and snowmelt. Sediment collects along the banks, vegetation flourishes and animals, in turn, are drawn to what are often the only strips of greenery for miles around across vast areas of Arizona and New Mexico. Rivers, furthermore, are long "edges," places where habitats meet and wildlife is abundant.

Nowadays, though, it is a rare river that flows free from head to mouth. Both the Colorado and Rio Grande reach their gulfs seriously depleted, because so much water has been diverted for myriad human uses. Dams, irrigation, flood control—all sap a river's natural vitalizing powers, including its ability to lay down nutrient-rich sediment. But spring cannot be held back. It warms the mountainsides and conjures the sweet trickle of water from the sleeping snow. Full, coursing rivers, like bird migrations and tree foliage changes, mark the seasons in the Southwest; and just like those other, more colorful signs of spring, water—at this time and in this place—means life.

HOTSPOTS

Most tributaries of the Southwest's large rivers experience peak water flow in late April and early May, allowing the rivers they flow into to peak about a month later. An unusually great snowpack can bring such a rush of water through stream and river channels that banks are gouged out and walls of mud come crashing down along with the churning water. When it happens, it is a spectacular sight, though just like the finest wildflower blooms, it may be a once-in-a-decade occurrence. River water is brown and silty anyway at this time of year, and the Colorado— the "colored-red" river—is perpetually chocolaty (except below its dams). The old settlers' lament about the Colorado was that it was too thick to drink, too thin to plow.

While the **Colorado River** is well dammed, it is still possible to sense its ancient and untamed power along certain of its stretches. One of the best—intimate, lengthy and beautiful— is along the road that runs east and north out of the town of Moab in Utah. Here the Colorado snakes through high red rock canyon country, creating a lush ribbon of green beneath the intensely glowing cliff walls. The road, State Road 128, follows the river on its east side, with numerous spots to turn off or drive down to the water. It is one of the loveliest drives in the Southwest as the highway twists and turns with the river, the raw scenery of the low canyon tending to draw the eye away from the river itself. Take US 191 2 miles north of Moab and turn right onto State Road 128 immediately before the US 191 bridge crosses the river. The first 15 miles parallel the river closely before moving away for about 7 miles and then returning to follow the river for another 12 miles. Here the road veers left—west—slightly, joining I-70 at Exit 202, 43 miles from the junction with US 191.

The **Rio Grande**, another heavily used river, has played a crucial role in shaping the history of Native American, Hispanic and Anglo peoples in the Southwest. Spring floods signal the beginning of planting season, as they have for generations of farmers and settlers along the river, making riverside land highly desirable. Several of the native New Mexico pueblos lie alongside the Rio Grande, and Hispanic farming communities cluster about it as it slides through the heart of New Mexico on down into Texas. From its start in the San Juan Mountains, the Rio Grande flows into New Mexico and doesn't hit a dam in that state until it comes to the Cochiti Pueblo, where the U.S. Army Corps of Engineers built a dam several years ago. The length of the river from the Colorado–New Mexico border down past Taos is officially designated "wild and scenic," meaning it is to remain free-flowing and natural. Beneath this is a great stretch paralleled by State Road 570, which follows the river through a deep and impressive gorge. The Rio Grande is at its best and most accessible here, as it rages through the steep bottom of the narrow gorge, covered with sage and boulders, that it created. To reach this area, head south from Taos on State Road 68 for about 4 miles, then turn west on State Road 570. The first 6 miles are paved, but the last 2 miles down to the river are not. Press on along this rough stretch. It's worth it. At the bottom of the gorge is a bridge— State Road 567—but stay on the east side of the river and follow State Road 570 for 5.8 spectacular miles to the junction with State Road 68. There are numerous campgrounds and turnouts along this drive. You can continue viewing the river, which may be swarming with rafters and kayakers at this time of year, by heading south on State Road 68. The road parallels the river for the next 6 miles, then veers off. At Embudo, 11.5 miles south of the junction of 570 and 68, there is a good bridge and a marker indicating that here John Wesley Powell, the man who first floated the Colorado, devised the U.S. system for measuring water flow.

One other river, the lovely **Animas**, is worth mentioning. From its head in the San Juan Mountains, it leaps right down to the town of Durango, Colorado, where it can be viewed most impressively at the Durango Fish Hatchery (the pools full of trout are also worth a look). The Animas positively boils here, fresh off the mountainside. The hatchery is in the town of Durango off Main Street (US 550), just north of the bridge over the river. Look for the sign to the right. Gateway Park, 0.8 mile south of the junction of US 169 and US 550 at Durango, is another great spot to see the

Animas. Riverside walkways, green lawns and a visitor center are all here.

One word of caution. At this time of year, most waterways will be moving dangerously fast, even those that may appear placid. Do not attempt to swim or wade in these waters, and avoid standing too close to their edges. Several feet of riverbank can give way without warning. Drownings are frequent at this time of year.

29

May Shorttakes

Thick-billed Kingbirds

The rest stop south of Patagonia (see chapters 67 and 30 for directions and comments on this rest stop) is renowned among birders for the thick-billed kingbirds that have nested here every year since 1962. The thick-billed is similar to its kingbird brothers but has an oversized bill and a darker head. It is extremely rare in the United States, nesting only in the very southeasternmost sliver of Arizona.

Golden Eagles

While nesting, golden eagles are highly visible around the cliff walls they call home. Good areas to check are at **Cedar Mountain**, 6 miles up County Road 7 off US 40 west of the town of Craig in northwestern Colorado; and **Burro Creek Campground** (see chapter 16) in west central Arizona.

30

Breakout: Birding in Southeastern Arizona

Roger Tory Peterson, the most renowned American birder of this century, once wrote of southeastern Arizona that "its magnetic pull cannot be denied. Here one finds a greater variety of nesting land birds than in any comparable area in the United States." When asked to name the top birding spots in the country, Peterson, whose wildlife guides have found a place in the daypacks of countless outdoors enthusiasts, included southeastern Arizona among the two or three finest.

Indeed, of all the places to see birds in the Southwest, maybe the whole country, the region of Arizona roughly south and east of Tucson, a corner occupying about one-sixth of the state, is indisputably the best. The Great Salt Lake area in Utah can be spectacular, and sections of the Rio Grande in Colorado and New Mexico are gems, but for variety, rarities and beauty, southeastern Arizona beats them all. May is the best month to go, though any season is outstanding. The last two weeks of May are considered the ideal time by most knowledgeable birders: the weather is not yet too hot, swarms of migrants are passing through and rare nesting birds such as the elegant trogon, the rose-throated becard and the sulphur-bellied flycatcher are beginning to arrive. The days are uniformly sunny, bright and dry, the nights cool and clear. And the birds are everywhere. More than three hundred species have been found here, including at least two dozen found nowhere else in the country and nearly three dozen that can be seen only in limited areas of Texas and New Mexico. The first-time visitor to the marvelously varied regions of southeastern Arizona is likely to be overwhelmed by the sheer number and variety of interesting birds to be seen.

And why is southeastern Arizona such a birding hotspot? First, with its proximity to Mexico, the area is visited by many birds from southern regions that rarely travel far north of the border. Mexican chickadees, broad-billed hummingbirds, yellow-eyed juncos, thick-billed kingbirds and a host of other infrequent visitors to the United States are found here and virtually nowhere else. The southeastern corner of Arizona is also the meeting place of several quite diverse land divisions: the Rocky Mountains, their high conifer forests dominating the vegetation at higher elevations; the Sierra Madres or "Mexican" Mountains, with their exotic, southern flora influencing the lower elevations; the lush Sonoran Desert from the south and west; and the vast Chihuahuan Desert to the southeast. This diversity of terrain has a dramatic influence on wildlife in the area, creating vastly different biotic communities within a few short miles of one another. Basin and rangeland is also the rule here, with towering sky islands surrounded and separated by broad spreads of desert scrub and grassland. Cut off from one another, the mountain ranges of the area stand as their own isolated habitats amid the rangeland below as surely as islands in an ocean. The "life zones" (see chapter 54) encountered on a drive to the top of any of the mountain ranges—the Santa Ritas, Santa Catalinas, Huachucas or Chiricahuas—are so definite and orderly that a 20- or 30-mile drive uphill is akin to driving from the deserts of Arizona to the mountains of Montana. From desert scrub, grassland and brushland to oak woodland, pine forests and spruce-fir highlands, even some riparian and wetland areas thrown in for good measure—it's all here, with a multitude of birds to attest to the variety of habitats.

Most of southeastern Arizona's famous birding spots are at their best in May. Madera Canyon (see chapter 21), the most often visited of all birding areas in Arizona and the most highly recommended for those with limited time in the region, has mobs of hummingbirds at the feeders by the Santa Rita Lodge. Look for rarities like the broad-billed and the violet-crowned along with more common sorts. Elf owls are here, as are flammulated owls; painted redstarts, verdin and a trogon or two can also be found. In the lower elevations leading up into the canyon, you will find northern cardinals, pyrrhuloxia, Gambel's quail, Crissal thrashers, rufous-winged sparrows and a multitude of desert scrub birds.

The Patagonia–Sonoita Creek Preserve (see chapter 67), as beautiful and refreshing a place as one can find in Arizona during spring, welcomes many birds to its cottonwood-lined creek in May. Gray hawks are more abundant here than anywhere else in the country during breeding season. More than twenty species of flycatchers and plenty of hummingbirds, summer tanagers, blue herons (nesting in the cottonwoods) and bunches of warblers can be found. For an extra treat, travel approximately 4 miles south on State Road 82 to a roadside stop (past the one with a memorial shrine). Rose-throated becards and thick-billed kingbirds have nested here, leading birders to dub it the most famous roadside area in America.

The Ramsey Canyon Preserve (see chapter 38), world-famous for its hummingbirds, is slightly past its songbird peak in late May, though still worth a visit. Hummingbirds will be buzzing around the many feeders near the cabins. Also keep an eye out for sulphur-bellied flycatchers, painted redstarts and Strickland's woodpeckers. Don't forget about the crowds here, either, or that reservations may be necessary.

In the Chiricahuas at Cave Creek Canyon (see chapter 26), the elegant trogon draws eager birders from around the country. While it vies with Madera, Sonoita Creek, Ramsey and others for the title of best birding spot in Arizona, it is generally a bit less crowded than those other hotspots, which are all much nearer to Tucson. Mexican chickadees are found almost exclusively here, particularly at the Rustler Park–Barfoot Park fork high up the road above the Southwestern Research Station. (See chapter 26 for more information about Cave Creek in May.)

Sabino Canyon (see chapter 19) may be the best place to visit if you only have a few morning hours to spend in the Tucson area. The cottonwood area behind the dam teems with birds in the morning. Look for typical desert scrub species on the walk there, then hummingbirds, flycatchers, orioles, lesser goldfinches, Abert's towhees and the very vocal Bell's vireo near the dam.

San Pedro Riparian National Conservation Area (see chapter 67) is fantastic for thousands of migrating birds as well as nesting gray hawks, an occasional green kingfisher and crissal thrashers. Mount Lemmon (see chapter 54) is always worth investigating for the wide variety of birds to be found in its five life zones, and Catalina State Park (see chapter 14) and the Arizona–Sonora Desert Museum (see chapter 31) are wonderful for desert scrub species. *Birds in Southeastern Arizona,* an essential guidebook by William Davis and Steven Russell, gives detailed information on seventy-two birding hotspots in the area; the detailed *Birder's Guide to Southeastern Arizona* by Harold Holt and James Lane outlines several half-day to two-day loop tours. Get one—or better, both—of these books; for the newcomer they are priceless. Also carry plenty of water, both in your vehicle and on your persons when hiking; wear sturdy footwear and long pants (this is cactus country); use sunscreen and wear your hat; and bring warm clothing for the cool nights. Above all, enjoy. Few places can compare to southeastern Arizona for great birding. "I found myself going back to the same valleys, the same canyons, and the same mountains," Roger Tory Peterson said of the region. After one trip to this birding paradise, you will probably find yourself returning again and again.

JUNE

31

Saguaro Flowering

To most people, just as the Eiffel Tower represents Paris or the Pyramids, Egypt, the stately saguaro cactus is the preeminent symbol of southern Arizona. It dominates vast stretches of the desert across the lower half of the state, its forests of pale green figures creating an eerie and haphazard pattern on the dry land. Alternately imposing and comical, the saguaro is as intriguing as it is omnipresent, inviting awe, respect and even a curious smile at an occasionally uncanny human resemblance. It is impossible to imagine the Sonoran Desert without its signature plant, whose correspondence with the land it blankets is perfect: both are tough, patient, mighty and, increasingly, fragile.

When you stand amid a thick forest of saguaros, it can seem as if the cactus must be among the hardiest, most resilient and most prolific of desert species. There are so many of them! The cactus, though, struggles greatly to reach a significant age. The saguaros we marvel at, the 30- and 40-foot giants, take decades to grow, needing about 15 years just to reach 6 inches and another 20 years to reach 6 feet. In 50 years a saguaro may reach 12 feet, while a 75-year-old may make it up to 20 feet, when it finally grows its first branching arm, a sign of maturity. The tall saguaros that seem to abound are at least 100 years old, and many may be well into the latter half of their second century. The saguaro, which grows to a height of 50 feet and weighs up to 10 tons, is the largest cactus found in the United States.

Clearly, the slow road to maturity is not easy. Saguaros are particularly vulnerable to destruction during their early years, when everything from extreme cold to having its protective ground cover eaten by grazing cattle can kill it. The latter threat was only recognized in the last few decades as contributing to an alarming decline in cacti numbers. If a saguaro can weather its first decade or two, though, its chances of survival are fairly good. But consider this: of the roughly forty million seeds a mature saguaro will produce in its lifetime, perhaps *one* will someday become a saguaro that reaches maturity.

The saguaro is an interesting case study in desert survival. Pleated up and down its cylindrical length to allow for the expansion it undergoes after drinking in the desert's infrequent rains, the cactus is essentially an enormous water storage tank. When a good monsoon rain briefly floods the desert, the saguaro's shallow web of roots sucks up all the moisture that falls in the 30- or 40-foot radius around the cactus. The plant's stem, the tall green cactus, expands, its spongy flesh soaking up and retaining as much as a ton of water a day during heavy rains. Since the 8 or 10 tons of a mature cactus could hardly be supported by the plant's watery flesh, the saguaro has a circle of woodlike "ribs" that run through its length on the inside. This "skeleton," incidentally, is often all that remains after a saguaro has toppled and died, the long sticks lying together on the desert floor like the wreck of some very lost and very small ship. Tohono O'odam Indians, formerly known as the Papagos, have used the sticks for generations for shelter, fences and, ironically, to reach up and knock the saguaro's red fruit from the top of its trunk and arms.

Because the saguaro retains so much water (its prickly spines reduce the water loss that leafy plants are subject to), it flowers annually regardless of drought. The first two weeks of June are usually the time to see the luscious white blossoms at their best. A crown of thick, greenish buds clusters about the tops of the trunk and arms, the yellow-centered, white-petaled flowers bursting out of them after sundown like fragrant stars popping out of the night sky. The flowers wilt by the next afternoon, a cycle that continues for roughly a month. As many as two hundred flowers a year can grow on the ends of a saguaro's arms, attracting bats, birds, moths and honeybees, all of which pollinate the flowers while drinking their nectar.

So lovely is the white blossom of the saguaro that Arizonans have declared it their state flower. But then, the saguaro has always been a popular plant, especially for wildlife. Gila woodpeckers and gilded flickers gouge out little nesting cavities in the cactus's skin, raising their young and then departing. The holes are then taken over by any number of birds, including kestrels, elf owls, purple martins and phainopeplas (and, unfortunately, starlings), which appreciate their new apartments' relative warmth in winter and coolness in summer. Wood rats, lizards and spiders may also inhabit the holes. White-winged doves feast on the seeds of the saguaro fruit; hawks make nests in the forks of the cactus's branches and sit atop the trunk to look for prey. With all its hustle and bustle, the saguaro is a veritable live-in mall.

And finally, while the saguaro's flowering draws us in what we consider to be nearly midyear, the Tohono O'odam so valued the cactus that their calendar was dictated by its cycle, specifically, by the cycle of the fruit it bears. Reddish and seed filled, this fruit, which grows after the flowering ceases, was (and is) highly coveted by native peoples, who ate it fresh, cooked it into a jam, dried it and even made an alcoholic beverage from it. For these people, the new year began when the fruit ripened. If ever a plant dominated the terrain, the wildlife and the people of an area, the saguaro is it.

HOTSPOTS

This one is easy. **Saguaro National Monument** is *the* place to see the magnificent saguaro and its pretty flower. Established in 1933 specifically to protect the saguaro cactus, Saguaro National Monument is similar to places such as Organ Pipe Cactus National Monument and Joshua Tree National Monument in that a type of vegetation led to the creation of a preserve. The east side of the monument, known as the Rincon Mountain District, is the larger of the two districts that make up the national monument and has several trails leading up into the

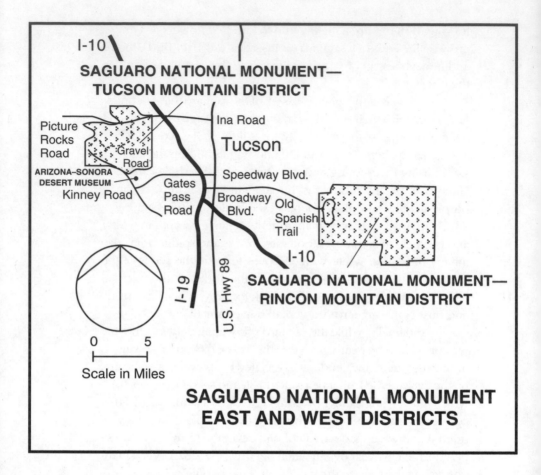

I-10

**SAGUARO NATIONAL MONUMENT—
TUCSON MOUNTAIN DISTRICT**

Picture
Rocks
Road

Gravel
Road

Ina Road

Tucson

ARIZONA–SONORA
DESERT MUSEUM
Kinney Road

Gates
Pass
Road

Speedway Blvd.

Broadway
Blvd.

Old
Spanish
Trail

I-10

I-19

U.S. Hwy 89

**SAGUARO NATIONAL MONUMENT—
RINCON MOUNTAIN DISTRICT**

0   5

Scale in Miles

**SAGUARO NATIONAL MONUMENT
EAST AND WEST DISTRICTS**

rugged Rincon Mountains. An 8-mile loop drive on a paved road takes you through one of the finest saguaro forests extant. Visit this area on a morning at the beginning of June and surround yourself with the sight of thousands of white flowers atop the branches of cacti all around. The loop drive is open from 7:00 A.M. to 5:00 P.M. daily; the visitor center is open from 8:00 A.M. to 5:00 P.M. There is a $3 entrance fee. To reach the Rincon Mountain District, take Broadway Boulevard east out of Tucson for 9 miles. Turn southeast onto Old Spanish Trail and follow it about 5 miles to the visitor center. Here there are books, displays, brochures and helpful rangers.

The west side of Saguaro National Monument, known as the Tucson Mountain District, is smaller and more rugged than the east side. No fee is charged here, you may drive the unpaved loop road any time of day and the saguaros are as thick and plentiful as on the east side and a bit more impressive. The loop drive here is about 6 miles long. There is a visitor center, with some of the same services as at the Rincon Mountain District. To reach the west side, take Speedway Boulevard, which becomes Gates Pass Road, west out of Tucson for 8.5 miles. Go right on Kinney Road (to the left is Old Tucson, a western theme park) and follow the signs 5 miles to the visitor center. You will pass the **Arizona–Sonora Desert Museum** on Kinney Road along the way.

Both the east and west districts are scenic and rugged areas, preserving classic Sonoran Desert habitat and, of course, exceptional stands of saguaro. Desert scrub dominates in the western district; desert scrub rising to pine forests is found in the east. At both, look for cactus wrens, Gila woodpeckers, white-winged doves and elf owls in, on and around the cacti. Remember also that the flowers are generally at their best early in the day.

32

A Sky Full of Bats

Bats inspire an irrational—and unwarranted—fear, accused of everything from spreading disease and diving into human hair to auguring death and sucking the blood from our necks. The truth is entirely different. These winged mammals are docile and beneficial creatures: they pollinate a number of desert plants (including the saguaro) and devour swarms of bothersome and destructive insects, and their droppings have long been used as fertilizer. Perhaps they are so intractably linked with things evil because they are nocturnal creatures and inhabit dim and gloomy places. Or perhaps it's just because they look a bit like flying rats. Whatever the reason, bats have suffered badly in the public relations department.

In the Southwest, the most common bat by far is the Mexican free-tail. With a population in the tens of millions, it is well known for its mass daytime clusterings in caves and its spectacular group departures at dusk when it sets out to hunt insects for the night. A typical free-tail bat can consume nearly a third of its weight in insects, primarily moths but also beetles and ants, each night.

Their method of hunting, indeed of traveling, is one of the bat's most remarkable and well-known characteristics. Instead of maneuvering by sight, bats do so by sound, specifically, echolocation. In what surely must have been a strange series of experiments, English scientists in the late 1700s found that bats who had been blinded could function normally but that deafened ones were all but helpless. By the 1930s, these findings, once scoffed at, were reconfirmed and explained. Bats, it was found, send out ultra-high frequency clicks and beeps through their mouths and noses. These sounds bounce off surrounding objects and are picked up by a bat's sensitive ears, allowing it to determine more about the objects in its environment—their size, shape, motion, even density—than we can with our eyes. Each bat is, in effect, a highly accurate sonar device.

Slow-motion examination of a hunting bat reveals that its apparently erratic flight is a purposeful darting about as it nabs insects. Remarkably, bats capture moths in the thin membranes that form their wings and scoop them into their mouths while in flight. And while bats are the only mammals that fly, their method of doing so, a sort of rapid swimming motion that allows their wings to beat up to twenty times a second, is vastly different from a bird's up-and-down wing flapping.

The Mexican free-tail bats of the Southwest are migratory, whereas bats in most of the rest of the country hibernate during winter. By October they depart for Mexico, only to return by early spring to their favored roosting spots. Here, in caves or hollow trees, packed in at over 250 bats per square foot, they dangle head downward during the day, give birth to their young sometime in June and make their hunting excursions nightly.

HOTSPOTS

Carlsbad Caverns National Park in southeastern New Mexico is not just the home of the wondrous and world-famous underground chambers; it is also the site of one of the most well-known and extraordinary of all wildlife shows in the Southwest: the bat flight. Although it is hardly a quiet or intimate experience—hundreds of people gather nightly in an outdoor amphitheater at the main cavern's entrance to watch the bats depart from the cave—it is undoubtedly among the premier natural spectacles this part of the country has to offer. In fact, it's said that the main cavern at Carlsbad Caverns was discovered when the thick stream of bats that emerged from it was followed back to its source, a big hole in the ground that is now known to stretch several miles in length.

Before World War II, as many as nine million bats were believed to roost in Carlsbad Caverns during the summer, a number now thought to have declined to something less than a million. Still, when the bats begin to stream out of the cave, the sight is staggering. Roused by the approach of dusk, masses of bats depart from their daytime roost, a chamber near the mouth of the main cavern, and head for the cave's entrance. With a loud, buzzing whoosh, swarms of bats circle about just in front of the entranceway, then charge off into the early night, forming a thick, dark river of skittering bats that obscures parts of the sky and can be seen for miles. The most impressive departures are those in which the greatest number of bats depart in the shortest amount of time, ten thousand or more bats per minute, at best. Some nights, for reasons unknown, the bats' emergence is slow and sputtery, taking two hours or more. Regardless, the event is always thrilling.

The bats filter out across the area up to 50 miles in any direction, descending on the Pecos and Black River valleys to consume insects. They return to their cave at dawn, plummeting down into the darkness like living bombs. Just like the sun—and in contrast to much else in nature—the bat flights at Carlsbad Caverns are predictable and reliable. Carlsbad Caverns National Park is reached by taking US 62/180 south from the city of Carlsbad 20 miles to Whites City. From here a well-signed, paved road winds 7 miles through yucca-dotted hills to the Carlsbad Caverns visitor center. There is no entrance fee for the visitor center and no fee to watch the bat flight, though there is a fee to enter the cavern.

If massive crowds aren't to your liking, even for the spectacular show at Carlsbad, travel to **Cave Creek Canyon** (see chapter 26) for a decidedly uncrowded bat show. Take the South Fork (see directions in chapter 26), and at a point about 0.1 mile before coming to the South Fork Forest Camp Picnic Area, look up on the cliffs to the right for a large dark cave with a prominent white rock visible on its floor. Find a spot with a good view through the trees, and at dusk watch the more than quarter of a million Mexican free-tail bats flow out of the cave and disperse.

You are much farther from the action here than at Carlsbad, but the huge number of bats compares favorably to the more well-known flight at the caverns. Besides, so few people know about the bats at Cave Creek, you may have the place all to yourself.

One other spot, which combines the proximity of Carlsbad with the elbow room of Cave Creek, is the bat cave at **El Malpais National Monument** in northwestern New Mexico. El Malpais, "the Badlands," is a fascinating region of blackened lava fields, ice caves, sandstone cliffs and arches and dense forests. The east side of El Malpais, reached by taking State Road 117 south from I-40 7 miles east of the town of Grants, skirts the edge of an enormous lava flow area. An overlook known as Sandstone Bluffs lies 10 miles south on State Road 117, and 8 miles south of this is La Ventana arch, a huge sandstone rainbow. But it is on the equally fascinating west side of El Malpais that the bats can be found. To reach the area, take State Road 53 south from Grants and follow it for 19.5 miles to a sign indicating "El Calderon" to the left. Drive 0.3 mile on a gravel road to reach a parking area. Lava fields, ice caves or "tubes," aspen, pine, sandstone—all are found in this region. Take the marked trail roughly 0.5 mile through rugged juniper–piñon land (the long Junction Cave is right next to the parking area) to reach the clearly marked lava cave that serves as a Mexican free-tail bat home during spring and summer. An interpretive sign is near the cave, and the best viewing is just west of it. Do not get too close or try to enter the cave. At dusk, watch as up to twenty-five thousand bats depart right in front of you, fewer than at either of the two other listed spots but just as thrilling. For some time now, the Bureau of Land Management has been offering interpretive talks at the cave on Saturday evenings. Call ahead (see the appendix) for specific details.

33

Northeastern Colorado's Grassland Birds

The short-grass prairie lands of eastern Colorado and New Mexico—the high plains—are more lifeless and monotonous than much of the Southwest's desert regions. Uninviting wastelands these prairies seem, best left alone to bake in the early summer sun. Northeastern Colorado, in particular, appears to be midway between remote and nowhere: it is overwhelmingly desolate and imposing at first glance. But if the region encompassed by the Pawnee National Grassland in this portion of the state is visited at the right time, it bristles with life. The number of grassland birds that come to nest here just as summer begins is mind-boggling, constituting what is acknowledged to be one of the most concentrated gatherings of nesting birds on the planet. If your image of the high plains has been shaped by old western movies and maps showing minuscule towns connected by ridiculously straight lines, the birds to be found here in June may make you realize what a treasure you have overlooked.

Over seventy million years ago, the grasses now characteristic of plains throughout the world first evolved, proving so successful that today they cover one-fourth of the earth's land surface. In terms of moisture received, grasslands lie somewhere between the humid forests and the dry deserts, though the short-grass prairie of northeastern Colorado is noted for receiving much less moisture than most other prairie regions. North America's natural grasslands are almost totally gone, of course, victims of agricultural expansion that, while demanded by a growing country, wiped out millions of years of evolution in a few short generations.

The wide-open spaces characteristic of grasslands have created some of the largest mass gatherings of animals ever seen by humans. The bison that used to number in the tens of millions just a century and a half ago are a prime example of this, as are the herds of pronghorn or the sprawling prairie dog towns found today. The ability to communicate easily and quickly, to move or take cover from sweeping fires or lurking predators, to not be singled out in the broad expanse of the prairie, has made wildlife here among the most sociable and widespread anywhere. Speed (the pronghorn is the fastest animal in the Western Hemisphere) and burrowing ability are common on the plains: here it is best to be able to outrun a predator or duck away from it.

Birds flock on the plains in enormous numbers, filling the air, calling from fence posts or high overhead, strutting on the ground. Horned larks, house finches, chestnut-collared longspurs, McCown's longspurs, lark buntings, mourning doves, phoebes, mountain plovers, swallows and sparrows flourish here, bringing the prairie to life with a wild frenzy of activity. Their calls seem to carry more clearly across the unobstructed landscape, as mating songs are performed in midair (there are few trees here) and nests are made—on the ground, of course. Raptors abound in numbers that have made northeastern Colorado famous nationwide. Rodents and small birds are sought by a variety of impressive hunters, including golden eagles, ferruginous hawks, Swainson's hawks, prairie falcons, great horned owls, red-tailed hawks and shrikes. The open spaces favor these birds—and the birders who make the trek to see the wildlife.

HOTSPOTS

Pawnee National Grassland is a spectacular bird-watching spot that is somewhat overlooked because of its remoteness. Despite the allure it holds for some, most people believe the area is a bit on the dull side. June is the best month. Any earlier than that and the roads may still be muddy; any later and the land will be hot and lifeless. The established grassland area sprawls across nearly 1,800 square miles, though about three-fourths of that land is private. While plains dominate the region, there are some creeks and potholes, some cottonwood groves, rocky cliffs and an interesting and popular butte area. Bring plenty of water, sunscreen, long pants and a full tank of gas.

It would be sufficient merely to point a birder in the direction of Pawnee and recommend driving on any road in any direction. The birding is good almost anywhere. Your best bet, though, is to visit the Pawnee National Grassland Headquarters at 2009 9th Street in the town of Greeley and pick up a map of the area and the fine brochure entitled "Birding on the Pawnee by Automobile or Mountain Bike." Bird lists are also available. It is highly recommended that anyone visiting Pawnee National Grassland stop by this office or at least obtain a brochure through the mail before traveling to the area. Many roads crisscross the region, much of the land is private and some roads may be impassable if there have been rains.

The basic route through the Pawnee is to begin at Crow Valley Recreation Area just north of the town of Briggsdale (roughly 35 miles northeast of Greeley) on County Road 77. Take 77 north for 3 miles, turn west onto County Road 96 and follow it for 4 miles. Turn north onto County Road 69 and travel for 4 miles, then turn west onto County Road 104 and continue on it for 6 miles. Here turn south onto County Road 57, take it for 4 miles, turn east onto County Road 96 for 2 miles, then turn south on County Road 61, which, after 3 miles, hits State Road 14. Eight miles east on 14 lies Briggsdale. This 35-mile loop, all on dirt and gravel roads, deserves a good three hours or more to cover well. At Crow Valley you may see great numbers of orioles, warblers, kingbirds, sparrows and more in the riparian area in the campground. Shrikes and kestrels dot the telephone wires and fences along County Road 77. Mountain plovers, long-billed curlews, larks, sparrows and longspurs can be found along County Roads 77, 96, 69 and 104. Raptors are good everywhere. Burrowing owls can be seen in the prairie dog towns near a windmill to the east at a turnoff 0.5 mile before County Road 69 hits 104.

This route is the one recommended by the Forest Service. Of course, you may drive any road you like as long as you don't trespass on private property. Another good nearby spot in Pawnee is known as Pawnee Buttes. Two massive sandstone towers, nearly 300 feet tall, loom high over the prairie, attracting prairie falcons, ferruginous hawks and golden eagles to their craggy faces. To reach the buttes, head out of Briggsdale on County Road 77 just as you did for the loop tour but continue 15.2 miles to County Road 120. Take a right here, travel 5.8 miles to County Road 87, and you will reach the small community of Grover. From here travel south on County Road 390 for 6 miles, turn east on County Road 112 for 8.3 miles, then look for a sign for Road 685 to the left. This leads to the buttes overlook. This route is known as the Pawnee Pioneer Trails Scenic and Historic Byway and is considered the most interesting route to the buttes.

One important word of warning: birds are easily stressed here and will abandon their nests if frightened off. Use binoculars to observe all birds. By approaching within even 300 yards of certain species, you may cause a nesting bird to temporarily leave its nest—thus leaving the eggs exposed to damaging temperatures—or permanently abandon it.

34

Yucca in Bloom

If you drive across certain southern New Mexico roads in early June, before long a strange sight begins to appear—over and over and over again. Shaggy, tough-looking little trees, like stubby palms, suddenly are everywhere. Atop each of them, shooting up from their green heads like tall, fleshy horns, stands a single graceful stalk adorned with clusters of what seems to be petaled snow. This is the soaptree yucca, bolder than the colorful desert wildflowers and more delicate than the hardy cactus blossoms.

The soaptree is most common in regions of the Chihuahuan Desert, though it can also be found in grassland areas and the Sonoran Desert. It is a short tree, with a stout trunk and a few branches. The stalk it sends up in spring may reach 15 or 20 feet into the air, however, and can become so heavy with flowers, it bends like some overburdened sapling. Its leaves—the yucca or palmlike part—are long, narrow spikes that slowly die and then form a sort of coat on the tree's trunk.

The flowers are the soaptree's glory. They burst out in creamy gobs along the upper portion of the yucca's long stalk, white flags of blossoms that sway in the breeze above an otherwise drab landscape, and then are pollinated by moths from May through July. While the flowers can be eaten raw or cooked—yucca salads are served in some southwestern restaurants—other parts of the plant are more frequently used. The fibers from the leaves were and are woven into baskets by many native peoples, and parts of the roots may be used as soaps and shampoos, something body-care companies have recently rediscovered.

The soaptree yucca may be the most famous of the yucca plants (it is New Mexico's state flower), but it has many related species and even a few popular lookalikes that often get confused with it. One, the lechuguilla, is actually an agave and, much like the Joshua tree in the Mojave, sagebrush in the Great Basin and the saguaro in the Sonoran, serves as the prime indicator of its desert. Agaves are related to yuccas and both store water in their leaves, but the former have thicker leaves and, with no trunk, grow on the ground. One agave in particular, the century plant, is worthy of mention not only because it may be found in some of the same areas as the soaptree yucca but because it is especially intriguing. While it doesn't take nearly as long to bloom as its name would indicate, it may take anywhere from one to two decades or more for the plant to blossom. It sends up a very thick stalk from out of its spread of tough leaves and then, in a fury of growth, throws all the strength and moisture it can gather into producing its thick reddish-yellow flowers. The stalk, as tall as 18 feet, stands like an enormous candelabrum, with jutting bunches of flowers sticking out and upward from it like low flames. Its energy expended in one dramatic flowering, the century plant dies. Yuccas bloom year after year, less urgently, more delicately. You need only drive south to discover them for yourself.

HOTSPOTS

If you drive I-10 in southwestern New Mexico, you will see plenty of soaptree yucca, particularly around Deming and Las Cruces. You could get off at a rest area and try to examine a tree or two, but for the best viewing, get off the interstate and head for the thicker and more accessible yucca stands.

The most unusual soaptrees are found at **White Sands National Monument** (see chapter 24), one of the unlikeliest places to find vegetation of any sort. Any plant that can survive in the shifting gypsum sand at White Sands must be able to grow quickly to avoid being submerged. The soaptrees on the dunes can grow more than a foot a year, keeping their heads above ground level, with their trunks a good 30 or 40 feet below the sand. As opposed to the soaptrees more commonly seen in New Mexico, the ones at White Sands have trunks that effectively stand 10 yards high, albeit mostly hidden underground. The green leaves still spread, and the stalks still flower; the plant has simply adapted to harsh conditions by growing very rapidly. A white flowering yucca above the pure white of the dunes at this monument is an eerie sight. Take the Heart of the Sands drive (again, see chapter 24) at least 3 or 4 miles into the monument and look for yucca on the dunes that have vegetation.

Several roads in southeastern and southwestern New Mexico offer access to the very best stands of soaptree yucca and agaves. The drive into **Carlsbad Caverns** (see chapter 32) on State Road 7 out of Whites City is great for both and could be combined with a trip to see the bat flight. There are several turnoffs and parking areas with trails along this 7-mile drive. Ocotillo and prickly pear cactus can also be seen here.

In the town of Carlsbad, the grounds of **Living Desert State Park** have abundant desert plants, including a number of blooming yuccas and a few century plants. This state park also has wonderful wildlife displays, something on the order of Tucson's Arizona–Sonora Desert Museum. Animals and plants representing New Mexico's Chihuahuan Desert areas are numerous here, in what is a combination zoological-botanical preserve and native desert. The short drive up to the state park also offers the opportunity to see yuccas and agaves as well as scores of other desert plants. For an introduction to Chihuahuan Desert vegetation, no place is better. To reach Living Desert State Park, turn west off US 285 at about 1 mile south of the northern edge of the city limits (if approaching from the south, this turnoff is 3.2 miles past the Eddy County Courthouse as you drive north on US 285 through the middle of Carlsbad). The road to the park is clearly marked and ascends in 1.1 miles to the parking area. The view from the top is superb.

North of Carlsbad about 35 miles lies the town of Artesia. Take US 82 west out of this town and drive through one of the best yucca stands in the state. Soaptrees in full bloom stretch in all directions along the first 20 miles of this drive, particularly 5 to 18 miles outside of Artesia. Few soaptree forests are this dense and expansive. Look for white-winged doves flitting about, and if you continue toward the lush Sacramento Mountains, you can see a few isolated stands of century plants.

State Road 80 south out of Road Forks (see chapter 26) has yucca stands nearly as thick as those near Artesia. They may be in bloom as you drive to Cave Creek Canyon to see the trogon (see chapter 26).

Northeast of here, State Road 90, the road between Lordsburg and Silver City, has equally extensive stands along its first 12 miles before climbing up into the Gila National Forest. To reach it, head north and then northwest on State Road 90 from Lordsburg, and after about 3 miles, you will reach a vast expanse of soaptrees that continues for the next 10 miles.

35

June
Shorttakes

Beavers

Frisky beavers can be active throughout the year, though mated pairs and their young are generally most visible by their dam lodges at dusk and dawn in summer (four or five kits are born by about mid-June). **Golden Gate Canyon State Park** (see chapter 8) has viewing sites along Ralston Creek. Other good beaver spots in Colorado include **Shadow Mountain Lake** and **Sugarloaf Campground**, both in the north central part of the state. At Shadow Mountain Lake, just west of Rocky Mountain National Park, the best place for beavers is at the Pine Beach Picnic Area. Look for beaver dams and the critters themselves, morning and evening, in particular. The lake is right off US 34 north of the town of Granby. The Sugarloaf Campground, which has plenty of beaver along the Williams Fork River, has a boardwalk that allows a visitor to walk through the marshes and ponds. Viewing areas and interpretive signs make this an outstanding and accessible viewing spot. It is reached by taking County Road 3 south out of Parshall, east of Kremmling (see chapter 57) on US 40. Take County Road 3 for 15 miles until it becomes Forest Road 138, then continue 9 more miles to the campground.

An osprey, perched in a tree, surveys its territory. Since osprey feed almost exclusively on fish, they need to live near water.

Osprey

These fish-eating birds of prey, impressive as they glide over open water, hunt at **Pine Beach** (see above) and can also be easily seen at **Big Creek Lakes** in north central Colorado. To reach the area, which is surrounded by conifer forest, take County Road 6W west out of Cowdrey (north of Walden on State Road 125; see chapter 13) 17 miles as it eventually veers north. Then turn left onto County Road 6A, following it for 6 miles as it becomes Forest Road 600 and then Forest Road 660.

36

Breakout: The Desert at Night

Midday in a summer desert is about as bad as it gets. From a wildlife standpoint, there is virtually nothing about—no birds, no reptiles, no mammals. And from a level-of-comfort standpoint, a bath in scalding water might prove more relaxing: the desert's temperature may be well above the century mark, the air is dry and the sun pulses in the sky with an intensity up to three times greater than in most other parts of the country. Go inside, visit a swimming pool, find a seat in a movie theater and come back out again after dark when the desert comes alive.

Like downtown nightclubs, summer deserts only get active after the sun sets. Most animals, reptiles and mammals in particular, simply aren't equipped to handle the extremes of temperature that torment the desert during the day. They retreat to holes and burrows and shady places to conserve moisture and keep their body temperatures down. Not only is it hot in the desert but the low humidity and generally nonexistent cloud cover mean that the heat intensifies throughout the day: ground-surface temperatures can be anywhere from 10 to 30 degrees (or more) higher than air temperatures. These same conditions that allow the desert to heat up so thoroughly during the day, however, also allow it to cool down considerably at night. Unlike more humid regions where temperatures aren't so prone to fluctuations, deserts radiate virtually all of their daytime heat back into the atmosphere, bringing temperatures down and night creatures out.

Snakes are among the most abundant—and feared—of the desert's nocturnal inhabitants. Look for a variety of rattlers and bull snakes if you plan to hike through desert land at night. While this may strike some as a bad idea, snakes—and almost every other animal—avoid humans. Just walk slowly, watch where you place your feet and wear boots and jeans—a good idea in cactus country anyway. Snakes show a marvelous adaptation to hot, dry land. Though deaf, many have an acute sense of smell (the darting forked tongue of certain reptiles is their way of detecting odors in the air) and can sense warm, living objects in their environment. The "pit vipers," or rattlesnakes, are called such because of the tiny holes or pits they have between each eye and nostril that can detect the body temperature of potential prey. In the dark, even with the poor eyesight many snakes have, their other fine senses make them deadly. Also look for the sidewinder in drier areas. Its distinctive J-shaped track results from its curious side-to-side style of locomotion.

Other reptiles you might find, depending on where you are and what the weather has been like, include the desert tortoise, gecko and Gila monster, best seen on wet, warm nights. Wildlife in general is more easily seen on those nights following rains. Many reptiles gorge on the insects that emerge from wet ground, frogs and toads become amorous and many plants go through growth spurts. Yuccas and agaves may send up flowering stalks at night after a rain, and the flowers of the saguaro and the fabulous night-blooming cereus open after dusk. The fragrant cereus, whose bloom may open before your eyes, is visited by the hawkmoth for nocturnal pollination; the white yucca moth does the same for the yucca.

The noises one hears in the desert at night are both spooky and fascinating: the eerie whistles, screeches and hoots of owls; the repeated chant of the whip-poor-will; the countless taps and rustlings and gruntings of creatures seeking protection or prey or mates. If something is zigzagging and flitting through the air, it's probably a bat; a darting through the grass may be a deer mouse; a leaping in grass or shrubs is most likely a rabbit or one of the ubiquitous kangaroo rats or pocket mice. A ghostly, near-silent something on the wing? Almost certainly an owl. A slithering, coiling on the ground? Snake! The desert is alive at night.

Mammals, far more active after dark than during the sweltering desert day, often turn up as a pair of glistening, curious eyes in the beam of your flashlight (which also sends most of them scurrying). The kit fox is frequently found hunting at night, while coyotes, badgers, deer, javelinas, bobcats, ring-tailed cats and the coatimundi, a relative of the raccoon, can be seen if you are patient. Skunks are often seen plodding along a path in the desert—and more frequently squished on the highway. For some reason these critters seem to dominate the roadkill statistics. It need hardly be added that if a skunk raises his tail while eyeing you, the time is ripe for departing—quickly. Sturdy boots won't protect you in this instance.

Because darkness—true darkness, the darkness of the outdoors—is foreign and frightening to most of us, the idea of tramping through the desert at night (not to mention the lurking creatures it hides) may be intriguing but undesirable. But there is more light than one would expect in the open desert. Moonlight, particularly around the time of a full moon, can be exceptionally illuminating. You can even read your field guide with it. Give your eyes time to adjust, too. The human eye can make out plenty of things in the dark if given at least 45 minutes away from a source of artificial light. Take a flashlight with you, tie it to your jacket so you don't drop it and tape some kind of red plastic over the top. This way the bright yellow light from it won't wipe out your patiently won night vision, and most animals will hardly even notice it. They will notice you, though, if you make a lot of noise or are overly panicky. Animals can sense fear and will avoid its source. Remain still, and remain calm. You needn't hike miles to see wildlife, and you needn't fear for your safety if you use common sense. (Refer to chapter 7 for desert safety tips.)

Still, if the idea of hiking at night doesn't appeal to you, stay in your car and drive along any lightly traveled desert road. This is an excellent and safe way to see wildlife, especially snakes, which seek the warmth of blacktop roads at night. Tarantulas and rabbits are frequently seen along roads, as are plenty of the creatures already mentioned. As with any desert travel, in a vehicle or on foot, take plenty of water, bring your flashlight and don't wander off too far if you have a poor sense of direction. A drive at night is a great introduction to desert land and a real eye-opener to the bustling nocturnal world.

JULY

37

The Night-blooming Cereus

Like a character from some bittersweet fairy tale, the flower known as the night-blooming cereus leads one of the briefest and most beautiful of all lives, blooming spectacularly after dusk on a midsummer's night only to fade by daylight the next morning. Its fleeting and fragrant existence makes it the most eagerly anticipated blossoming plant in the desert. "Cereus parties" are held in backyard gardens to celebrate the annual display of Arizona's "Reina de la Nocha," Queen of the Night.

The night-blooming cereus is yet another example of the amazing adaptive powers of desert plants. As with many other cacti, the night-blooming cereus plant stores its own water, waits for a stimulating rain, then blooms quickly in an attempt to attract insects that will pollinate it. In the case of the cereus, it is the hawkmoth, an insect so large it is occasionally mistaken for a hummingbird (its flight pattern is like that of a hummingbird), that is the primary agent of pollination. Drawn to the waxy white flowers, the hawkmoth uses its long tongue to suck nectar from the cereus, coating itself with pollen in the process. When it moves on to drink from another flower, it coats the second bloom with pollen, unwittingly aiding the cereus's reproductive cycle while feeding itself.

Other night-flying insects are also attracted to the cereus, whose rich, heavy perfume sweetens the air—overly sweetens the air, according to some noses—more than 30 yards from the flower. The buds open spasmodically and quickly in early evening, with anywhere from two or three to twenty or more flowers unfolding on a single plant when the proper conditions converge for but a single night in late June or, more likely, early July. And because most cereus plants are stimulated uniformly, it is not uncommon for all cereus plants in a given area to bloom together.

The flower is a fleshy white, with many petals and a halo of stamens that rise like strands of thread from the flower's center. It is nearly half a foot long and just shiny enough, some say, to reflect the light of the moon and the stars. Soon after the following morning's dawn the flower wilts and dies, not to be seen again for another year.

What is so odd about the Queen of the Night's brief annual appearance is that she is bred in the humblest and most inconspicuous of homes. The stems on which she grows appear so gray and lifeless that they could easily be mistaken for withered branches. The plant generally grows intertwined with a creosote bush or some other desert shrub, almost totally hidden by the larger plant and nearly invisible to all but the most trained eyes. At 2 to 5 feet tall, the twiggy-looking cactus known as *Cereus greggii*, with its few stems and feeble spines, seems all but dead. And then, like Cinderella, the night-blooming cereus escapes her drab dwelling and reveals her true beauty.

As with most desert plants, there is a bit more to the cereus than meets the eye. Beneath the ground, the plant has an enormous lump of a root that can hold as much as 80 pounds of water. More typically the root holds 10 or 15 pounds of moisture to sustain the plant through times of drought. Native peoples would dig up the root when water was scarce, though nowadays it is illegal to disturb a cereus in the wild—if you can find one. The Queen of the Night is nearly impossible to discover, too preoccupied, one might suppose, in making certain she is at her most radiant for her one-night outing.

HOTSPOTS

For a flower that's immobile, fixed, rooted, not going anywhere, the night-blooming cereus is extremely difficult to locate. In fact, of all the attractions listed in this book, the night-blooming cereus may be the most difficult to see. While it is certainly possible for a knowledgeable naturalist to locate a cereus in the wild, the best suggestion I can make is to seek out an established botanical garden. The best for the night-blooming cereus is the **Desert Botanical Garden** in Phoenix (see the appendix). This desert preserve has a fine cereus collection and offers an outstanding range of summer programs with titles such as "Moonlight Desert Discovery Experience" and "Taste of the Desert Sunrise Tour." A simple call to the office will let you know if the cereus is about to bloom. The hours—7:00 A.M. to 10:00 P.M.—make it possible to admire the flower. If you want to see the cereus in bloom and you aren't good friends with a backyard gardener or a knowledgeable botanist, the Desert Botanical Garden isn't merely your best bet for locating the cereus; it's probably your only bet.

38

Hummingbirds

"The hummingbird," wrote an English visitor to the American colonies in 1634, "is one of the wonders of the country, being no bigger than a hornet, yet hath all the dimensions of a bird, as bill, and wings, with quills, spider-like legs, small claws: for color she is as glorious as the rainbow." Found only in the New World, the hummingbird, the world's smallest bird, was a strange sight to early American settlers in the East, who generally were treated to only a single species, the ruby-throated. The West, nearer the tropics, is regularly visited by fifteen of the world's more than three hundred species of hummingbirds, and while the sight of one no longer elicits meditations on the rare and marvelous, it is always exciting. No other bird is so zealously sought after by backyard birders, who adorn their trees with vials of sugar water just to attract them. Instantly recognizable and equipped with the most unusual and most rapidly moving wings to be found, hummers remain the one bird nearly everyone delights in.

Hummingbirds are found virtually anywhere in the Western Hemisphere where there are flowers, from deserts and plains to mountains and forests. Because they are primarily creatures of the equatorial regions, it is more common to encounter them in southern latitudes, though summer finds them as far north as southern Canada and abundant in some northern states. Arizona is the best place in the United States to find hummingbirds; the climate and terrain of the state's southeastern corner provide ideal nesting habitat for eleven species. Madera Canyon alone has been visited by all fifteen of the West's hummingbird species at one time or another.

While hummingbirds are among the most readily identifiable of all birds—tiny, brightly colored body; needlelike bill; blur of wings—the enormous amounts of energy they consume and expend are equally noteworthy, if less well known. The average hummingbird has a metabolic rate roughly one hundred times greater than an average human's and a heart rate of about 1,200 beats per minute. If a slightly larger than average-sized human male led as lively an existence as a hummingbird, he would have to consume more than 150,000 calories a day and drink enough fluids to offset losing nearly 25,000 pounds of sweat daily! Hummingbirds fuel themselves by consuming half their own body weight in sugars each day, feeding on flower nectar up to six times an hour.

Much of the energy a hummingbird takes in is devoted to powering its wings. As anyone who has ever seen a hummingbird knows, its wings are a mere buzzing haze, beating more than fifty times a second in many species and allowing the bird to hover, keep its body still in midair and fly straight up, straight down and sideways. When a hummingbird hovers, its wings describe a sort of horizontal figure eight, rotating and flipping over at the top of the figure eight so that each wing's front edge slices the air going both forward and backward. The muscles that power a hummingbird's wings account for one-fourth of the bird's weight. With so great an emphasis on its wings, a hummingbird's legs are almost an afterthought, used almost entirely for perching and not for walking.

For all its structural uniqueness, however, and the darting grace of its flight, the hummingbird's primary beauty lies in its rich coloration. Bright patches of green and red and purple and blue glimmer on the hummingbird's body; males have an iridescent throat patch, called a gorget, that sparkles brilliantly when sunlight strikes it at certain angles. These throat feathers are noteworthy because their iridescence derives from the structure of the feathers themselves, not their pigment. It is the difference between, say, the color one sees in a rainbow and the color of a shirt. To male hummingbirds, these scientific details are of no concern. They use their gorget as a means of display, swooping about in front of prospective mates while flashing their alluring hues. They appear to be, as John James Audubon wrote, "glittering fragments of the rainbow, ... lovely little creatures moving on humming winglets through the air, suspended as if by magic."

HOTSPOTS

The best area to find hummingbirds in midsummer is southeastern Arizona. Among the most common hummingbirds found in July in Arizona are the broad-billed, with its greenish body and forked tail; the blue-throated, whose "seep-seep" call and relatively large size (at more than 5 inches it is bigger than most other American hummingbirds) are distinctive; the black-chinned, with its dark gorget and wide western distribution; the magnificent, whose dazzling colors and relatively slow wing beat help to identify it; and the broad-tailed, whose most distinctive trait is its loud, whistling wing beat. The black-chinned, in fact, has been unofficially designated the "summer hummingbird" in Tucson because it is so common. Remember, of course, that hummingbirds are drawn to flowers, using their long tongues to suck nectar from the blooms into which they have dipped their bills. Hummingbirds seem also to be very attracted to the color red and often approach humans very closely. Curious and seemingly friendly (though a hummer defending a nest will viciously dart and stab at far larger birds), hummingbirds apparently have little fear of being harmed by larger creatures. Their speed and maneuverability make them as uncatchable as the proverbial greased pig.

Of all the places frequented by hummingbirds in Arizona during summer, the most renowned is the Nature Conservancy–owned **Ramsey Canyon Preserve** in the Huachuca Mountains, about 90 miles southeast of Tucson. Few birders are unaware of Ramsey Canyon, a lush, scenic area with a perennial stream, abundant wildlife and pine–fir forest. Sycamores and maples shade Ramsey Creek, while songbirds abound.

Unfortunately, Ramsey Canyon is, like many other birding spots in Arizona, being loved to death. For such a small area—less than 300 acres—Ramsey Canyon is visited by over thirty thousand people a year, making it one of the most heavily used birding areas in the Southwest. The Nature Conservancy's official regulations concerning Ramsey Canyon are as follows: visitor hours are 8:00 A.M. to 5:00 P.M. daily; preserve capacity is very limited—parking reservations are required for weekend and holiday visits, and weekday parking is on a space-available basis only; group visits require prior arrangements; no buses, trailers or large RVs; all visitors who are not members of the Nature Conservancy are asked to consider making a $3 donation; day visitors must obtain trail permits in the bookstore before walking. This should not deter you. Simply come early on a weekday and enjoy. The trail along Ramsey Creek, a 0.5-mile-plus loop, is outstanding for riparian species, while the longer Hamburg Trail leads to a great forest overlook and may bring sightings of white-tailed deer and a variety of birds. The feeders at Mile-Hi Reserve, though, are the big draw for the hummingbirds and the people who want to see them. The Mile Hi, with its six cozy cabins and fine bookstore, serves as the headquarters for the Nature Conservancy at Ramsey Canyon Preserve. As many as a dozen different types of hummingbirds may be seen feeding here as July wears on, including less common species such as the white-eared and violet-crowned. Despite its sometimes crushing popularity, Ramsey Canyon is a deservedly great birding spot, and its beauty rivals that of any of the other popular sky island canyons to be found in southeastern Arizona. To reach Ramsey Canyon, head south out of the town of Sierra Vista on State Road 92 for 6.1 miles, then turn west on Ramsey Canyon Road and travel 3.8 miles to the parking area at Mile Hi.

The feeders near the Santa Rita Lodge in **Madera Canyon** (see chapter 21) are every bit as productive as the ones at Mile Hi. Hummingbirds swarm here throughout summer. Although Madera can also get fairly swamped with visitors, it is often a good alternative to Ramsey Canyon on a weekend, though Sundays may be crowded. The best option of all is to find a way to visit both Madera Canyon and Ramsey Canyon on weekdays.

One other spot, mentioned hesitantly because it is not truly a natural area, is the hummingbird aviary at the **Arizona–Sonora Desert Museum** (see chapter 31). This is a remarkable walk-in enclosure in a uniformly remarkable zoo museum. As many as ten species of hummingbirds dart all about you as you walk through the small building in which they nest, feed and display. It is the best chance most people will ever have to view so many hummingbirds in such close quarters, as the tiny birds swoop about and occasionally move within inches of one's shirt or hat. Young children get positively giddy in the place, and even those who prefer their wildlife completely wild can get lost admiring the dazzling little birds.

39

Summer Flowers of the Rocky Mountains

After the bitter cold chill of a Rocky Mountain winter has passed and the blankets of snow have faded from the meadows and forests, even the brisk mountain air seems ready to burst into color. So ripe and anticipatory does this whole high land become after its winter slumber that when it finally awakens—when columbines, paintbrush, lupines, lilies and scores more explode in lush, full bloom—it seems the entire mountain world might join in. And just as in the desert in spring (see chapters 9 and 15), when the land turns from brown to neon bright, the wildflowers that sprinkle and splash across the Southwest's high country can be literally breathtaking.

Mountain wildflowers are at their best from June through August, with many peaking in July, roughly a three-month shift forward from peak bloom season in the desert. Although wildflowers in the Rockies can be elusive at times (but not as difficult to find as Sonoran Desert blooms), they are more predictable than their desert cousins. Whereas the location of goldpoppies and lupines in southern Arizona depends almost completely on rainfall and temperature, the type of wildflowers one encounters in the Rockies depends largely on elevation and soil.

From the small monument at the Four Corners, that point where Utah, Colorado, New Mexico and Arizona meet, it is possible to drive on paved highways roughly two hours to the northwest and rise from an elevation of about 4,500 feet to nearly 11,000 feet. Thus, beginning amid piñon and juniper, one ascends through bands of scrub oak and ponderosa pine, Douglas fir and aspen, and then subalpine fir and spruce until reaching nearly timberline. The montane forests of the Rocky Mountains, that region roughly between the lower grasslands and the subalpine forests, are the best wildflower areas. These forests of ponderosa pine, Douglas fir, lodgepole pine and aspen are found on all of the major mountain ranges in Colorado and northern New Mexico, as well as mountainous regions of Utah and Arizona. At an elevation of roughly 6,000 to 9,000 feet, montane forests avoid the extreme cold that lies above and the periods of drought that lie below, and the associated wildflowers are delightful.

In areas dominated by ponderosa pine, look for the yellow sulphur flower and one-sided penstemon, whose lavender flowers grow along just a single side of the plant's stalk. Lodgepole pine forests may turn up lovely bloomers like fairy-slipper orchids or heartleaf arnica, though both tend to be early summer bloomers. And in aspen forests, where wildflowers may be particularly abundant, look for the sego lily (Utah's state flower), the Colorado blue columbine (Colorado's state flower), the perky lavender and yellow showy daisy, the common wild geranium and the delicate, nodding meadowrue. It is in the meadows, though, those gently swaying, brightly painted fields, where the finest blooms are found, their names rolling off the tongue with a sort of poetic grace: scarlet paintbrush, trumpet gilia, whiskbroom parsley, penstemon and orange sneezeweed abound in the drier meadow areas, while fringed gentian and the abundant and wondrously pink western shooting star are more often found in wet meadows. Think of a mountain wildflower scene, and more than likely some of these species are populating the meadow in your mind's eye.

One of the nice things about wildflower hunting in the Rockies and nearby areas is that every change in elevation and location can bring about wonderfully different populations of flowers to discover, and the scenery is spectacular. From Hovenweep National Monument, say, along the Utah–Colorado border, where four o'clocks and sunflowers bloom, up into the Rio Grande

National Forest, where columbine, shooting star, lupine, aster and gilia abound, or the San Juan National Forest, which has everything from alpine tundra flowers to lower montane species, the Rockies have blooms in a startling variety of size, shape and color. July, when the passes are clear of snow and the meadows are fresh with color, is the time to visit.

HOTSPOTS

Of all the great wildflower spots in Colorado, the one that will be found near the top of almost any list is **Yankee Boy Basin**. Tucked deep in the mountains just southwest of the town of Ouray, this area is famous for its fields of columbine and paintbrush; and while the drive up into the basin is scenic and rich in history (old mines and townsites dot the slopes), its ruggedness presents a bit of a challenge for those seeking the meadows above. Start just south of Ouray at County Road 361, also known as the Camp Bird Road, just off US 550. This is the same turnoff to Box Canyon Falls, an attraction in its own right. Drive through aspen and pine, cross Canyon Creek at 1.9 miles and travel along a couple of steep ledges at the 3- and 4-mile marks. At 4.8 miles above US 550, stay right at a signed fork in the road. The large Camp Bird Mine is to the left. From here up, the road gets progressively rougher; a four-wheel-drive vehicle becomes a necessity, and jeep rentals are available in Ouray. Another fork lies 1.3 miles beyond, with Imogene Pass to the left. Stay to the right and forge on past the ghost town of Sneffels a quarter-mile ahead, then stay to the right at yet another fork 0.6 mile past Sneffels. The last mile up to Yankee Boy Basin is the steepest and roughest of all, and many people park near this last fork and walk the final stretch of road. However you get there, by the time you reach the basin, you will be surrounded not only by acres of brilliant wildflowers but also by tall spruce and magnificent snow-draped ridges and peaks, Mount Sneffels to the north in particular. This is a spectacular and scenic area, and the sheer magnificence of its wildflower spreads cannot be overstated. Photographers and wildflower lovers come from all parts of the country to enjoy the lupine, primrose and wild iris in Yankee Boy Basin. If you don't mind a little bit of rough road and perhaps a bit of a hike, the best wildflower show in the Rockies awaits in the San Juan Mountains.

The San Juans contain what is considered the most ideal montane forest in the entire southern Rockies. Situated just enough to the west to receive winter storms from the Pacific and just enough to the south to receive summer rains from the Gulf of California, the lush San Juan Mountains feature luxuriant wild-flower fields. If the drive up to Yankee Boy Basin is too intimidating, try portions of the **San Juan Skyway** (see chapter 55) for good meadow access.

Farther north and east, **Mount Evans** (see chapter 42) offers wonderful tundra flowers, especially along the 4- or 5-mile stretch below Summit Lake. The most spectacular tundra of all, though, is found in **Rocky Mountain National Park** (see chapter 49), where a rich diversity of wildflowers can also be found in the meadows and glades below. One of the nicest things about hunting for wildflowers in Rocky Mountain National Park is that, despite the inevitable crowds, staff at every visitor center or station can easily direct you to the best spots for wild iris or columbine or, higher up, the alpine sunflower and forget-me-not. For scenery, accessibility and diversity, Rocky Mountain National Park is the spot.

Utah, to the surprise of some, is a great state for Rocky Mountain wildflowers. The Wasatch Mountains, the westernmost branch of the Rockies, are tall—over 11,000 feet in many spots—and scenic but seem "un-Rockyish" to those inclined to think of Colorado as the sole Rocky Mountain state in the Southwest. All such misconceptions will be put aside at the Alta/Snowbird ski area in the **Albion Basin**. High above the Salt Lake Valley, this fir and aspen basin is rimmed by several towering peaks and is nearly as popular in summer for hiking, biking and wildflower viewing as it is in winter for skiing. Little Cottonwood Creek trickles through the bottom of the canyon, while the meadows just above the tram building at Snowbird are a wildflower delight: arnica, lupine, sego lily, paintbrush and columbine, among others. It is even possible to take the tram to the top of Hidden Peak and wander through alpine meadows back down to the visitor center area. To reach Albion Basin, take I-15 south from Salt Lake City, then get on I-80 just outside of town. After 4.5 miles on I-80, take US 215 south 6 miles to Exit 6, looking for the "Snowbird Ski Area" sign. The rest of the route is clearly signed. Take State Road 190 for a brief 1 mile, then follow the signs onto State Road 210 headed south. The road turns east and climbs steadily through oak, aspen, fir and pine, reaching the main resort area 12.5 miles after getting off US 215. There are plenty of signs along the way. The most popular and accessible hiking trails start right at the tram building, where a wooden bridge crosses over the creek. From here you can climb all the way to the peaks above.

40

White-tailed and Mule Deer in Summer

A fawn's first few weeks of life in the Southwest are about as idyllic as can be. It is the doe who does all the work foraging for food for her young, while the fawn does little more than rest, stay well hidden where its mother has left it and wait to be fed. Because deer are the most numerous large mammals in the United States, the opportunity to see fawns, does or sizable bucks in summer—all at the peak of health or at the fresh beginning of their lives—is outstanding in a variety of habitats.

Deer are found throughout most of North America. Mule deer (see chapter 70) are common in much of the West; white-tailed deer, slightly bigger than mulies, are more widely distributed across the continent. The rough boundary of white-tail distribution, in fact, corresponds fairly closely with much of the territory covered in this book, so that an island of land uninhabited by them includes Utah, parts of western Colorado, parts of northern Arizona and much of western New Mexico, as well as California and Nevada. Outside of this area, "deer" means "white-tailed deer," and at about fifteen million strong, its preeminence is indisputable. Here in the Southwest, those areas uninhabited by white-tailed deer are generally inhabited by mule deer, with considerable overlapping range.

Found in habitats ranging from forests to swamps and from

farmland to Texas cactus country, the white-tail is perhaps more abundant today than ever and certainly many times more numerous than the half-million or so it had dwindled to over a century ago. Though larger and more abundant than mule deer in general, white-tails are more elusive and hence can be difficult to find. Unlike mule deer, who are curious to a fault and will often linger in the open, white-tails dart out of sight at the first hint of danger, seeking to put as much distance as possible between themselves and the perceived intruder or searching out a nearby covered area for retreat. When startled, the deer's tail, pure white on its underside, raises up like a flag, signaling alarm to any nearby companions.

Agile, fast runners who can leap over fences at least 6 feet high, the white-tail's wariness accounts in part for its success as a species. It has thrived despite human encroachment, finding a niche in the "edge" environments where forests meet open expanses—fields, streams, lakes and, not so incidentally, subdivisions. The white-tail prefers to stay away from open spaces, remaining on the fringes of forests that offer thick cover and traveling along these same protective corridors.

White-tails generally don't travel too far. While mule deer may migrate from low to high elevations in summer, white-tails are content to find relatively safe areas and stay in them if enough food can be found, at times remaining within very small areas for lengthy periods.

White-tailed bucks are not as sociable as mule deer bucks, summering by themselves and, like most bucks, playing no part in the family life of does and fawns. Does are bred over a three-month period in autumn and thus give birth to fawns throughout the summer—white-tails after a six-and-a-half-month gestation period, mule deer after seven months. The doe gives birth in solitude, then leaves her baby bedded down in some well-concealed spot of her choice. She forages—early morning and late afternoon are the most common mealtimes for deer—and then returns frequently to nurse her young with a thick milk rich in fat and protein. The fawn's spotted coat, which some retain well into autumn, is excellent camouflage, as it breaks up the defenseless animal's outline as it lies motionless on the ground, a position it instinctively assumes when alarmed. Fawns grow rapidly in summer, quadrupling their weight in the first month alone, which is also around the time they begin following their mothers. Look for does and their young together, foraging at the edge of meadows throughout summer.

Be sure to keep an eye out also for sturdy bucks. In summer, white-tailed deer are a reddish-tan above, as opposed to grayish-tan during the rest of the year, with thin, fairly short hair. By midsummer, while fawns are beginning to lose their spots, mature bucks are growing antlers that will reach their full glory by early to midautumn. If the weather has been fairly mild in winter and if enough food has been available during that season on into spring, by July most bucks will have a substantial growth of sturdy antlers covered with a velvety coating. Their solitary summer days, spent gaining strength for the autumn rut that will perpetuate the species, are a neat contrast to the gentle and quiet lives of the does and fawns. Together, they reveal the vibrant heart of nature's cycle, as the longest days of the year begin to pass and the most abundant animal of its size on the continent endures.

HOTSPOTS

The best place in Utah to see mule deer during summer is at **Big Flat**, a broad meadow area in the Tushar Mountains. This range in the southwestern part of the state boasts a few 12,000-foot-plus peaks, plenty of fir and aspen and the rich meadows that lure foraging deer. Plenty of deer can be found at Big Flat, including does with their young and even some mature bucks. Big Flat also has a reputation as a fine spot for photographing deer, since the animals remain fairly tame during their carefree summer. In winter the deer are nowhere to be found—over 300 inches of snow fall in this region of the Fishlake National Forest and skiers flock to the nearby Elk Meadows ski resort—but in midsummer, with aspen shimmering and the open grasslands green and lush, Big Flat is a haven for deer.

To reach the area, take Exit 112 off I-15 at the town of Beaver. Get on State Road 153, which intersects the business loop through Beaver, and head east up into national forest land. Stay on State Road 153 along the entire route, keeping straight at a

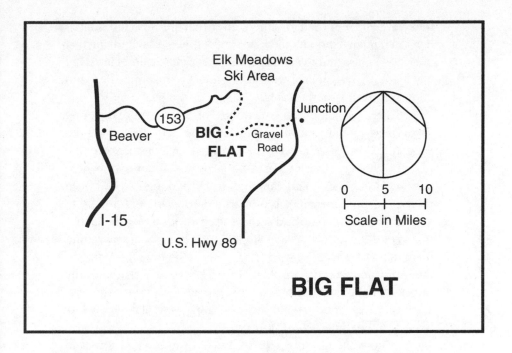

BIG FLAT

junction 10.9 miles from where 153 began in Beaver. The route travels through meadows and white fir and aspen. Keep right, following State Road 153 17.4 miles from Beaver, then keep straight 0.7 mile beyond this. The ski area lies 2.1 miles ahead. Puffer Lake is on the left at the 22.3-mile mark, but stay on 153 by following a sign reading "East 153." The pavement ends just beyond the sign, and the gravel road twists and climbs through conifers for 2 miles to a sign that reads "Wildlife Viewing Area." Here the vast, grassy, aspen-ringed meadows of Big Flat begin. Drive slowly, scanning the trees and fields for deer, before reaching a sign for the end of the designated viewing area 2.9 miles from the first sign. State Road 153 actually continues east, but the road gets rough in spots. It's best to return to Beaver from Big Flat.

Mule deer abound at **Great Sand Dunes National Monument** in south central Colorado (see chapter 24). All animals here are protected, as they are in all federal parks and monuments, and as a result the deer have become remarkably tame, even bold, begging for food from campers and cleaning up around picnickers. The Colorado Division of Wildlife has occasionally had to remove deer from the monument after they became too dependent on human handouts and leftovers. It goes without saying that deer need grass and twigs more than sandwiches and chips and that feeding a wild animal "unnatural" foods is both unhealthy and improper. Staff-issued fines help reinforce the message.

Deer aren't found on the dunes, of course, those towering mounds of brown sand that rise more than 700 feet along the Sangre de Cristo Mountains (see chapter 24 for a discussion of the region's geology). But they can be seen just about everywhere else, including picnic and camping areas, parking lots and even roads. The monument area is primarily piñon–juniper forest, with a bit of ponderosa pine and some cottonwoods along the creeks that skirt the dunes. To reach Great Sand Dunes National Monument, take US 160/285 14 miles east out of the town of Alamosa, then turn north onto State Road 150. The route is flat, with the dunes looming ever larger as you approach the monument area. The visitor center lies 19 miles after turning onto State Road 150. Access to the dunes is just beyond.

The white-tail subspecies found in southern Arizona and parts of western New Mexico is the coues, a big-eared scamperer smaller than every other white-tail except those found in the Florida Keys. Mature bucks may be no more than 100 pounds. Their range seems to be expanding a bit more to the east in New Mexico, and their numbers—roughly 850,000—are on the rise. **Cave Creek Canyon** (see chapter 26) has plenty of them around the campgrounds and areas where the elegant trogon can be found. Above Cave Creek Canyon, **Rustler Park** is an ideal spot for white-tails. Open meadows that draw broad-tailed and rufous hummingbirds, thick stands of conifers, including the most southerly stand of Engelmann spruce in North America, and spectacular views on the way up to the 8,500-foot campground area highlight the cool, pleasant Rustler Park area. The trails around the campground and picnic tables generally turn up white-tails on a July morning. The main trail is a full-day hike all the way up to Chiricahua Peak. Rustler Park is reached by taking the road from Portal into Cave Creek Canyon 1.4 miles past the ranger station. The road forks here. Take the paved road to the right for 1.8 miles. Here the pavement ends at the turnoff to the Southwestern Research Station, an idyllic spread of cabins and offices for professional wildlife researchers from around the world. Continue up the gravel road, climbing through oak woodland. The turnoff to Paradise, an old mining site, lies 3.8 miles after the Southwestern Research Station, with spectacular views of western New Mexico just beyond. Onion Saddle, at 7,600 feet, lies 3.2 miles beyond the Paradise turnoff, with ponderosa pine and more great views along the way. You will reach a fork 1.9 miles after going left at Onion Saddle. Barfoot Park is to the right, Rustler Park to the left just 1.1 miles up the road. At Rustler Park, a ranger station lies along the left fork; the camping area and hiking trails are to the right. **Mesa Verde National Park** (see chapter 61) is another good spot to see deer in the summer.

41

July Shorttakes

Desert Bighorn Sheep

Desert bighorn sheep (see chapter 5) can be found in summer at **Willow Beach** south of Hoover Dam, though boat

A female bighorn sheep, showing the characteristic slender, sickle-shaped horns of ewes.

viewing is best. One of the better congregations of desert bighorns gather here in summer, drinking at the Colorado River's edge. To reach Willow Beach, take US 93 northwest out of Kingman for 60 miles, then turn west on the Willow Beach turnoff and travel 4 miles.

Rocky Mountain Bighorn Sheep

One of the best chances to see Rocky Mountain bighorn sheep in summer, when they retreat to remote mountain highlands, is by traveling the **Mount Evans Road** (see chapter 42). They can often be seen close to the road and are as beautiful in summer as in late autumn, even if they aren't ramming heads. **Rocky Mountain National Park** is the other outstanding spot for bighorns in summer. Look for them in the meadows on the east side of the park, the same areas in which elk can be seen in September (see chapter 49).

42

Breakout:
The Mount Evans Road

If you glance at a road atlas of Colorado, you may notice, just
southwest of Denver, a small written note almost lost amid the
jumble of town names and labyrinthine roads that cluster about the
great city. "Highest road in the U.S.," it reads, an accompanying
arrow indicating State Road 5, which leads almost to the top of
14,264-foot Mount Evans. A paved road higher than 14,000 feet?
Believe it. While only three other states in the Union have mountains
that poke above the 14,000-foot mark, Colorado has a blacktop
that leads cars and bikes, trucks and trailers up and into the very
heart of what is known as the Front Range. Here, along the eastern
slope of the Rockies, peaks such as Mount Evans retain a strong
hint of winter even in July. At this elevation there is nothing but
tundra land, a veritable patch of the Arctic north, its alpine
meadows, ice-crusted lakes and vast snowfields accessible for
only a few short weeks during the summer and offering one of the
most dramatic mountain views in the lower forty-eight states.

The road begins at Echo Lake, a small, crystal blue spread
of snowmelt that, at 10,700 feet, is plenty high itself. Actually, the
drive up to Echo Lake is scenic in its own right, starting at the
Arapaho National Forest Information Station/Clear Creek Ranger
Station in Idaho Springs (30 miles west of Denver on I-70) and up
State Road 103 13.5 miles through lodgepole pine and aspen. The

ranger station at Idaho Springs, incidentally, has a fine display on forest and tundra environments, making it a good first stop on the way to Mount Evans. Just past Echo Lake lies a gift shop and the turnoff to State Road 5. Look for the sign here declaring it "North America's Highest Auto Road."

Engelmann spruce, with a few lingering aspen, dominate these first few miles above Echo Lake. The Hudsonian or Subalpine Region, as this life zone is called, is surpassed in harshness only by the alpine tundra that lies just above. In the southern Rockies, Engelmann spruce and subalpine fir dominate from roughly 9,000 feet up to timberline, their ability to withstand bitter cold and fierce winds beneficial even in July, when the average daily temperature is just slightly above 50°F. Spruce forests, like the one the Mount Evans road winds through on its first 3 miles upslope, are generally thick and dense, with some 120-foot-tall giants and an occasional old-timer of four hundred years or more.

The real Methuselahs of this region, however, are the twisted bristlecone pines found just at timberline, which is roughly 11,500 feet in the southern Rockies. Here the hardy limber pine, more prevalent on Mount Evans's rockier ridges, gives way to the tough, gnarled bristlecone pine, a tree whose relatives in the Great Basin region routinely live to be three thousand years or older. Bristlecones in the southern Rockies commonly surpass the thousand-year mark. Strong winds, low temperatures and uniformly severe conditions leave them as stubby and twisted as anything from a lonely Arctic grove. Decades of exposure to wind and ice leave the bristlecone pine's sapwood almost entirely exposed as these white-trunked wraiths, surprisingly common on Mount Evans's open, southern slopes, eke out an existence along this thin strip of elevation. A particularly fine stand of bristlecones—more than 10 acres in size—can be found by taking the trail from a parking area at the signed Mount Goliath Natural Area just at timberline. It is here, 2.5 miles above Echo Lake, where the trees begin to thin out, disappearing entirely 0.7 mile beyond this. Here one enters the fascinating, desolate land of near-perpetual winter—the tundra.

Any tundra land found south of the Arctic Circle is designated "alpine tundra," though the original meaning of the word—*tundra* is Russian for "land of no trees"—holds as well here as it does far north. In the southern Rockies, tundra is found at an elevation of roughly 11,600 feet, give or take about 400 feet. It is a "land of no trees" because, simply, it is too cool even in summer for them to grow. Tundra in the Rockies stays frost-free for only about forty days, and temperatures rarely crack the 60-degree mark.

But this hardly means the region is lifeless. Just as gray jays, Clark's nutcrackers, pine grosbeaks, chickadees, blue grouse and numerous mammals abound in the regions just below timberline, so do an intriguing cast of critters thrive on the barren upper slopes of Mount Evans. Smallish mammals especially—shrews, pikas, pocket gophers, voles and marmots—are found on the tundra throughout summer, most of them after spending a good part of the rest of the year in hibernation. The small pika, found skittering over fields of broken rock, makes loud squawking sounds or high-pitched cries that echo across the tundra. The yellow-bellied marmot, a chunky, lumbering, ground-dwelling squirrel roughly as long as a cat, may cross the road in front of you or may be basking on some rocky outcropping in full view.

The most impressive mammals up here, however, are the Rocky Mountain bighorn sheep, the elk and the mountain goat. Bighorn sheep (see chapter 64) generally summer at extremely high elevation, seeking both the remote, rocky areas where their natural defenses are best served and the nearby meadows of grasses and herbs—spartan fare but sustenance bighorns thrive on with little competition from other large mammals. They also have remarkably well-adapted hooves, which are sturdy and hard along the outer edges and soft and rubbery in the center, allowing them to virtually grip the rocks over which they race. Mountain goats, too, though introduced from outside the southern Rockies, are well suited to the terrain and rarely venture below timberline in summer or winter. Both of these large mammals, as well as small herds of elk grazing on the open slopes, are seen with surprising frequency on the road up to the summit of Mount Evans.

Birds are rarer the higher up one goes, but a nice variety nest on Mount Evans's upper slopes before departing in autumn. Rosy finches, horned larks, rock wrens, water pipits and others can be found easily in July, while a more strenuous search may turn up a white-tailed ptarmigan, the only bird to remain at alpine levels throughout the year. In summer the white-tailed ptarmigan is coated with brown and black feathers on top; only in winter is it found in its all-white glory.

Just as the tundra is not devoid of life in summer, neither is it devoid of color. Alpine wildflowers—small, low growing and fragilely beautiful—can transform tundra meadows into palettes of swirling hues. What the flowers lack in height and size gives them an advantage in the fight for survival: by staying close to the ground, they avoid cold and wind as much as possible. Adapted to the very brief frost-free season, alpine wildflowers are perennials almost across the board; only a handful of hardy annuals are capable of germinating and producing seeds under such arduous conditions. Look for alpine avens, sky pilots, American bistorts, alplilies and alpine wallflowers in the open meadows of Mount Evans anywhere from 4 or 5 miles above Echo Lake all the way up to Summit Lake. The signed Alpine Garden Trail established by the Denver Botanical Gardens lies 4.8 miles above Echo Lake.

At the 9-mile mark exactly, one reaches the picturesque alpine water hole known as Summit Lake. Ice crusted and rimmed with snow throughout the summer, the slopes on the far side of the lake rise straight up to the summit of Mount Evans. A trail leads around the right side of the lake, offering the best chance on the whole mountain to see rosy finches and water pipits. The brown-capped rosy finches one finds at Summit Lake commonly search for seeds and insects near the edges of snowbanks, while water pipits hunt for insects on the snowbanks themselves. Both will almost certainly be found darting over the waters of the lake or on the slopes just above it. The trail around the lake's edge also leads to a low pass that reveals, far below, two shimmering alpine lakes. As with all paths on the mountain, stay on the established trail; tundra vegetation is fragile.

The real adventure still awaits above, as the road rises up from Summit Lake through snow patches and fields of rubble rock. Over 5.5 miles of tightly winding, narrow road leads to the 14,200-foot mark of the mountain. Park here, admire the already stunning view, then hike up the short trail to the top of the peak 64 feet above. Here, atop the large boulders that lie strewn on the mountaintop, one can look out into the bracing wind in all directions and see a horizon painted with jutting bulks of brown and white. It is the very epicenter of a world of high mountains, far distant, it would seem, from civilization—until one looks down and sees the small parking lot below. That is, if it's possible to look away from the 360-degree view the peak offers. Longs Peak, 50 miles to the north, and Pikes Peak, nearly 60 miles to the southeast, are but two of the more prominent mountains one sees from the top of Mount Evans. It can be bitterly cold up here even in midsummer, so take a sweater or a jacket. Clouds can roll in quickly, obscuring the view and possibly threatening lightning— a distinct danger at this high, exposed elevation. On a clear day, the drive to the top of Mount Evans is a spectacular and rare glimpse at a world as awesome as it is remote. It is a strange feeling to drive back down the road to Echo Lake and then down to the interstate—returning to summer, in effect, when a land of winter lies peacefully far above, revealing itself for but a few brief weeks before the snows reclaim it.

AUGUST

43

Late Summer Desert Wildflowers

With the spectacular spring wildflowers of the desert a distant memory and the fresh mountain wildflowers of early summer already starting to fade, August would seem to be the time to begin dreaming about next year's blooms. But just when it seems as if all color will be drained from the desert, a group of hardy flowers gives one last showy gasp. Spurred by monsoon rains, flowers like the Arizona caltrop and the desert zinnia as well as bright blossoms on some barrel and pincushion cacti make late summer almost as beautiful, at least in certain areas, as spring.

Particularly in the central and southeastern portions of Arizona, storm clouds begin pelting the land with ferocious rains by midsummer. Carried up from the Gulf of Mexico, these thick, moisture-laden clouds bring torrential downpours to both the Chihuahuan and Sonoran deserts, raising the humidity and flashing spectacular displays of lightning. These short, heavy rains kick up the seeds of both annuals and perennials that have lain dormant in the soil. Shortly—within hours, even—these seeds germinate, producing flowers most profusely along roads and arroyos. The vast fields of blooms so common during the earlier months don't usually appear at this time of year; late summer flowers are more likely to appear in patches.

Generally, the wildflowers that grow best in late summer

are those most tolerant of the almost tropical conditions that can prevail at this time of year. Many are close relatives of tropical species and prefer the hot weather, high humidity and long days of August. Many are also fairly leafy, able to produce green leaves quickly and in direct response to high temperatures and violent rains. Above all, the wildflowers of late summer are beautiful, colorful and varied—just like their spring cousins.

Keep an eye out for the five-petaled Arizona caltrop, a quick bloomer with a rich orange color that makes it look almost like the goldpoppy; the desert zinnia, which displays bunches of little yellow blooms; the dainty, purple morning glory; and curiosities such as the devil's claw. Some cacti do well at this time of year also. Look for the pinkish flowers of the pincushion cactus, which can bloom after nearly every good summer rain; the barrel cactus, whose orange flowers practically glow; and the jumping cholla, with its tiny but pretty pink flowers. In some of the mountain canyons, certain shrubs do well, including wild cotton, which has a delicate, pinkish-white flower; the desert senna, a golden yellow perennial; and the desert willow, whose orchidlike flowers attract hummingbirds.

Just as in spring, late summer wildflowers are unreliable, unpredictable and sometimes hard to find. The principles governing their blossoming—the drought-evading tactics that explained February's and March's blooms—remain essentially the same. But perhaps even more than these early season flowers, the blooms of August are easy to appreciate. More subtle and less concentrated than their spring relatives, late summer flowers are the last explosion of fine desert color one finds before heading into autumn.

HOTSPOTS

The best places to find wildflowers in late summer are the same as those where wildflowers are found in spring. Only the time of year has changed. Check any of the recommended spots listed in chapter 9 and chapter 15, particularly the more southeasterly locations. For the best up-to-date information on any given year's showier blooms, always call ahead before visiting an area.

44

Spadefoot Toads

The deserts of southern Arizona and southern New Mexico seem to be the least likely places to find toads, those warty amphibians who would seem better suited for areas with plenty of water. But the desert is deceptive. When the summer monsoon season arrives (see chapter 48), enormous numbers of spadefoot toads shake off their prolonged torpor and, revitalized by the rain, emerge from their underground burrows to crowd the pools that have accumulated. As if this hydration process weren't amazing enough, spadefoots are equally renowned for their raucous mating calls. The sound of groups of spadefoot toads in full, amorous cry is common on some of the less-traveled desert roads following a summer rain. And so it is that like so many of the desert's creatures, the spadefoot is expert at avoiding the harsh conditions of its environment, timing its life cycle to take advantage of the one, brief time of the year when it can thrive.

The American toad best adapted to its desert environment, Couch's spadefoot is common throughout the Sonoran and Chihuahuan deserts. Spadefoots are plump and small, about 3 inches or so, with an overall greenish- or brownish-yellow coloration decorated with meandering dark lines. When the summer water holes begin to dry up, the spadefoot, true to its name, digs an underground burrow for itself by using the horny, sharp-edged "spade" that projects so conspicuously from its hind foot. The toad backs into the ground, moving its body in a sort of rubbing or digging motion with its feet—think of someone vigorously stamping out a cigarette—loosening enough soil to create a burrow as deep as 2 feet below the surface. Here it remains dormant for perhaps ten months, though if there are insufficient rains, the spadefoot can remain dormant underground for an additional year. And just how does the spadefoot go without water for such prolonged periods? Several ways. The spadefoot's body is about one-third pure moisture by weight even before the toad enters its burrow. Some of that moisture is in the form of diluted urine in the spadefoot's bladder, and some is a sort of concentrated urine spread throughout its body. By storing and concentrating bodily fluids, the spadefoot dramatically slows their loss. To further help retain moisture, the spadefoot also sloughs off protective layers of skin that effectively entomb it within a dry shell underground. Spadefoots, like many other desert toads, can lose up to half their body weight in moisture and still survive.

All of the moisture spadefoots lose during their months underground is replenished when the vivifying rains return. After a good, hard downpour, the toads dig out of their burrows and expose themselves to the night's heavy rains. A patch of vein-packed skin between its legs accounts for a good percentage of the water a spadefoot soaks up. And then the noise begins. As if to compensate for their months of inactivity, spadefoots gather in ditches or temporary ponds and call to potential mates so loudly they can be heard miles away. Thought to be a device for bringing toads together in large numbers for genetic diversity, the spadefoot's call sounds uncannily like the quick bleat of a distressed sheep. Strangely, the cries of countless spadefoots can actually add up to a sort of pleasant din—for a short while!

Spadefoots breed quickly, usually within the first night or two after emerging, and the eggs that are laid can hatch after a mere half-day. These tadpoles, in turn, can transform into small toads in anywhere from two to five weeks—in time to avoid the dry weather that descends on the desert.

HOTSPOTS

Spadefoots can only be found—and heard—after a good, hard summer rain. August's monsoon season is ideal spadefoot time, when the critters are abundant across southern New Mexico and southern Arizona in mesquite and creosote regions and desert grasslands. In Arizona, try **Saguaro National Monument** (see chapter 31) and the **San Pedro Riparian National Conservation Area** (see chapter 67).

In New Mexico, try **Oliver Lee Memorial State Park** (see chapter 19). The best area of all, though, is the **Mesilla Valley**, south of Las Cruces down to the New Mexico–Texas border. This fertile oasis in an otherwise dry region is one of the few genuine garden areas in all of southern New Mexico, producing well over $100 million worth of crops annually. Plentiful water makes the valley wondrously lush, particularly when contrasted with the parched mountains to the east and the dry desert to the west. For spadefoot toads it is a veritable heaven. After a good rain, their cries can be deafening along the roads that wind through the valley's orchards and fields.

The easiest way to travel through the Mesilla Valley, one of New Mexico's greenest and most pleasant areas, is by taking Exit 140—the Mesilla exit—off I-10 in Las Cruces. This puts you immediately on State Road 28, otherwise known as the Don Juan de Oñate Trail. Look for the 29-mile marker immediately. State Road 28 winds southeast, skirting mile after mile of irrigation channels and passing through farm fields, orchards and several small towns. Roads turn off to the east and west—east, especially—at frequent intervals; during the monsoons, nearly the entire drive seems to reverberate with the cries of spadefoots. The road is level and flat throughout and crosses the Rio Grande 6 miles after leaving the interstate. A brief 3.1 miles beyond this, open fields take the place of the dense pecan orchards that dominate the first stretch of the route. Drive, stop, listen and even get out and watch the suddenly lively toads in a brimming pond. It is possible to take any of a number of roads east to State Road 478 or I-10 (both of which lie parallel to State Road 28), or continue a total of 22.6 miles from your start at I-10 to the turnoff to the town of Anthony, which lies half in New Mexico, half in Texas. From Anthony, complete the long, skinny rectangle back northwest to your starting point on I-10 by traveling 21.2 miles on State Road 478. This road parallels the railroad tracks immediately to the west instead of the irrigation canals found on State Road 28. The entire trip is approximately 45 miles of fertile land—and numerous spadefoot toads on a wet summer night.

45

Kokanee Salmon Spawning

Salmon in the Rockies? As improbable as it may seem, they are actually quite common in some mountain lakes of the high Southwest. While the sockeye salmon, whose seasonal runs from the ocean to freshwater streams provide huge quantities of commercial fish annually, is the better-known American salmon, its landlocked brother, the kokanee, is just as admired by fishermen far inland. For those more interested in viewing the kokanee than eating it, the very end of August and on into September is the kokanee's spawning season, when it is at its most colorful and is most easily seen.

As summer begins to fade into autumn, kokanee begin migrating upstream from the lakes they have been inhabiting and head for shady pools or even the shallow and more protected areas of lakes. While kokanee generally resemble rainbow trout during most of their lives, during the spawning season they undergo a transformation. The male's head turns green, his body turns a bright red, his back grows humped and his jaw begins to hook so severely that his overbite would strike the finest orthodontist as uncorrectable. The female, whose coloration is far less gaudy during the spawn, pairs off with a male, builds an underwater "nest" of rock and gravel, then lays her eggs—five hundred or so, usually, though numbers in the thousands are not unusual. After the male fertilizes the eggs with his sperm, or milt, and the eggs are buried, the pair defends the nest and then both adults perish within about two weeks. This is an especially popular time for fishing in those lakes where it is allowed. Many streams are off-limits to fishing during the spawn.

While it generally takes four years for a kokanee to reach spawning age, the young hatch in less than seven weeks, then move to deeper waters. Here they can find the zooplankton and insects they need to grow. A foot and a half is about maximum for a kokanee, with most growing to a foot in length.

Kokanee are exotics, or imports, in the lakes of the Southwest, though they have done exceptionally well here and can now be found in lakes throughout the West. Kokanee were first introduced into Colorado in 1951 and into New Mexico twelve years later.

Because kokanee live most of their lives in deep lake water, the spawn offers a unique opportunity to see them up close. In some spots it is possible, if you move slowly and quietly along the bank of a stream, to watch kokanee just 5 or 10 feet away as they form pairs and the males defend their territory. Their brilliant red coloration and frenzied activity make them easy to spot.

HOTSPOTS

Whenever viewing spawning kokanee—or any fish, for that matter—it is important to avoid fast movements and loud noises. Both will frighten the fish away. Also, of course, never swim or wade in an area where fish are spawning, and never throw anything into the water.

Northern Utah offers the two best spots to witness kokanee spawning close up. At both sites, the spawn usually begins in late August and may peak a couple of weeks later, though this can occur a bit earlier. Start keeping an eye out for kokanee by the fourth week of August at the very latest.

The **Little Bear River** just above Porcupine Reservoir has a spectacular kokanee run that may peak any time from late August to mid-September. To find out about a particular year's run, contact the Utah Division of Wildlife Resources, which has been holding a "Kokanee Salmon Day" on the second Saturday in September, though that date may change in the near future.

Porcupine Reservoir, created by a small dam, lies in a basin of steep hills and may be fairly brimming over, diminishing the length of the inlet on public land and thus decreasing the accessible viewing area. This is because the Little Bear River flows through private property before emptying into Porcupine Reservoir. The gate on the far side—the inlet side—of the reservoir leads into private property, and although it may be possible to enter this area with the landowner's permission, it's better to limit viewing to that part of the inlet on public land. Since the kokanee move as a group, if their spawn is caught at just the right time, it is possible to stand on the bank of the Little Bear and watch them cavort en masse. The Utah Division of Wildlife Resources traps kokanee here to collect their eggs to stock other areas.

To reach the reservoir, take State Road 165 south out of Logan to the town of Hyrum. The town of Paradise lies 4.2 miles farther south, and State Road 165 ends 1 mile beyond. The community of Avon lies 2.2 miles past the point where State Road 165 ends. Continue through rolling hills and farmland to the "Porcupine Dam" sign 1 mile past Avon. This is Road 11200 South. Look also for the "Big C Ranch" sign. Go east on this road, which becomes gravel after 1.6 miles, skirting the river and passing several turnouts. The road eventually climbs up to the dam, reaching it after 3.9 miles. Go left, following the rough, winding road 2.4 miles around to the far side of the reservoir. The inlet lies just below this point.

Far more scenic and just as productive for kokanee is the **Sheep Creek Geological Loop** near Flaming Gorge Reservoir. The dramatic rock formations here are an exposed portion of the Uinta Fault, which stretches for nearly a hundred miles along one of the few east–west oriented mountain ranges in the United States, the Uintas. Eggs from the kokanee that spawn in Sheep Creek supply hatcheries throughout Utah. The potential viewing area here is far larger than at Porcupine Reservoir. The sheer cliffs and towering spires in Sheep Creek Canyon are a visual treat as well. Several interpretive signs in the canyon point out strata and particularly interesting formations.

At the heart of the geological loop road lie some of the best and most accessible spawning sites. This area is reached by taking

State Road 44 west from US 191 just south of Flaming Gorge Reservoir. At 15 miles, turn left onto Forest Road 218 at the "Sheep Creek Geological Loop Road" sign. This road is paved along its entire length, a bit poorly in spots as the loop ends; turnoffs to places such as Deep Creek or Sheep Creek Lake are dirt roads. After passing through pine and aspen, at 6.8 miles the road begins to drop down into the canyon, passing enormous jutting banks of red rock before reaching the Palisades Picnic Area 7.4 miles after leaving State Road 44. A sign here explains that overnight camping is prohibited from May through October due to flash flood danger. For the next 2.6 miles, the road follows alongside the river, with many turnouts for kokanee viewing and magnificent rock formations all along the route. A bridge over slow-flowing water lies 3.5 miles beyond Palisades. Check the creek here for kokanee, or try the broad waters at the Carmel Picnic Ground 1.5 miles past the bridge. This pleasant cottonwood and juniper turnout provides great creek viewing, as does the Navajo Cliffs Picnic Ground 0.7 mile beyond Carmel. A scant 0.2 mile past Navajo Cliffs, the road hits a junction with State Road 44. The town of Manila lies 5.9 miles to the north.

46

Buffalo in Rut

The story of the American bison, commonly known as the buffalo, is so familiar and so all-encompassingly tragic, it has transcended the realm of history and become almost allegoric. In its way, the near-extermination of the buffalo tells us more about ourselves and this country than nearly any other comparable episode, replete, as it is, with issues of land, freedom, genocide and greed; it speaks of some of the best and much of the very worst of our past. The buffalo that remain today are but a minuscule fraction of the multitudes that once gathered on the plains—perhaps the largest aggregations of sizable mammals ever seen by modern man anywhere on earth. But what also remains to us, aside from the bison itself, is a creature forever attended by the ghosts of the past, a creature that very well may be the archetypal American animal.

Everyone knows that buffalo once roamed the American plains. What may be less well known is that great areas of eastern New Mexico and Colorado constitute the western fringe of this prairie land. Buffalo historically did not abound in these short-grass prairie regions, preferring instead the mixed prairie to the east, that vast, treeless ocean of grass commonly referred to as the Great Plains. Nowadays, as a means of preserving the remaining buffalo, they have been transplanted and live in well-managed or semidomesticated security throughout the West, everywhere from Dakota grasslands to semidesert sage flats.

Before 1870 there were, by most estimates, at least sixty million buffalo gathered on the plains at any given time. They were, in actuality, very destructive animals, herding in such enormous numbers that they grazed and trampled the land bare for miles around. But when the herds moved on, the grass would return, having been well clipped by buffalo teeth and fertilized by buffalo manure. The fires that naturally swept across the plains also stimulated new growth, providing fresh bluestem grass for millions of bison. Anglo encroachment ended all this, as cattle began eating the grass, land was cleared, fires were kept in check and buffalo were slaughtered both indiscriminately and as part of the effort to demoralize those Indian tribes for whom the buffalo was the very core of economic and spiritual life. By the 1890s, the animal whose numbers had surpassed all exaggeration but who proved too slow and too large a target to withstand bullets was reduced to only a few hundred remaining beasts. The bountiful West had been plundered.

At present there are roughly sixty-five thousand buffalo in North America, all in protected areas and all owing their existence to emergency conservation efforts undertaken in the early part of this century. In the Southwest, whose more arid regions they never occupied historically, bison can be found in small pockets of public land, including a few river valleys and even some forests. Buffalo travel quite far, always searching for good grazing, so in those areas where they are not primarily sustained by human-provided feed, they remain fairly mobile. Only a few of the larger preserves or ranches can tolerate such wear and tear.

Although buffalo can be seen year-round, late summer is the time of their rut, a rarely observed and deeply stirring event. Like most male mammals, bison bulls fight over the females. By the end of July, having grown increasingly restless, the males become aggressive toward one another as they attempt to claim cows. When two bulls reach the full-blown confrontation stage, they will face each other, paw the ground, kick up dirt, then lunge headfirst at each other like slower, bulkier bighorn sheep again and again until one gives up. It is a brutal, pounding affair, one that shook the prairie floor for countless ages until little more than a century ago. To see it today is to be transported back to that time— and to feel a great loss for the untold millions of these animals who once dominated the plains.

HOTSPOTS

Most of the places buffalo roam nowadays are public lands where the herds are strictly managed. Two of the very finest are found in northern Arizona on sagebrush–saltbush land administered by the Arizona Game and Fish Department. The **House Rock Ranch**, northeast of Grand Canyon National Park on the eastern edge of the Kaibab Plateau, is situated in the low, rolling hills of House Rock Valley. The aptly named Vermilion Cliffs lie to the north, deep Marble Canyon to the east, the Grand Canyon to the south and forests to the west. Buffalo have wandered the Kaibab Plateau since 1905, brought to the area by Charles "Buffalo" Jones, who hoped to crossbreed bison with cattle; he eventually gave up his sizable herd. The state bought the roughly 100 remaining buffalo in 1927 and has continued to maintain a herd of approximately 125 since then. The ranch is enormous—over 65,000 acres of sagebrush and scrubby piñon–juniper woodland— though only 30 acres are actually the property of the Game and Fish Department. The rest is leased U.S. Forest Service land. Your odds of seeing buffalo by simply showing up are only fair. Be sure to call the Game and Fish Department in Flagstaff (602-774-5046) before embarking on a trip to the ranch; at the very least, they may have recent information on buffalo sightings. The best bet is to try to arrange your visit for when the ranch manager will be at the on-site headquarters. The manager may be able to direct you to the likeliest viewing areas.

To reach the ranch, cross the Colorado River on US 89A southwest of the town of Page and, 22.7 miles after the river, look for a turnoff to the left for Forest Road 445. A sign here reads "House Rock Buffalo Ranch—22 miles," and another one directly behind it reads "House Rock Buffalo Ranch—21 miles—Forest Road 445." The gravel and dirt road passes through monotonous short-grass prairie, reaching a fork after 10.9 miles. Follow the sign to the left, keeping the low, juniper-dotted ridge to your right. At

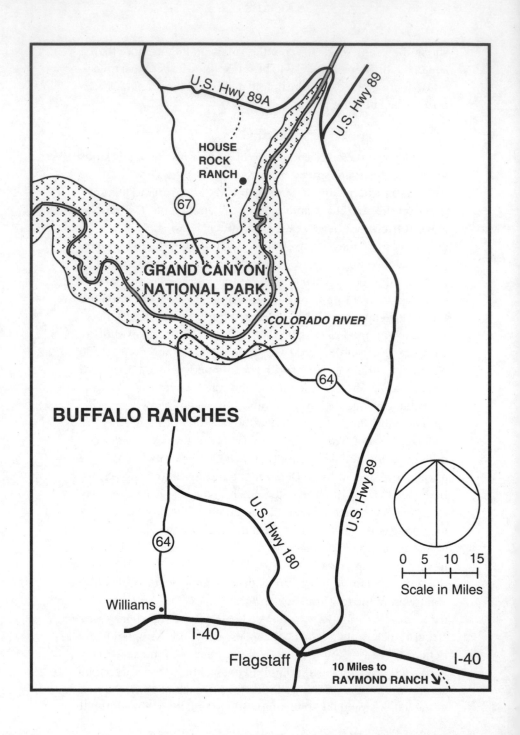

U.S. Hwy 89A

U.S. Hwy 89

HOUSE
ROCK
RANCH

67

GRAND CANYON
NATIONAL PARK

COLORADO RIVER

64

BUFFALO RANCHES

U.S. Hwy 89

64

U.S. Hwy 180

0   5   10   15
Scale in Miles

Williams

I-40

Flagstaff

10 Miles to
RAYMOND RANCH

I-40

the 12-mile mark the road enters the Kaibab National Forest, then enters the House Rock Wildlife Area 3.1 miles after this. Clearly marked signs for various turnoffs appear soon after; stay on Forest Road 445. Nineteen and one-third miles after leaving 89A, a sign directs you to the left; the headquarters area lies 2.1 miles ahead. If no one is here, or if you don't have a brochure and map from the Game and Fish Department, the only way to see buffalo is to drive the ranch roads. Get back on 445, drive south and take any of a number of roads that snake off east and west; be certain to stay only on established roads.

On the other side of the Grand Canyon and east of Flagstaff lies another state-operated buffalo area, the **Raymond Ranch**. The terrain here is very similar to that at the House Rock Ranch— low hills and open plains of sagebrush, juniper and piñon. The buffalo herd, numbering roughly eighty animals, was begun in part with transplants from the House Rock Ranch nearly fifty years ago. Raymond Ranch, only 10 miles off I-40, isn't nearly as remote as the House Rock Ranch, and though it is far smaller, just under 15,000 acres, the buffalo have plenty of free, open space. Take Exit 225, roughly 25 miles east of Flagstaff, off I-40 to go south on Buffalo Range Road. Look immediately for a sign that reads "Raymond Ranch Wildlife Area—10 miles." The road becomes dirt right away (and can be muddy following a rain), passing through nearly treeless sage and saltbush land all the way to the ranch. Enter ranch property, marked with a sign, after 8.3 miles; the headquarters is 2.1 miles beyond this. Just as at House Rock, the two best ways of locating buffalo are to have contacted the Game and Fish Department in Flagstaff beforehand or to talk to the ranch manager in the headquarters house. If no one is at the on-site headquarters, the best road to travel can be entered through a white gate just west of the house near the hay shed.

The **Philmont Scout Ranch** in northeastern New Mexico has a herd of 135 buffalo easily seen by pulling off State Road 21 beginning 2.1 miles after leaving the town of Cimarron. For 1 mile, look to the right to see buffalo in a vast piñon–juniper area.

In Utah, the **Henry Mountains** are home to a free-roaming herd of roughly two hundred buffalo. Unfortunately, the roads into this area are extremely rough and the viewing is difficult, though if you can brave the obstacles, the thrill of seeing one of the most natural herds in the country may exceed that of seeing the animals on a sagebrush plateau. Do not search for these buffalo on your own. Stop at the Bureau of Land Management office in Hanksville, clearly signed, off State Road 24, which runs through this small town in south central Utah. Here you can get up-to-date information on road conditions and buffalo locations. The area is simply too large and the animals too elusive to have much luck otherwise. If you plan your trip into the Henrys just right, this might be the most satisfying buffalo viewing of all.

> *A warning: Buffalo may charge if angered, and rutting season is hardly the time to try to get a closeup photograph of one. Never move toward a buffalo on foot. Better yet, stay in your vehicle.*

47

August Shorttakes

American White Pelicans

These impressive birds (see chapter 51) gather in large numbers during the summer in some wetland areas of Utah and Colorado. Try **Bear River Migratory Bird Refuge** (see chapter 56) in Utah. **Lake John** (see chapter 13), windswept and open, is

A flock of white pelicans take flight from a body of water.

a great and relatively unknown spot for summering pelicans in Colorado. Colorado's best-known pelican hotspot in summer is at **Riverside Reservoir** west of Jackson Lake (see chapter 10). An island visible from the south side of the reservoir is a major nesting area for pelicans. Bring binoculars. To reach the reservoir, take I-76 to Exit 66, then take US 34 west for 12 miles up to County Road 87. Turn north, travel 4 miles, park next to the road and walk the trail to the viewing area. The other fine pelican spot in Colorado is the **Adobe Creek Reservoir State Wildlife Area** north of the small town of Las Animas in the southeastern part of the state. Hundreds of pelicans spend the summer at this large reservoir, situated in open prairie land. To reach it, head north for 12 miles on County Road 10 from the point just west of where State Road 194 and US 50 intersect.

48

Breakout: Monsoon Rains

Traditionally, the Navajo people call the relatively mild storms of winter "female rains," a name suggestive of the gentle precipitation that is more the rule than the exception from November through March. After June has passed, and heat and drought have reached their bone-drying extremes, the "male rains" descend on the deserts of the Southwest in all their temperamental, violent fury. An August afternoon across much of Arizona and portions of southern and western New Mexico and southeastern Utah often sees vast, angry armies of dark storm clouds gathering ominously in what was a crystal blue morning sky, preparatory to lashing out at the desert with incredible ferocity. The Southwest's monsoons—for that, in fact, is what these storms are—can be counted on each and every late summer to impart to the region not only torrential rains but also skies washed marvelously free of dirt and dust, skies so pure and fresh they seem to sparkle. After a hard rain even the driest of desert horizons glistens like a wonderland beneath the brilliant blues and pinks of the dusk air, itself streaked with shreds of the departing storm.

The word *monsoon* usually brings to mind those storms in southeastern Asia that pour rain on the land as if some incessant, heavenly fire hydrant had been opened. Storms of the American Southwest are not as severe or lengthy as Asian storms, but they are called monsoons nonetheless because they are created by winds that alternate directions seasonally and occur over a vast area. American deserts happen to lie in that region of the Northern Hemisphere where there are definite seasonal shifts in storm paths. The cooling and warming of the earth's surface combined with the prevailing wind patterns cause these seasonal shifts, so that during winter the Southwest is visited by storms moving eastward from the Pacific Ocean, while in summer the storms move west and northwest from the Gulfs of Mexico and California. During summer, the east-moving storms from the Pacific have "migrated" too far north to have an influence on storm patterns in the Southwest.

How do these various convergences of temperature and wind go about creating the "male rains" of summer? When the warm, wet air presses in from the Gulf of Mexico, it rises quickly above the desert, buoyed by the hot air that has prevailed in early to midsummer. Massive, billowing clouds, some swelling to 7 or 8 miles in height, gather above the desert, expanding and darkening as they cover the sky. These are cumulonimbus clouds, huge puffs of moisture, frequently anvil shaped or at least flat on their "bellies," with the characteristic dark undersides that indicate imminent rainfall. Eventually, of course, the clouds reach a breaking point. No more moisture can be held, and a violent but usually brief thunderstorm ensues.

While roughly half the annual rain that falls in most desert areas of the Southwest comes during winter, it usually occurs in steady and small doses. In the summer, though, a place like Phoenix can receive as much as an inch or more of rain in a twenty-four-hour period—this in an area that only receives 8 or 10 inches of rain a year. City streets flood, streams and rivers swell and desert arroyos or washes overflow with rain after sitting dry and empty for nearly the entire year. Flash floods are an ever-present danger at this time of year, as storms can arrive with little or no warning and seem to descend in an instant. Tragically, drownings become common during monsoon season—often during storms that last just an hour or two. Stories of children being swept away while playing in waterways in cities such as Albuquerque and Phoenix are sobering reminders in evening newscasts.

But, as is often the case, where danger lurks, so lies beauty. After the hot months of May and June, when it is not uncommon to have absolutely no rain at all and the relative humidity drops to single digits, the rains of late summer are more eagerly welcomed than a two-week vacation. After June's wind and sunshine have sucked all the color and water from the land, storm clouds signal the return of life. By as early as the Fourth of July, though often not until a week or two later, monsoon season begins. The rains usually occur over an eight-week period, peaking in August, with an average of just under sixty days officially falling under the Weather Service's category of "monsoon days." In 1984, Phoenix had ninety-nine monsoon days, seventy-three of them in a row. It is not unusual for there to be more than thirty consecutive monsoon days during a typical Arizona summer.

Facts and averages can't relate the feel of a summer storm in the desert. It can only be experienced. There is the oddly ripe, electric smell of the approaching storm; the sight of the enormous, hulking clouds blotting out the sky with a heavy inevitability; the first light taps of rain, followed by a downpour that can cover several square miles and literally soak a person in seconds. And then there is the lightning and thunder, certainly the most dramatic and frightening players in the drama that is a desert monsoon. Huge cracks of light burst across the sky, while the accompanying booms rattle the land—and the ear—for emphasis. And finally, after the peace of the still, sweltering desert has been almost irrevocably shattered, a sort of gentler peace offers itself up as a replacement. It is a peace of subtle yet brilliant color—blues and yellows and reds paint the sky—and of a green that begins to reclaim the land from the brown that had held it for so many months. It is a peace of passing, tattered clouds and rainwater that runs in sheets and then begins to slow to drips and trickles. It is, at last, a peace of clear air, of pure sky and of a land once again blessed with water.

SEPTEMBER

49

Bugling Elk

The call of a mature bull elk during its rut is, like the howl of a coyote or the screech of a hawk, both haunting and unforgettable. It begins with a low moan, then quickly ascends to an eerie, anxious squeal that trails off in several thick barks. To hear this "bugling" on a crisp early evening in September, the surrounding aspens a brilliant gold and the pine-rimmed meadows a still-lush green, is to listen in on one of the most stirring, primal dramas of the Rocky Mountains. The elk rut is a raw, restless time for these, the wildest of our continent's deer; and it seems appropriate that its call is at once strange, majestic and defiant.

Few people would deny that the elk is the most impressive mammal in North America. Only the moose is larger among antlered animals, but the elk is unmatched in its fine proportions and regal bearing. It's often called "the Monarch of the Forest," and it's not hard to see why. Bulls routinely weigh well over 700 pounds and may hit the half-ton mark; they can reach speeds of over 30 miles an hour and can run for miles when spooked, possessing an uncanny ability to move quietly through dense brush; and, finally, mature bulls carry a massive, spectacular rack of antlers. This magnificence becomes more pronounced during the rut, when bulls become as edgy as a creature can get. Their necks swell; they cake themselves in mud and their own urine; and then, with noses running and eyes wide, they gather harems and attempt to fend off other bulls. A bull elk is polygamous, with some champion bulls corraling sixty or more cows for the mating season, though less than half that is more common. Like some harassed, fugitive sultan, he spends the rut protecting what he's got and breeding incessantly. Fights between bulls are generally brief and rarely result in any serious injury. There may be a bit of antler clashing and shoving and twisting, and then one will back down. Usually a smaller bull will be frightened off by one who simply displays his more massive antlers and body. Elk also give off a strong, musky odor that, it is believed, indicates rank just as much as do large antlers.

The most characteristic element of this frenetic rut is the bugle. It seems to serve as a sort of tension release, indicating everything from anger to challenge to insult all at the same time. The sound of one elk bugling can infuriate another bull, who seems to believe that here is some fellow who has either got what he wants or wants what he's got. At dawn or, more likely, dusk on into evening, bugling may echo throughout the forest like a volley of heckling screams.

A herd of elk travels through a forest. Elk feed on forest browse and, in open land, on grasses.

Bull elk start preparing for the rut in August, separating from the one or two male companions they may have had during their leisurely summer to begin polishing their antlers. Consumed with an as-yet-unfocused energy, bulls scrape the dried velvet from their antlers by "sparring" with saplings and lashing out at bushes and trees. Small trees stripped of bark are one of the sure signs of elk in early autumn. Their energy turns to mating and fighting, and after the frenetic rut is completed, the exhausted bulls, who probably ate little or not at all for a period of about three weeks, are left dangerously depleted of strength. Only good grazing before the snows begin will allow them to replenish themselves well enough to survive the long winter.

When Lewis and Clark made their way west, elk were abundant in the plains and treeless foothills. Indeed, their still-present herding instinct indicates that, like buffalo or pronghorn, elk were once more of an open country animal. Now they are found mostly in the high country of the West: above timberline in summer, down into spruce, aspen, fir and pine forests primarily, and the lower foothills and valleys in winter. Elk graze in meadows and on grassy slopes, though during winter, hunger can drive them to start taking chunks out of aspen for nourishment. Nearly extinct a century ago—or at least reduced to well under 1 percent of the ten million or more that once roamed parts of the upper two-thirds of the United States—elk today constitute a healthy and safe population, particularly in the Rocky Mountains. Elk do so well at present that hunters annually take as many animals—roughly seventy-five thousand—as once existed just over ninety years ago. September in the mountains will forever resound with the eerie and magical call of the elk.

HOTSPOTS

Rocky Mountain National Park in north central Colorado is one of this country's finest national parks. Its 414 square miles are filled with so much spectacular scenery and so many wildlife viewing opportunities that the park is, year in and year out, among the most popular in our nation's system, drawing nearly three million visitors annually. Trail Ridge Road, the highest paved through-road in the United States, climbs through four different life zones on its journey across the Continental Divide—the park is almost cut in half by the Divide—beginning in foothills and topping out in tundra above 12,000 feet. This is one of the most scenic drives in all of America. Pine, fir and aspen, meadows and tundra, streams and marshes, nearly one hundred mountain peaks taller than 11,000 feet—all of this lies within the park's boundaries, as do Rocky Mountain bighorn sheep, deer, moose and the small mammals and birds associated with the tundra and subalpine regions here. And, of course, there are the elk, abundant in the region well over a hundred years ago but reduced by about 1890 to only a handful. In the winter of 1913–14, about fifty elk from Yellowstone Park were transplanted to the area that would become Rocky Mountain National Park a year later. Predators such as wolves and grizzlies were killed off, enhancing the recovery of the elk. Today, between four and five thousand summer in the park, and about one-third that number can be found at the park in winter, the rest preferring to spend the colder months at lower elevations.

Rocky Mountain National Park is snow-covered in winter, providing a complete contrast to the flower-rich meadows and sunny forests of summer.During the autumn rut, there is no better place to hear elk calling. The best spots in the park are Horseshoe Park, Upper Beaver Meadows and Moraine Park, though at Rocky Mountain the elk provide such a fine show there is actually a group of volunteers on duty during September and October to direct visitors to the better spots. Created in the early 1990s as a means of dealing with the problem of overeager wildlife viewers, the Elk Bugle Corps, a group of roughly sixty-five volunteers, staffs the park solely to help visitors see and hear elk. The corps directs traffic, provides interpretive information and even passes out brochures from roughly 5:00 P.M. to 8:00 P.M. each evening through the end of October. It makes for one of the finest combinations of wildlife viewing and accessibility imaginable.

The best elk areas are on the park's east side and are reached by entering through either the Fall River Entrance Station for Horseshoe Park or the Beaver Meadows Entrance Station, though the two areas are also connected by road within the park. Both entrances are reached easily from the town of Estes Park on

US 34 and US 36. Strictly enforced park rules concerning elk viewing are as follows: stay by the roadside and out of the meadows to observe or photograph elk; stay out of the signed off-limits areas during the rut; turn off car lights and engine while observing and talk quietly; and do not call, whistle or imitate bugling. There is a $5 entrance fee for the park.

New Mexico's premier elk viewing area is the **Valle Vidal**. This enormous park area, surrounded by hills thick with aspen and fir, supports nearly two thousand elk, most of whom live in the area year-round. Hunters know the valley as the finest elk spot in the state. For wildlife observers, this makes September all the finer for seeing and hearing elk here, since most of the hunting is allowed only in October when the rut has concluded. Obviously, when the rifles come out, the elk become more skittish.

The Valle Vidal area is fairly remote, lying roughly 45 miles up a good dirt road off the highway. To reach it, head 5.4 miles east from the town of Cimarron on US 64, then look for a sign for the Valle Vidal Unit–Carson National Forest. A dirt and gravel road heads north, climbing through piñon, juniper, scrub oak and then ponderosa pine for many miles. You will reach the boundary of the Carson National Forest after 22.9 miles, where a sign indicates the Valle Vidal. The wide-open park area doesn't begin for another 20 miles, after passing McCrystal Creek Campground, the Shuree turnoff and the Cimarron Campground, all fine wildlife areas where there are elk as well as deer and even a rarely seen buffalo herd. In the valle area, elk viewing is at its best in the late afternoon or early morning. It is possible to drive all the way through on this dirt road and come out at Costilla on State Road 522 almost at the New Mexico–Colorado border; or, of course, you may just drive 50 miles or so into the Valle Vidal, see dozens of elk, then turn around to come back out on US 64. No place in New Mexico is better. **Mount Taylor** (see chapter 50) is another fine elk spot, with viewing possible right from the road through some of the higher meadow areas.

Northern Arizona is outstanding for elk. Pine and aspen forests, vast meadows and ideal temperatures make the Mogollon Rim area ideal elk habitat. This rim, which cuts diagonally across the state from roughly Springerville west to Lake Mead, is the southern edge of the Colorado Plateau, and its elevation creates a wonderland of forests and streams. Two of the region's best elk spots are near the town of Flagstaff. The first, **Kendrick Park**, lies northwest of Flagstaff on the way to the Grand Canyon. Take US 180 north out of Flagstaff, passing the Museum of Northern Arizona on the left just at the edge of town. From here, continue for 18.1 miles to the park area. The road passes through thick ponderosa forests with patches of aspen, only to open up into a vast meadow on either side of the highway. The San Francisco Peaks loom to the southeast, while the park, rimmed with pine, aspen and even some fir and spruce, will almost certainly reveal groups of elk in the morning or evening. At the 18.1-mile mark, a road travels to the right just in front of the Kendrick Indian Crafts store. This is Forest Road 514, and it passes through the heart of the vast meadow. At 1.8 miles, a sign for Kendrick Park is visible just before the road enters the forest. Back on US 180, continue north for another mile to the "Coconino National Forest Picnic Ground—Kendrick Park" sign and picnic area on the left side of the road. This pleasant ponderosa area offers good views of the west side of the meadow.

Just south of Flagstaff, fifteen minutes from the heart of town, lies **Rogers Lake**, a shallow, intermittent lake whose surrounding meadows are prime elk habitat. In wet years the lake covers several hundred acres; by late summer it may just be an open park. To reach it, take the I-40 Business Loop 3 miles west from the middle of Flagstaff to the turnoff to Woody Mountain Road, or get off I-40 at Exit 191 and travel east on the Business Loop for 2.5 miles to the turnoff. Woody Mountain Road turns to dirt after 1 mile, then reaches the Rogers Lake area 5.5 miles beyond this. A sign here indicates the lake in case there is no water visible. Look for elk anywhere—in the meadows, in the ponderosa pines that surround the low basin and along the road as you drive in. It is not unusual to see herds of twenty-five or more.

50

Piñon Nuts

Few things are as distinctively Southwestern as the tasty piñon nut, and few trees are as abundant throughout the region as the piñon. The state tree of New Mexico, the piñon dominates southwestern terrain from roughly 4,500 to 7,000 feet so that this belt is known as the Piñon–Juniper Woodland. The tree's appeal, however, stems from its ability to produce, in early autumn, nuts with a soft, creamy-white kernel coveted by humans and animals alike.

Piñon trees are common in what can be called the "in-between" region: higher than the deserts below but not as high as the more lush forests above. Piñon is common in New Mexico and Arizona virtually anywhere north of the southern deserts and can be found in Utah's lower half and Colorado's western third. Junipers share the same range, mixing with piñons on mesa tops, rocky plateaus and lower mountain slopes. On over 40,000 square miles, piñon trees, interspersed with berry-spangled junipers or, at higher elevations, vanilla-scented ponderosa pine, are representative of the Southwest, just as the aspen characterizes the forests 2,000 feet above.

The piñon is not, however, a particularly attractive tree. It is usually just about 15 to 35 feet tall, although an occasional giant of 50 feet may be found; its many branches twist and angle oddly; and its crown appears scrubby and ill-formed, though infrequently a straight, tall tree will grow. Its production of nuts, not its appearance, is the piñon's claim to fame.

With all the attention the piñon nut receives—highway vendors and trading posts sell nuts in abundance, and autumn pickers, often families of Native Americans, can be spotted collecting nuts off the ground or shaking them out of trees onto spread blankets—it would seem that the trees themselves would have long ago revealed all their secrets. And yet, the mystery of how and why the trees produce nuts persists. The woody piñon cones occur at the tips of the branches, passing through a cycle that comprises nearly three growing seasons. Nuts form within the cones during the second year and mature, along with the cone, during the third year. If all has gone well, with no disease or insect infestation or poor weather, the dark brown shells will hold within the small and tightly packed kernels.

The odd part is that none of this occurs with regularity. Some stands may produce little or none in any given year, while a 10-mile drive up the road might put a nut hunter in the midst of a bumper crop. But there are always good piñon crops some- where. If rainfall and sunlight were the deciding factors, predicting piñon crops would be easy. Forecasting nut production, though, is notoriously difficult. Generally, a given stand of piñons will have one or two outstanding crops in a ten-year period, with fair crops every two to four years in between. In about six years out of the ten, there will be no production.

Once the growth process starts, nut crops can be roughly predicted two years in advance, with fairly high accuracy one year in advance. When the green, pitchy cones, each holding about ten to twenty seeds, begin turning brown by mid-September and then, spurred by cooler weather, open up to reveal their dark brown shells, piñon season is in full swing. During good years, the nuts, as much as 20 pounds per tree, blanket the ground, providing food and winter caches for a variety of birds and rodents. Cracked nuts and animal droppings reveal the presence of squirrels and wood rats, and a variety of jays can frequently be seen collecting nuts and flitting from tree to tree. Blue scrub jays, Stellar's jays and piñon jays, as well as the gray and white Clark's nutcracker, are colorful, frequent and occasionally pesky companions of the piñon picker on a brisk autumn day. These birds, almost wholly responsible for disseminating piñon seeds, are the most voracious of the nut eaters, followed by rodents, turkeys, deer and even some bears. It's estimated that humans get less than 15 percent of the nuts produced.

But what a treat they are! It's easy to understand why so many southwestern Native Americans collect the almondlike nut and have references to its sustaining, even motherly, power in some of their legends. The piñon nut, harvested in autumn amid fragrant forests, cooling breezes and the rustlings of squirrels and jays, is a welcome prelude to the long winter ahead.

Here are a few tips for picking piñons. After the cones open, the entire crop of nuts falls within about a month, making late September and much of October prime picking season. Although—or perhaps because—piñon trees grow plentifully, trespassing on private property has become a major problem in many areas. The surest, safest and most courteous way to gather piñon nuts is to visit one of several national forests, where incidental nut picking is permitted. Bear in mind that nut crops are usually poorer at the fringes of the Piñon–Juniper Woodland, and always call ahead before trekking to a site. The local forest supervisor's office will know for certain by August if a nut crop is imminent, and they will know where nuts can be picked. Remember, there's always a good crop somewhere nearby!

HOTSPOTS

One of the best spots to find piñons is in the **Mount Taylor Ranger District** of New Mexico's Cibola National Forest. Mount Taylor is an extinct volcano, and now, at 11,301 feet, it looms over the San Mateo Mountains and surrounding woodlands. A graded dirt road passes just below the top of the mountain, affording a fine view of the area. The many dirt roads lower down or over the top of the high lookout point offer the best paths to the abundant piñon trees. Easily traveled when dry, the dirt roads cut through acre after acre of piñon stands. As they begin to climb higher and ponderosa or aspen appear, the chances of finding producing piñon trees decrease.

To reach the piñon stands on Mount Taylor, follow Route 547 north out of Grants, New Mexico. Approximately 2 miles up the road is the Ranger District Office, where maps that show the maze of dirt roads above can be obtained. Continue on Route 547, and just past the 13-mile marker, the asphalt turns to gravel. Well before that lie several dirt roads, including numbers 193 and 239, which can be taken to find seemingly endless stands of piñon. Call ahead to the Mount Taylor Ranger District (505-287-8833) for information. The number for the Cibola National Forest, which includes the Mount Taylor district and three others in New Mexico, is 505-761-4650. Another fine site for piñon nuts near Mount Taylor is west of Grants in the national forest region south of **Bluewater Lake**. Take I-40 approximately 25 miles west of Grants to Thoreau, and head south on Route 17 for 13 miles to Bluewater Lake. Continue south until, just past the lake, the road enters national forest land and vast tracts of piñons.

Other prime spots include the Jicarilla Ranger District (505-334-2876) of the Carson National Forest, accessible by Route 64 east of Farmington, New Mexico; the Camino Real Ranger District (505-587-2255) of the Carson National Forest, accessible by Route 518 south of Taos, New Mexico; and the entire Santa Fe National Forest (505-988-6940) in north central New Mexico. Roughly one-third of the national forests in northern Arizona and New Mexico and southern Utah and Colorado will have good piñon crops in a given year. See the appendix for a complete listing of telephone numbers.

51

Migrating Pelicans

The American white pelican is an odd mixture of the elegant and the peculiar. Imposing and resplendently white, the pelican also has oversized feet, an outlandishly long bill and a flabby throat patch. There are several great places in the Southwest to find large concentrations of pelicans in summer, but during their early autumn migration, their numbers peak.

Pelicans nest comfortably in marshy areas by lakes and reservoirs, flying dozens of miles daily to scoop up several pounds of fish to feed their young. They are efficient "dip" fishers, slurping up fish with their bills while swimming, rather than diving down to the surface to pluck out their prey. At times they work in teams, joining together to shepherd fish into shallower water where the feeding is easier. When September arrives, it is time to head south, the warmer Gulfs of Mexico and California being their prime destinations, though many pelicans also can be found throughout winter in the Lower Colorado River Valley.

Pelicans on the wing are an unforgettable sight. The black on their wing tips and outer secondaries provides a stark contrast to the rest of their white bodies. Their heads are drawn in rather than extended; and they fly with a heavy, almost sluggish determination, flapping several times, then gliding powerfully. Pelicans seem to enjoy soaring and circling high overhead, sparkling white in the afternoon sky, though when migrating in flocks they usually travel in a single line. And it is in flocks, whether on the wing or clustered together on some windswept, autumn lake, that the American white pelican is most impressive. As anyone who has ever seen a large group of snow geese or tundra swans knows, there is something pure and pleasing in seeing a collection of white birds, and the pelican is as impressive as they come. When dozens or even hundreds are bunched together or slicing through the sky, it's difficult to imagine that a century ago experts believed the bird would soon become all but absent in North America. It has persevered, providing us with one of the showiest of all autumn migrations.

HOTSPOTS

Fifteen miles north of the town of Carlsbad in southeastern New Mexico lies **Brantley Lake**, created after the completion of Brantley Dam in 1988. Huge flocks of American white pelicans use the lake as a migratory stop in September and October, just as they used to stop at Lake McMillan, now a playa-like area north of Brantley. The lake, which fluctuates between 300 and over 2,800 acres in size depending on how the Pecos River is flowing or how much water is needed downstream, sits in dry Chihuahuan Desert country, creosote covered and sunbaked. Brantley's waters attract plenty of visitors in summer, while autumn's mild-to-warm temperatures make for very comfortable bird-watching.

Bird-watching data on Brantley Lake are still being gathered, though it seems that the pelicans have continued to return to the area in undiminished and still-impressive numbers. Some of the best birding seems to be on the northwest side of the lake, with perhaps equally productive viewing from Brantley Lake State Park's day use area, which has easier access. To reach Brantley Lake State Park, travel north on US 285 from Carlsbad. The turnoff to the state park, County Road 30, lies 8.4 miles north of the turnoff to Living Desert State Park in Carlsbad. At the 2.4-mile mark along County Road 30, the road crosses the Pecos River, then passes through vast creosote flats. The visitor center and pay station ($3 daily fee) lie 2.2 miles beyond the Pecos. The day use area is 1.8 miles from here. It offers good views of the lake and the dam on the far side. By walking through the day use area, it is possible to see a good portion of the lake or walk right down to it. Gulls and terns are common, and there is an opportunity to see many other waterfowl on most days. More of the shoreline can be reached by taking the road to Rocky Bay just before the day use area. This gravel road leads to the park's primitive camping spots right beside the lake. Avoid mud here, or you may end up bird-watching longer than you intended!

Bitter Lake National Wildlife Refuge (see chapter 62), an hour and a half north of Brantley Lake State Park, attracts numerous migrating pelicans. It and **Bosque del Apache National Wildlife Refuge** (see chapter 62), along with Brantley Lake, are the three best spots in New Mexico to see pelicans. In Utah, the **Bear River Migratory Bird Refuge** (see chapter 56) can turn up flocks of four hundred or more, making it very nearly the best of all spots in a good year. Colorado's **Barr Lake State Park** (see chapter 2) northeast of Denver is visited by fair numbers of American white pelicans in September, though the state's best spot of all is farther to the northeast at **Jackson Lake State Park** (see chapter 10). Flocks of more than three hundred pelicans may stop over here in September.

52

Migrating Raptors

In late September, just as autumn begins to chill the high Southwest, a mountain lookout can be an uninviting spot. The sun, scorching hot one moment as it stares down on the exposed ridge, becomes suddenly ineffectual, overwhelmed by fierce breezes that chap the skin and shiver the bones. A novice bird-watcher, stories of legendary migrations still ringing in his or her ears, begins to wonder why he or she didn't take a picnic in the quiet pines below. And then a black dot appears to the east, growing larger and closer in a matter of seconds, wings suddenly coming into focus as the bird—a sharp-shinned or red-tailed hawk, perhaps—soars effortlessly, majestically, just overhead before sailing off into the clear afternoon sky to the west. Maybe another one follows just after it, and then two together, or five or six in a row. Maybe a merlin breaks up the parade of red-tails, or a flock of Swainson's hawks appears out nowhere. Binoculars poised, eyes scanning the horizon, all thoughts of discomfort disappear, lost in the growing excitement of tracking the mightiest birds of all, the raptors.

Hawks, eagles and falcons can be found almost anywhere in the West if you search hard enough. They feed on passerine birds, insects and rodents and, in fact, help to control the populations of the latter two. In some agricultural areas, raptors

A Swainson's hawk perches on a branch. Trees and telephone poles provide good vantage points for these sharp-eyed hunters.

such as the northern harrier (formerly the marsh hawk), the kestrel and the ubiquitous red-tailed hawk are very common. It is usually during migration, however, that raptors can be seen in large numbers, since they are almost always fairly solitary creatures.

Many raptors migrate south in the fall just like most other birds, seeking the warm winter temperatures in places as far away as Peru, though plenty are found in the United States during winter. A hawk may travel more than 200 miles a day in a migration that spans several thousands of miles, and so, like any smart traveler, it will try to get the best mileage possible. To this end, raptors seek the updrafts created on mountain ridges when prevailing winds press against a steep slope and then push up to the sky. These buoyant, invisible "highways" provide lift for the birds, who return to them year after year, so that when they migrate, raptors are commonly found following the windward side of mountain ranges. Great numbers of them can then be seen when they reach, as inevitably as salmon returning to the mouth of a river, some convenient and narrow ridge oriented along a north–south line. Here they pass over the ridge to continue their flight south, and it is at these points that raptors can be seen, often in staggering abundance.

While there are not many known lookouts in the Rockies—certainly nothing to compare to the world-famous eastern sites, such as Pennsylvania's Hawk Mountain—there are some outstanding ones. HawkWatch International, a nonprofit organization dedicated to studying and preserving raptors, staffs several of these lookouts during both spring and autumn migrations, counting birds to get a fix on raptor populations. It is intriguing work, based not only on an aesthetic appreciation for raptors but on the belief that these birds of prey, residing atop the food chain, can indicate much about a given ecosystem. Everything from drought and deforestation to disease and pollution may be reflected in fluctuating or declining raptor numbers.

Because the migration patterns of raptors in the Rockies are more diffuse than in some areas in the East, it is difficult to assert very much in the way of absolute patterns. Certainly, Cooper's, sharp-shinned and red-tailed hawks, kestrels, golden eagles and turkey vultures usually prevail numerically. The average for the two HawkWatch hotspots listed in this chapter is about 4,800 raptors over a six- to eight-week period—roughly 150 a day with peaks of more than 300 on better days. Less frequently seen raptors, which may fly through almost anytime during September, range from peregrine and prairie falcons to osprey and northern goshawks.

One encouraging finding amid all this raptor watching is that most species seem to be increasing in number. Why this is so is something of a mystery still, though if it is true, it says something good about the state of the West in general. The true interest in raptors, beyond any data or conclusions to be derived from their viewing, resides simply in their alluring combination of beauty and power. Just find a lookout in September and see for yourself.

HOTSPOTS

The two best and most-studied raptor hotspots in the Southwest are the HawkWatch sites in New Mexico's Manzano Mountains and Utah's Wellsville Mountains. The **Manzano Mountains** site hits peak numbers in late September, and early afternoon generally offers prime viewing time on any given day. Ideal weather is clear and sunny with good western winds. In September and October, there will be plenty of avid and knowledgeable birders at the site, as well as a HawkWatch staffer or two. The lookout is spectacular, with great views to the west as you approach by vehicle and even finer views to the north, east and west after taking the short hike to the lookout site. The rocky outcropping that serves as the lookout directly faces a north–south ridge that the birds pass over, and the cottonwood-lined ribbon of the Rio Grande appears far down and off to the west. Expect up to two hundred birds per day at this site, many more at season's height. To reach it, travel 15 miles east of Albuquerque on I-40 to Exit 175, the Tijeras–State Road 337 exit. Take this road south for 29.7 miles, then take a right on State Road 55. Follow this 12.1 miles to the 75-mile marker in the small town of Manzano. An adobe church lies to the left of the road; take Forest Road 245 on the right. A sign here reads "New Canyon Campground and Capilla Peak Lookout—12 miles." This bumpy road passes through piñon, juniper, oak and ponderosa pine, passing the New Canyon Campground after 5.3 miles, then getting steeper before reaching an area with radio towers and great views to the west 3 miles farther on. Less than a mile beyond this, a total of 9 miles from State Road 55, look for a sign to the left of the road indicating the Gavilan Trail. Stop here! Ahead of you just a short way up the road and to the left is the Crest Trail—don't take this one—and then an observation tower and camping area. Follow the Gavilan Trail an easy half-mile to the lookout.

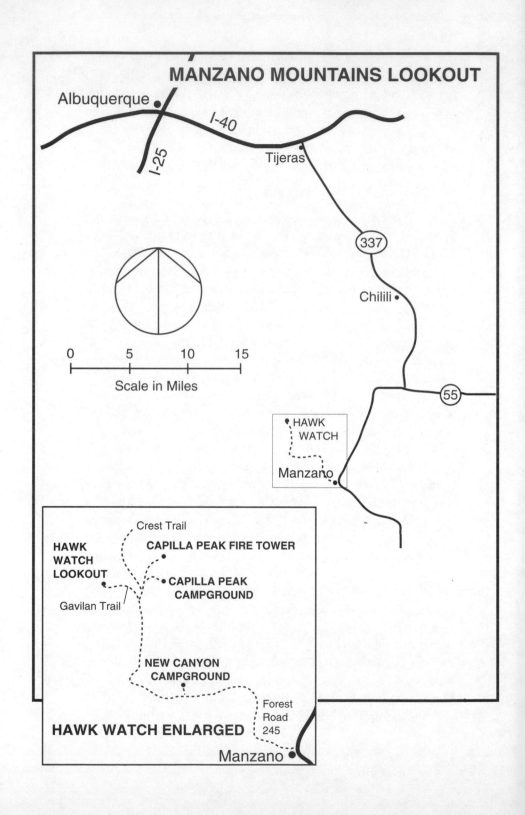

MANZANO MOUNTAINS LOOKOUT

Albuquerque

I-40

I-25

Tijeras

337

Chilili

55

0   5   10   15
Scale in Miles

HAWK WATCH

Manzano

Crest Trail

HAWK WATCH LOOKOUT

CAPILLA PEAK FIRE TOWER

CAPILLA PEAK CAMPGROUND

Gavilan Trail

NEW CANYON CAMPGROUND

Forest Road 245

HAWK WATCH ENLARGED

Manzano

In northern Utah lies the Southwest's other premier raptor viewing lookout in the **Wellsville Mountains**. The Wellsvilles are an isolated branch of the Wasatch Mountains, surrounded almost entirely by towns, farm fields and roads. From the lookout, the view is outstanding: Willard Bay and the Great Salt Lake lie far away through the haze to the southwest; the Bear River winds through the land to the west; squares of farmland are scattered everywhere, with mountains and foothills both east and north; and a spread of buildings and roads can be seen far below on three sides. The birds are fantastic: sharp-shinned, red-tailed and Cooper's hawks predominate, with plenty of golden eagles also.

The one thing most people remember best about the lookout, however, is the difficulty in getting there. Of all the sites listed in this book, none is more physically demanding to reach than the Wellsville site. Be forewarned: the 3-mile hike to the saddle below the lookout is tough! It passes through brush, too, so be prepared to get your clothes damp if the morning has been wet. The aspen and greenery are pleasant, but it is a genuine relief to finally reach the saddle near the top. Suddenly, the whole west side of the area is revealed and the vistas become staggering. Even for a good hiker, the trail will take about an hour and a half to cover. Start early in the day before it is too hot, and take plenty of water. From the saddle, turn right to hike along the top of the ridge for about half a mile to the lookout. A HawkWatch staffer or two will be here, but you won't find nearly as many birders as at the Manzano site.

To reach the Wellsville lookout, take Exit 364 off I-84 in Brigham City and travel 17.8 miles to the town of Wellsville on US 89/91. In Wellsville, go north on State Road 23 for 6.1 miles to the post office in the town of Mendon. Travel two more blocks and then turn left onto North 3d Street. The road curves, then straightens, traveling a total of 2 miles up steep gravel to a parking area. An old sign here reads "Deep Creek—3 miles." Walk up the half-road/half-trail, staying left at a fork. The "road" narrows to a definite trail shortly thereafter, then continues up and up and up.

At both of these sites, but particularly at Wellsville, bring good boots, water and sunscreen. If you plan to stay for any length of time, as you surely will want to, bring food also. Binoculars are essential, of course.

53

September Shorttakes

Butterflies

In southeastern Arizona, butterflies are at their best in September. Both in their numbers and variety, the butterflies of this part of the Southwest are astonishing, particularly because of the presence of some Mexican species found nowhere else in the United States. Look for California sisters, pipevine swallowtails, dog-faced sulphurs, red-spotted purples, marine blues, painted ladies, monarchs and up to two or three dozen more. **Ramsey Canyon Preserve** (see chapter 38) is the region's premier butterfly site.

54

Breakout: Arizona's Mount Lemmon

If you were to drive from southern Arizona all the way up to Montana, the inevitable latitudinal changes reflected in the plant and animal life along the route would be gradual. If you take the road to the top of 9,157-foot Mount Lemmon just outside of Tucson, though, the same changes in vegetation and wildlife become evident in a scant 30 miles. It is an axiom of biology that plants and animals are distributed in fairly well-defined groups and, furthermore, that these groups can be found at predictable latitudes and elevations. That is to say, traveling up a tall mountain will reveal the same changes in the biotic community that a several-hundred-mile drive north would: it's all the same to the flora and fauna.

A 300-foot rise in elevation is roughly equal to a 1°F drop in temperature. Climb high enough, and vast gradations of temperature and humidity become apparent, so much so that a 1,000-foot increase in elevation is about equal to moving 300 miles closer to the North Pole. The length of the growing season decreases, rainfall increases and winds become stiffer. When conditions alter, so does the vegetation that is able to survive. All plants and animals have in their genetic makeup information on the environmental conditions that will allow them to survive. Vegetation and wildlife are thus naturally sorted into what are called life zones or biomes—those communities or groups (of plant life, especially) that can almost always be found together.

The connection or equating of elevational zones with changes in latitude was first formally made by C. Hart Merriam, a biologist of the late nineteenth century who came to his conclusions after spending some time studying the San Francisco Peaks near Flagstaff in northern Arizona. Merriam's life zone theory has been criticized as too general and hence, has been abandoned by most biologists, but for the amateur naturalist it provides a handy means of grouping and understanding communities. Starting at the lowest elevations in the Southwest, there is the Lower Sonoran Zone, generally 4,000 feet and below where desert scrub—mesquite, creosote, palo verde—dominates and Gambel's quail, Gila woodpeckers, cactus wrens and Gila monsters can be found. Next one reaches the Upper Sonoran Life Zone of oak woodlands and desert grasslands. Above this, at roughly 7,000 to 9,000 feet, lies the Transition Zone where ponderosa pine forests are alive with the sounds of flickers, jays and nuthatches. Next comes the Canadian Life Zone, at 9,000 to 11,000 feet. Here one finds Douglas fir, white fir, black bears and yellow-eyed juncos—all more characteristic of America's more northerly latitudes. Higher still is the Hudsonian Life Zone, where Engelmann spruce and more fir can be found. Above that lies the Tundra or Arctic Zone, unknown in southern Arizona. North-facing slopes, because they receive less sunlight, are cooler and retain snow longer; thus their life zones tend to occur at lower elevations than those on southern slopes. On the northern side of a mountain, for instance, the Canadian Zone can be found at roughly 8,000 to 10,000 feet, about 1,000 feet lower than on a southern slope.

But the best way to gain a true understanding of the life zone concept is to drive to the top of a mountain, preferably one that shows off as many zones as possible. For this, nothing is better than the "sky islands" of southeastern Arizona, those ranges that are surrounded by an ocean of desert while peaking out at elevations of over 9,000 feet. Mount Lemmon, the tallest peak in the Santa Catalina Mountains northeast of Tucson, is ideal for discovering the four most common life zones in southeastern Arizona.

Take Speedway Boulevard east out of the middle of Tucson, and turn north onto Wilmot Road, following it as it becomes Tanque Verde Road. Four miles ahead, this road turns left to become the Catalina Highway. The road here passes through the Lower Sonoran Zone, with plenty of saguaro, mesquite, brittlebush, creosote and ocotillo. The road climbs quickly after passing the "Coronado National Forest" sign (all mileage given here will use this sign as a starting point) and affords fine views of the city. Saguaro gives way to scrub oak after about 4 miles, with open, grassy areas and even some willow in the draws. Evergreen oaks and grassland are found at Molino Basin, a popular camp-ground area at 4.8 miles, firmly in the Upper Sonoran Life Zone.

Oak dominates for the next 4 miles, with some yucca and agave also apparent. Pines begin to appear at the 9-mile mark. The Bear Canyon picnic area is reached after a total of 10.3 miles. The ponderosas of this Transition Zone area will dominate most of the rest of the route. Fine view points await just above, with Windy Point Vista at 12.8 miles and 6,300 feet offering an outstanding look at the Tucson Valley below.

After 14 miles, the ponderosas become noticeably denser and the road continues to climb up and up. At 18.3 miles, the Palisades Ranger Station lies just off the road; 2.3 miles beyond this is the turnoff to the 7,600-foot Bear Wallow Picnic Area. The life zones get a bit scrambled here in this area of ponderosas, Douglas fir, white pine and Engelmann spruce. After more fine vistas, you will reach the turnoff to the ski area at 23.1 miles, after passing through some aspen and white fir, along with the other mixed-conifer species found at Bear Wallow. One and a half miles up the road lies the ski area—and the end of the drive at a locked gate. This is a thickly forested area, and by late November the slope here may be jammed with skiers. The Tucson area is one of those unique places where it is possible to walk through a scorching desert at noon and then go skiing two hours later.

If you are a bird-watcher, you will undoubtedly notice the variety of species encountered during the journey from the lower Sonoran Desert to Canadian spruce and fir forest. Gambel's quail, verdin, curve-billed thrashers and Abert's towhees give way to acorn woodpeckers and scrub jays. Higher up, Stellar's jays, pygmy nuthatches, evening grosbeaks and pine siskins in the Transition Zone lead to yellow-eyed juncos and red-breasted nuthatches. It is a singularly fascinating and varied trip, this 30-mile lesson in life zones, and it's a lot easier on your gasoline bill than driving all the way to Montana.

OCTOBER

55

Fall Foliage and the Quaking Aspen

October in most of the West lacks the colorful brilliance of a New England autumn; we do not have the vast forests of deciduous trees that, spurred by late summer's shortening days, cool nights and good rains, explode in such dramatic colors in fall. But what we are denied in vast, general brilliance is more than compensated for by one delicate, bright, almost ethereal tree whose colors make it the equal of any New Englander's maple or oak. This is, as any good Rocky Mountain dweller knows, the remarkable quaking aspen.

As if to celebrate its own fresh, youthful spirit, the aspen stands in defiant contrast to the surrounding firs and spruces and pines. And, indeed, it is found in groves alongside all these others, populating open slopes in any region from the foothills to subalpine zones. Though not nearly as common in the East, the aspen has the widest distribution of any tree in North America.

Aspens play an interesting and protracted sort of leapfrog with conifers. When an area has been heavily logged or decimated by fire, disease or avalanche, the aspens quickly replace the previous evergreen tenants. Open spaces with plenty of sunlight and poor topsoil cry out for an aspen invasion. The graceful, white-barked trees oblige quickly, usually through a process known as "root suckering": a single aspen will send out surface roots, which develop shoots that grow their own root system. These "suckers" grow into 10-foot-tall aspens within seven or eight years, allowing the trees to thrive in large, unbroken groups. Meadow edges, high mountain slopes, exposed ridges—any place with abundant sunlight and moisture just below the surface is perfect for aspen.

For a few decades, maybe even the better part of a century, an aspen grove buzzes with activity and color: birds, mammals and insects seek food and cool cover in wet aspen glades; grasses grow high while wildflowers are at their Rocky Mountain best; and the delicate leaves of the aspen trees sparkle pale green in summer and gleam yellow-gold in fall. In time, though, nourished by the rich soil the rotting aspen leaves create, conifers move inexorably in and up, eventually casting a life-sapping shade that spells doom to aspen. Disease and age claim the once-vital trees; what had been aspen forest turns to fir or pine or spruce, until these trees are wiped out and the process begins anew. This does not occur inevitably and everywhere, however. Some aspen stands have endured for a century or more, young shoots continually replacing dying trees.

The adjective *quaking,* as applied to the aspen, is not difficult to account for. Winds that puff the slightest of breaths cause the aspen's leaves to shiver and shimmer, fixed, as they are, at the end of stalks longer than the leaves themselves. These stalks are also flattened at right angles to the plane of the leaf, serving as relatively fixed pivots to the easily disturbed leaves.

Like all deciduous trees, the aspen's colorful transformation in autumn is caused not by the introduction of some new pigment but by the withdrawal of chlorophyll, whose green dominates the leaves as they make food in spring and summer. When the nights get colder and longer, leaves stop production, chlorophyll breaks down and other colors already present blare forth. Because of the aspen's sucker system, it is not uncommon to see vast numbers of the tree change in color together; they are, after all, genetically identical.

Aspen are more abundant in the southern Rockies than anywhere else in the West, especially from roughly 6,500 feet to 10,000 feet and on the west side of the Continental Divide. Colors generally peak in early October, having begun to change in early September in the higher subalpine regions and a week or two later in the lower montane zones. On the right weekend, the sun bright in the crisp mountain sky, entire slopes are coated with glimmering gold as the gentle aspen announces the end of summer.

HOTSPOTS

It would be difficult to find an autumn drive more scenic than the **Nebo Loop Scenic Byway** south of Salt Lake City in the Wasatch Mountains. Utah, to the surprise of many people, has spectacular mountain scenery, and the drive around Mount Nebo showcases the best the state has to offer. Thirty-eight miles of glowing aspen, wondrous views and a stunning, closeup look at Mount Nebo, the tallest peak in this westernmost range of the Rockies, add up to one of the most rewarding fall drives in the Southwest.

Begin at the town of Payson, Exit 254 off I-15, where signs indicating the loop drive direct you up Main Street. Hit US 6 1.1 miles after leaving the interstate, still following the signs, then turn right after 0.5 mile to get on 600 East Street. Low hills, oak and cottonwood usher you up into the Uinta National Forest, with a sign marking the forest's boundary after 4.9 miles. After 2 more miles, the road climbs up into white fir and then aspen, fir and willow 3 miles farther on. Turnouts, trails and signs for camping areas become common, and the view begins to broaden. Aspen become thick and spectacularly colorful for the majority of the rest of the route, dominating the road, slopes and many meadows all around. The road continues to climb, cutting through picturesque meadows to reach the Payson Lakes Guard Station 8.9 miles after passing the Uinta National Forest boundary sign. After the Blackhawk Junction, 1.3 miles beyond the guard station, the views get even better, with broad vistas to the east and west. The road is over 9,000 feet here. The Utah Lake Overlook, 2.8 miles after Blackhawk Junction, offers a great view of mountain-rimmed Utah Lake, open to the west. It is the rich color of aspen in early October that is the finest sight of all, even atop this winding ridge with its overlooks of the Utah Valley and fine views of the Wasatch Mountains. Seven and a half miles after the Utah Lake Overlook is the Nebo Mountain Overlook, an impressive turnout that allows a reach-out-and-touch-it look at the mountain. From here the road winds and descends, returning eventually to oak, juniper and cottonwood, then crossing Salt Creek 10 miles after the Nebo Mountain Overlook. Two and a half miles beyond this, the road leaves the national forest. An information booth here may be stocked with maps. The road hits a stop sign 0.8 mile after the information booth. Turn right here onto State Road 132 and hit I-15 4.9 miles ahead at the town of Nephi.

The **Logan Canyon Scenic Byway** to the northeast of Salt Lake City in the Wasatch National Forest rivals the Nebo drive for outstanding fall foliage. From Garden City along the western shore of Bear Lake (see chapter 4), US 89 climbs to over 7,700 feet, allowing fine views of the lake below. The autumn colors lie ahead, though, as the road winds through scrub oak and then some pine and aspen to reach the "Logan Canyon Scenic Byway" sign 5.7 miles after leaving Garden City. There is a dramatic overview of Bear Lake 0.4 mile after the sign, and then the road descends into rolling hills, spruce and pine and miles of blazing colors created by aspen, willow, maple and cottonwood. The canyon's sheer limestone walls and rock formations provide an intriguing backdrop for the autumn leaves. Beaver Creek runs through the canyon, and the road passes through several meadows and then over the Logan River 17.6 miles after Garden City. The canyon area becomes more hemmed in with cottonwood and willow roughly 10 miles after crossing the river, and there are several turnouts for campgrounds and picnic areas. A national forest sign indicates the forest's western boundary 37.2 miles from Garden City. Main Street in the town of Logan is 3.4 miles ahead. The mouth of Logan Canyon, just east of Logan, lies at 4,700 feet— a drop of more than 3,000 feet from the hills above Garden City. Whether you begin on the east or west side of this drive, the route has color enough to satisfy even a New Englander.

New Mexico offers some great fall foliage. Try **Sandia Crest** (see chapter 25) for an outstanding drive up and into stands of aspen just outside of Albuquerque. At the crest, take the walk north from the cluster of communication towers. North of North Sandia Peak there are fine aspen areas, and the entire north-facing slope of the range is blanketed with a spectacular stand of aspen.

The best is last. Colorado is renowned for its aspen, and no place is better than the San Juan Mountains, where aspen grow in dense groves from roughly 8,500 feet to 10,500 feet. The **San Juan Skyway,** a 236-mile Scenic Byway loop, is difficult to praise too highly, as it delivers mile after mile of rich scenery and fabulous golden aspen. The road ascends to over 10,000 feet in some places, and even when you have climbed higher than the aspen, distant ridges gleam with color, while clear mountain views, alpine lakes and cozy valleys await. Some stretches of the road, particularly the "Million Dollar Highway" south of Ouray, seem to slice right through the mountains and then rise up to touch the sky.

The San Juans, the largest range in the U.S. portion of the Rockies, are uniformly beautiful. Deposits of sediment and millions of years of volcanic activity have crafted a range with more acreage higher than 10,000 feet than any other mountains in the country. Many of the first roads were laid down during the gold and silver mining days of the 1870s, and most of the area is just as rugged today as it was then.

Begin in Durango on US 550 and head north up into the San Juan National Forest. After 15 miles, ponderosa pine and some scrub oak dominate, and the mountains above sparkle with aspen gold. Just beyond this, the road passes through miles of thick aspen, turning to fir and spruce before 10,640-foot Coal Bank Hill Summit and then 10,910-foot Molas Pass. The best aspen thus far lie along the first 25 miles of US 550 out of Durango. You will reach Silverton after a total of 49 miles, with a bit of oak and aspen on the descent to the town. Ouray lies 23 miles ahead, after crossing 11,018-foot Red Mountain Pass; at roughly 8 miles before reaching Ouray, the road passes through a vast and outstanding aspen "bowl."

After the alpine heights of the Durango-to-Ouray portion of the drive, the already outstanding autumn colors become even finer. Continue north to Ridgway, 10.3 miles from Ouray, then turn west onto State Road 62. The next 24.7 miles grow more stunning by the mile, particularly after about 10 miles, when you reach the

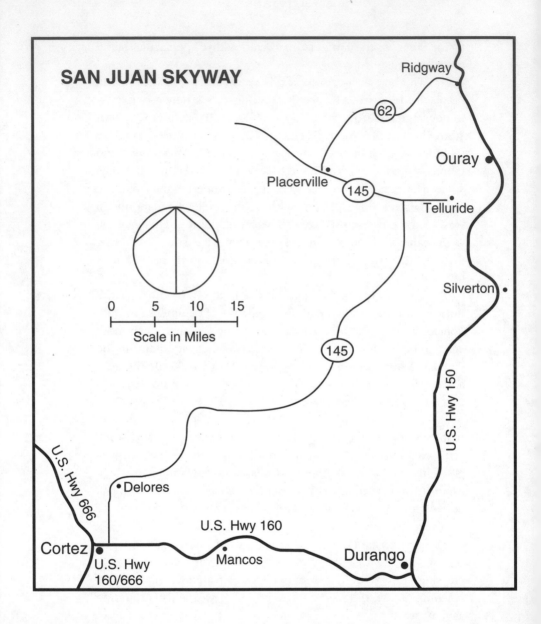

SAN JUAN SKYWAY

Ridgway

62

Ouray

Placerville

145

Telluride

Silverton

145

U.S. Hwy 150

0   5   10   15
Scale in Miles

U.S. Hwy 666

Delores

U.S. Hwy 160

Cortez

U.S. Hwy
160/666

Mancos

Durango

Dallas Divide. Meadows and ranchland are ringed with the massive mountains of the Mount Sneffels Wilderness. Aspen and some oak will be in full color. Cottonwoods appear just before the small community of Placerville, where a turn to the southeast puts you on State Road 145. The road parallels the San Miguel River in the canyon of the same name, a pretty drive lined with aspen, oak and cottonwood. At the 13-mile mark along State Road 145, take a brief 3-mile side trip up the box canyon in which the town of Telluride sits. Surrounded by mountains and aspen, Telluride is a full day of autumn color in itself.

Get back on State Road 145 for more of what may begin to feel like aspen overload. Within 5 miles of Telluride, the road passes through aspen-fringed meadows, then keeps climbing to awesome Lizard Head Pass before dropping down to follow the Dolores River through more aspen. The delicate tree dominates the area from roughly 20 to 60 miles after leaving Telluride, ending about 15 miles before the town of Dolores. Cortez lies 73 miles away from Telluride on State Road 145. In Cortez, turn east onto US 160 and travel 42.7 miles back to Durango, passing through smooth, rolling hills covered in areas with aspen and oak. At the end of the long day, with so much scenery and beauty behind you, the words *autumn* and *San Juan Mountains* may seem as perfectly linked as *quaking* and *aspen*.

One final note: The U.S. Forest Service operates a Fall Colors Telephone Hotline that offers recorded information about the best autumn foliage across the country, including national forest land in the Southwest. This unique and comprehensive information, updated each week, is available by calling 1-800-354-4595.

56

Waterfowl Migration

Waterfowl—ducks, geese and swans—are abundant in the Southwest in autumn. Actually, "abundant" hardly describes the startling numbers of birds that gather at some of the Southwest's refuges, lakes and reservoirs come October. At Bear River Migratory Bird Refuge in northern Utah, for instance, half a million ducks may be found, including tens or even hundreds of pintails and green-winged teals. The Southwest attracts so many birds during the autumn migration, when birds funnel south to warmer wintering grounds, that a birder visiting the right places at the right times may get some sense of what the West was like when such numbers were the rule rather than the exception.

Bird migrations in autumn differ from those in spring (see chapter 18) and not merely in terms of their direction. Most birds have their new flight feathers and some summer fat, and plenty of young are traveling also, making autumn numbers greater than those in spring. Waterfowl migration in fall is also much more concentrated, with large "fronts" arriving in the Southwest by October, then staying for a time (or even all winter, in some areas) before continuing south. Waterfowl, incidentally, will fly day or night during migration, whereas a majority of other species travel at night only. And again, just as with spring migrations, what prompts birds to migrate remains a mystery. The shortening of days, certainly, is a key factor, though conflicting theories abound. Whatever it is, birds depart, destined, along the Pacific and Central flyways, for California, Arizona, New Mexico and Texas and even a few temperate spots in Colorado. Many, of course, head for Mexico or even farther south, to parts of Central or South America.

While waterfowl migrations in autumn are undeniably impressive, they are nowhere near what they once were and have even declined dramatically over the past few decades. By best estimates, roughly one hundred million ducks, geese and swans depart from their summer breeding grounds at season's end, with less than half of these returning in spring, though much depletion is due to natural causes. Habitat destruction throughout the Americas—the transformation of the northern prairies from wetlands to farms, the deforestation of southern regions—has wiped out considerable numbers of waterfowl, however, and prospects for recovery remain uncertain. Some of the duck flights recorded in the late 1980s by the U.S. Fish and Wildlife Service were among the lowest ever, and since the mid-1970s some duck numbers have been cut almost in half.

In October, though, look for substantial numbers of mallard, pintail, green-winged teal, canvasback, redhead, cinnamon teal, scaup, bufflehead, goldeneye, gadwall, Canada geese and snow geese. The largest gatherings of tundra swans (formerly known as whistling swans) in the United States, roughly twenty thousand strong, may pass through the Bear River refuge in October. These magnificent, snow-white birds, who linger into winter some years, pierce the cool air with their mysterious, high-pitched yodel. Long-necked and possessed of a 6-foot-plus wingspan, the tundra swan is one of the most conspicuous and beautiful of all waterfowl migrating south in October. There were once so many of them at Bear River that just under a century and a half ago, early explorers told of thousands of acres covered with the birds. Those days, regrettably, have passed. But on a perfect autumn day, beside a lake busy with ducks, the sky above streaked with lines of geese, it may seem as if they've all returned again.

HOTSPOTS

It has been said that **Bear River Migratory Bird Refuge,** west of Brigham City in Utah, is the best place in the entire United States for seeing huge numbers of beautiful, captivating birds. Surely no one would dispute that the refuge is one of the few remaining spots where birds still gather in numbers even approaching those described by early settlers across much of America, or that the refuge is one of this country's prime breeding grounds for waterfowl and shore- and marsh birds. The Bear River refuge is one of the best birding spots in the country, ranking among the top twelve on Roger Tory Peterson's list of favorites.

Broad and treeless, the expanse of marshland, canals and impoundments that is the refuge is just one small fraction of the massive Upper Great Salt Lake Basin formed by the Wasatch Fault. The impoundments, some more than 5,000 acres, provide ample food for autumn waterfowl. These shallow, marshy areas attract throngs of birds throughout the year, making a spring, summer or fall visit endlessly fascinating. In fact, if you come in May or June, you are bound to see thousands of grebes, swallows, egrets, white-faced ibises, coots, killdeer, sandpipers, avocets, stilts and red-winged blackbirds, with many of these species numbering in the hundreds of thousands. Nearly 225 species have been counted at the refuge, with over 60 nesting in the summer. You may see half a million birds easily during your visit. Sometimes you can see half a million swallows alone. By October, when many of the shore- and marsh birds have departed, equally numerous groups of ducks, geese and swans take their place, drawn to the open, fresh water of the refuge's tens of thousands of marshy acres. The sight of three hundred thousand pintails is nothing short of amazing.

To reach the refuge, take Forest Street west from where it intersects with Main Street in Brigham City. Forest Street crosses over I-15 2.3 miles after leaving Main Street, continuing west across the flats to skirt the Bear River on the left 3.4 miles after the overpass. A mile beyond this the road turns to gravel before becoming pavement again 1.5 miles later. After this, the road alternates gravel and pavement and is fairly unmaintained. The road keeps skirting near the winding river; look for plenty of birds on the water. A sign reading "Bear River Migratory Bird Refuge" stands 15.1 miles from the Main Street–Forest Street intersection in Brigham City, with signs just beyond this one indicating the route for the 12.5-mile tour loop. A bird list and map are available at an information booth by the river and just as you begin the loop route. Interpretive signs have been posted along the way as the road winds through marshy flats and open water. At one time there were observation towers for viewing, but a severe flood in 1983 destroyed them. Not to worry, the birds are still there.

There are other outstanding sites farther south on the Great Salt Lake, making the entire lake area one of the nation's outstanding spots for waterfowl as well as other wetland birds. The **Harold S. Crane Waterfowl Management Area** at Willard Bay northwest of Ogden is visited by vast numbers of waterfowl in October, though its large mudflats give it a different feel than Bear River. This major stopover point for waterfowl, the southern portion of the Bear River Bay, can be reached by taking Exit 354 off I-15 (look for the sign for Willard Bay). You will be on State Road 126, but look immediately to the right for a sign reading "Willard Bay State Park—2 Miles," and turn right here. This is 4000 North Street. Follow it straight for 2.4 miles (do not turn right at 1.4 miles; this road leads to the state park), where the pavement ends. Look for the "Willard Bay Wildlife Management Area" sign and continue on the dirt road to a fork 0.3 mile ahead. Stay left to head west through mudflats and a marshy reservoir area. The massive impoundment to your right contains the waters of Willard Bay Reservoir. At 2.7 miles beyond the fork in the road, look for the "Harold S. Crane Waterfowl Management Area" sign and proceed just beyond it to the parking area. A vast pond and marsh area here, surrounded by mudflats, hosts many of the same species seen at the Bear River refuge. Watch out for muddy roads; even safe-looking flats can be dangerously spongy.

Farther south along the Great Salt Lake lies the **Ogden Bay Waterfowl Management Area,** known as one of the finest wetland areas in the United States and a near-equal to Bear River. At roughly 20,000 acres, the management area sits squarely in the delta created by the Weber River as it flows into the Great Salt Lake. With shallow, marshy areas, open water and sophisticated water control systems, it attracts hundreds of thousands of ducks by late

September into October, as well as plenty of geese and swans. Just as at Bear River, much of the Ogden Bay area is still trying to recover from the flooding that occurred over a decade ago. Gates into the management area may be locked at times, and some road alterations have been planned for many years. Nevertheless, foot traffic along the dikes is allowed year-round. Waterfowl numbers generally peak during the first week of October, with pintails and green-winged teals leading the charge.

To reach Ogden Bay, take Exit 341 off I-15. Turn right onto State Road 97 and head west for 2.1 miles. State Road 97 ends here, so turn right onto State Road 108, take it for 0.2 mile, then turn left—west—onto State Road 98. This is also 5500 South Street. Travel west for 5.2 miles, then turn right onto a gravel road (7500 West Street), following it past the "Dead End" sign to the "Ogden Bay Wildlife Management Area—South Access" sign just beyond. If this gate is locked, you will need to get out and do some walking. Straight ahead 0.5 mile along the paved road lies a parking area with marshland and ponds just to the north and west; the south run of the Weber River is next to the parking area. Dikes wind around and through the pond areas. From this first parking area, four more lie scattered along the 1.5-mile road to the southwest, which is where the largest of Ogden Bay's vast ponds lies. Of course, if the first gate is open, drive to any of these parking areas. It is a vast, open place, alive with a constant babble of bird "talk."

Bosque del Apache National Wildlife Refuge and **Bitter Lake National Wildlife Refuge** (for both, see chapter 62) in New Mexico are outstanding waterfowl hotspots in October. In Colorado, the **Monte Vista National Wildlife Refuge** (see chapter 63) can be equally productive.

57

Pronghorn Antelope

The pronghorn is the fastest mammal in the Western Hemisphere, perhaps in the world over any long distance, and yet it races across the plains with such grace and fluidity that it hardly seems to be exerting itself. Suddenly, within a minute of being spooked and taking flight, a herd of pronghorns is a mile distant, outrunning danger and the chill October wind with complete, instinctive ease. The animals move together, flowing and shifting like a flock of birds, until they are out of sight or safe—just long enough for a human spectator to realize how fast the creatures were moving. Indeed, the wonder of seeing such pure speed embodied in such a handsome and agile form takes getting used to.

At one time, there existed creatures in the New World that could challenge the pronghorn's speed. Those others died out and the pronghorn survived, its speed a lingering but now vastly disproportionate advantage. The pronghorn, in fact, is the only remaining member of its family and is the only hoofed animal native to North America. Deer, elk and all the other more popular big game animals are "immigrants." The pronghorn evolved here millions of years ago and has no other close relatives anywhere in the world, making it a true native of America and a true creature of the West. Thus, it is odd that, in spite of its exotic beauty and near-supernatural speed, the pronghorn is a relative unknown outside of those regions it occupies. Perhaps this is because the buffalo, the only other big animal that historically shared the pronghorn's range, has grabbed most of the glory associated with the West's wide-open plains. Or perhaps it is because pronghorns seem so insubstantial. Whatever the reason, the pronghorn endures, more than the buffalo ever will again, as a vital part of the West.

Like the buffalo, the pronghorn was able to thrive on the open spaces at the middle of this continent, and its numbers swelled to well over fifty million, according to early settlers. But also like the buffalo, the pronghorn proved attractive to hunters, if more for its meat than its bristly hide, while the inevitable fences that ranchers laced across the plains disastrously impeded its free-ranging habits. By 1900, pronghorn numbers were at roughly fifteen thousand and dropping. Sound game management practices wrought a miraculous comeback, and pronghorns at present number at least half a million. Their range may be smaller now than it once was, but pronghorns are in no danger of dying out. They graze successfully on browse plants common in ranching areas—sage and chamisa are among the favorites—thus avoiding competition with cattle. Ranchers don't mind them, and hunters kill them in reasonable numbers. Furthermore, predators rarely catch them, and when they do, the pronghorn proves a vicious fighter, kicking and scraping with its powerful legs, as more than a few coyotes have found. The pronghorn is here to stay.

Aside from its speed, the most striking thing about the pronghorn is its handsome coloration. The pronghorn is tan on most of its upper body and white on its underside, the inside of its legs and its rump. Two white bands across its throat and swaths of white on the face complete its sharply defined honey-and-milk beauty. It looks so unique and exotic that settlers called the pronghorn an antelope, a name that has fairly well stuck, despite its inaccuracy: no true antelopes are native to any regions outside of the Old World. The male's horns—true horns, not antlers—curve backward, and a single, flat "prong" bends inward on the front of each. At roughly 3 feet tall, the size of a small deer, the pronghorn presents a well-proportioned, handsome form. At a full run, the animal is nothing short of pure grace.

A portrait of an uncommon pronghorn antelope doe, with horns.

Because the pronghorn lives in open land, it needs speed—and the strong, tendon-tough legs to go with it—as well as acute eyesight, estimated to be as powerful as an 8-power telescope. While this may or may not be true, the pronghorn can certainly detect even slight motion on the horizon several miles off. In the sage flats, plains and foothills it inhabits, the pronghorn's eyesight is of incalculable value, and the animal will avoid entering even lightly forested areas at all costs. Always alert and curious, the pronghorn's sleep is fitful, and during the day it moves through a jittery, constant cycle of graze-scan-run.

If you are lucky enough to come across a group of pronghorns as you are driving in their range, you may have what is a somewhat common but undeniably odd encounter with them. Running parallel to you, the small herd will slowly accelerate, pushing up to 30 or 40 miles an hour easily, a speed they can maintain for miles. Then, when the angle is right, they will begin to slant toward you, gaining just enough speed to leap across the road directly in front of you with a split second to spare. For some unknown reason, pronghorns have a habit of doing this—to horses, trains, cars. Sometimes the animals will pause to look back after they have "bested" you, almost as if they were gloating. It is as if some ancient spirit had, however briefly, triumphed.

HOTSPOTS

September through October is the heart of the pronghorn rut, when the bucks attempt to gather small harems by tussling with one another and nervously minding their does. By the time mating has ended, pronghorns gather in herds more than they do during their leisurely summer, making October an ideal time to see perhaps a bit of rutting activity and certainly larger groups of the animal than you would be likely to see in summer. And while Wyoming and then Montana are the best pronghorn states nowadays, there are pockets of the Southwest that are every bit as good.

The northeastern corner of Utah, Flaming Gorge Reservoir country, has some of the finest, up-close pronghorn viewing on the **Lucerne Peninsula.** This is sage and juniper land, a broad, open plateau that overlooks the crystal blue waters of Flaming Gorge and is rimmed in places with interesting red rock formations. This is a protected area with a nearby campground and marina, and the pronghorns are so accustomed to human presence they can often be found in the camping areas. Look for the animals at water's edge, on the road and in the sagebrush grasslands all around. To reach the area, head east out of the small town of

An alert herd of pronghorn antelope does and fawns on the grass-lands. When only four or five days old, fawns can outrun a human.

Manila on State Road 43 from the intersection of State Road 44 and State Road 43. The road can be momentarily confusing just ahead as it enters Wyoming. Look for the sign for Lucerne Valley Road (Forest Road 146) at 4.2 miles and turn onto it. Reenter Utah 2.4 miles ahead and look for pronghorn everywhere. The campground and marina lie 1.9 miles after returning to Utah. This is a scenic spot, and the pronghorn viewing is among the most guaranteed anywhere.

Classic pronghorn terrain lies to the east in the semidesert sagebrush areas of western Colorado. Outside of the town of **Kremmling,** enormous rolling hills covered with sage provide ideal habitat for large numbers of pronghorn. By early to mid-autumn, large herds of pronghorn gather in the vast, wide-open spaces here, making it possible to see good numbers of both bucks and does. The best area for viewing can be reached by traveling 1 mile east of Kremmling on US 40 and turning north onto County Road 22. This well-maintained dirt road passes through broad and immense sage hills. Look for pronghorn to the east, especially. The best viewing is within the first 2 to 3 miles. Beyond this there are ranches and homes. The first few miles off US 40 is private land also, but there is no human presence. In Colorado, also try the **Pawnee National Grassland** (see chapter 33), in particular, the Pawnee Buttes.

Outside of Wyoming and Montana, the largest concentrations of pronghorns are found in northeastern New Mexico. This is short-grass prairie and badland country, with plenty of grass and low brush covering the rugged ground created by long-extinct volcanoes. As far as scenery and landmarks go, there really is nothing much to speak of. There are open grassland, soaring hawks and plenty of pronghorn. The region's best pronghorn area is along State Road 120 west out of the small town of **Wagon Mound.** The road passes through private land, with the Sangre de Cristo Mountains looming to the west as you drive to Ocate, 20.5 miles west of Wagon Mound. Low hills and flat grasslands offer ideal pronghorn habitat. Drive all the way to Ocate, or go as far as you like before returning to Wagon Mound, which lies along I-25 about two hours northeast of Santa Fe. If you want to see pronghorn—and plenty of them—this is the Southwest's prime spot.

Just north of Wagon Mound and to the east, US 56 between **Springer** and **Clayton** can be equally productive. This 80-mile drive through prairie land can turn up hundreds of pronghorns on a good October day, morning or late afternoon being the best viewing time, as it is in any pronghorn area. Springer is 25 miles north of Wagon Mound on I-25. This corner of New Mexico is exceptional for pronghorn, and though the roads pass through broad ranching areas that offer little in the way of spectacular scenery, the pronghorn viewing is second to none.

58

Moose

Many people are surprised to learn that moose inhabit some of the forests of Utah and Colorado. These mighty creatures, the largest antlered mammals ever to live on earth, are generally thought of as creatures of the far north. And, indeed, while they are found across almost all of Canada and Alaska, one wide branch of their range swings down through Idaho, Montana and Wyoming into the northern parts of Utah and Colorado. Here, in habitat generally less boggy and muddy than that found farther north, the moose has thrived, pushing its range even more southward in recent years.

Bull moose and elk have many points of similarity, particularly during their ruts. Like the elk, a moose stirred by the impending mating season will scrape clean his massive antlers, thrash small trees and shrubs to blow off some steam, create wallows in which he cakes himself with mud and his own urine and posture or fight with other bulls to establish dominance. Unlike elk, however, moose gather no harems, preferring instead to stay with only one cow for a week or so before moving on to a new mate. The cow moose also plays a fairly active role during the rut, playfully inviting bulls to her and answering a bull's grunting call with her own loud wail. October is the heart of the four- to six-week rut; at its conclusion, the moose, like his elk cousin, is ragged and depleted.

The Shiras moose, the species found in the Rockies, is smaller than his northern brothers but still plenty big—roughly half a ton for a mature bull. Moose prefer the cold conifer and aspen forests of the north where there are plenty of lakes and streams, but it is clear that any similarly forested region with nearby meadows and bogs will serve (moose territory dips down into Minnesota and parts of New England). Throw in plenty of shrubs and deciduous trees for browse (willow is a particular favorite), and moose can thrive.

Despite its impressive size, in any comparison with the elk, the moose will usually come out looking less favorable. With its long snout and droopy upper lip, humped shoulders, big feet and long legs, a mature moose looks ungainly and ill-formed. On further consideration, though, each apparently awkward part serves an exact and refined purpose. The moose's long snout allows it to browse both underwater and high up on tasty tree limbs; the oversized shoulders and chest house massive lungs for strenuous running and swimming; and its thin, gangly limbs and large feet give it balance and strength for traveling through snowy, muddy terrain. If the sum of its parts is less than its whole, it is of little concern to the moose, who is as regal-looking as any animal alive come autumn. With its distinctive, broad rack of antlers, over 4 feet from tip to tip on a Shiras, the moose stands alone as the largest deer in the world.

HOTSPOTS

Many of the last few chapters have featured large animals in rut, not out of some voyeuristic preoccupation but because during their mating season, most of these animals become far less cautious and can usually be seen with more ease. The moose is no exception. While these horse-sized animals are usually content to stay most of their lives within very limited areas—5 square miles is big enough, if sufficient food is available—the rut finds them at the peak of activity and movement. They also become dangerously and recklessly aggressive, occasionally charging anything from a human being to a car or even a train. Exercise considerable caution and good sense when in the presence of a moose.

During the early 1990s, the Colorado Division of Wildlife and the U.S. Forest Service transplanted thirty-one moose to the upper Rio Grande area about 25 miles west of the town of Creede in south central Colorado. Despite plans to release more in the near future and the hopes of biologists that someday the area will support hundreds of moose, at present they are tricky to find. At **Clear Creek,** the primary initial release area, the few moose in the region now roam over several hundred square miles of national forest land. To reach Clear Creek, take State Road 149 from the small town of South Fork 22 miles northwest to Creede. From Creede, the road winds and climbs through meadows, aspen and fir, with peaks all around and the Rio Grande often in sight to the south. The road dips south, then north, and at 20.5 miles beyond Creede, look for Forest Road 510 to the east. This road winds 4.5 miles through mountain riparian area; with plenty of willow and surrounding pine and fir, this is ideal moose habitat. One of the original release sites was right near the campground along Clear Creek. Because of the high degree of variability in moose movement here, you would do well to contact the Colorado Division of Wildlife before searching for moose in this area.

While the Creede area is the southernmost location of moose in Colorado, others have been living in the northern portion of the state for more than fifteen years. The Colorado Division of Wildlife introduced moose to the North Park area of north central Colorado in 1978, and this remains the best spot in the state to see them. The verdant basin that is North Park, surrounded by impressive mountain ranges to the east (Medicine Bow), the west (Park) and the south (Rabbit Ears and the Never Summer Mountains), is laced with several meandering creeks and rivers, including the North Platte and the Canadian. It is along the **Illinois River,** however, which eventually joins the Michigan River near the town of Walden, that moose viewing is at its best. To reach the prime viewing area, head north on State Road 125 from its junction with US 40 3 miles west of the town of Granby. Follow this quiet road through pine and fir, up and over the Continental Divide at Willow Creek Pass, then down into North Park territory. Seven miles past the Divide, still in heavily forested terrain, look to the right for the few cabins that comprise Old

Homestead. This is the turnoff to County Road 21. Follow the road downhill and cross the Illinois River, then turn east, keeping the river to your right, and follow the road 6 miles straight ahead to the river. Eventually the county road becomes Forest Road 740 and then Forest Road 750, but there are clearly marked signs at each junction, and at the fork of 740 and 750 a sign indicates "Illinois River—2 miles" to the right. When the road finally veers south and hooks back up to the river, an "Illinois River" sign indicates you have arrived. Park by the sign and walk or drive very slowly along the road that skirts the low ridge above the river. It is a marshy, willow-choked stretch here, perfect browse habitat for moose. After 0.3 mile, the road turns to the right into dense forest, making viewing more difficult.

If Colorado seems like an unlikely state for moose, Utah seems even more unlikely, though the hardy creatures actually thrive there. In the Fishlake National Forest at the center of the state, which has some of the highest peaks and most scenic forests in Utah, there is a growing moose population, one more accessible than those in the northern parts of the state. **Fish Lake,** nearly 9,000 feet high and rimmed with aspen, is a center for moose activity, though they range over a large area. State Road 25 makes a loop through the heart of ideal moose range, beginning a few miles southwest of the lake. To reach State Road 25, get off I-70 at either Exit 48 (Sigurd) or Exit 40 (Richfield), depending on whether you are approaching from the north or the south, respectively. From either town, get on State Road 24 and follow it south past its junction with State Road 119 for 24 miles to the signed turnoff to Fish Lake. This is State Road 25. The lake lies 7.6 miles ahead, the Forest Service Lodge 1.2 miles farther. Definitely make a stop at the lodge, where recent moose sightings are documented and maps and information are available. Actually, many moose sightings occur in the surrounding camping areas along the road by the lodge and even next to the ranger station. The best time to look for moose is in the morning.

Continue on State Road 25, which runs alongside the lake. There are pullouts, picnic and camping areas and thick stands of aspen. A nice trail rims this side of the lake. Willow bottoms in the area attract moose. Two and a half miles beyond the lodge, the road moves away from the lake, then enters more marshy meadows. Climb up to the Johnson Valley Reservoir, 8 miles beyond the ranger station, and to more meadows 3 miles beyond this. Trailheads for Splatter Canyon and Ivy Canyon follow, with plenty of streams and willow flats all along the route. While Fish Lake is home to plenty of moose, many are also sighted in these more remote but equally accessible areas.

The road curves to the southeast after rounding Johnson Valley Reservoir. At 11 miles past the reservoir, look for a sign to the right for Wayne City. Stay on State Road 25, with the Mill Meadow Dam to the right just a mile ahead, then reach a junction with State Road 72 1.5 miles past the dam. To the north, State Road 72 meets I-70 after 32 miles; to the south, State Road 72 hits State Road 24 in the town of Loa after 10 miles.

59

October
Shorttakes

Kokanee

These salmon (see chapter 45) have a spectacular run in **Navajo Lake** in northwestern New Mexico that is most visible near the dam on the lake's southwest end. Fishermen converge on the lake in droves, and the fish are easiest to see near the spillway or near the rocks southeast of the dam. The lake, situated in picturesque canyonland, is reached by taking US 64 east out of Bloomfield for 20 miles, then State Road 539 north for 5 miles.

The **Roaring Judy Hatchery** along the East River in Colorado north of the town of Gunnison also has a kokanee spawn in October. While this is not truly a natural area, the viewing is first-rate. To reach the hatchery, take State Road 135 north out of Gunnison for 11 miles to the town of Almont. Then continue north on 135 for 4 miles to the hatchery.

60

Breakout:
Canyonland Colors

Of all the scenic canyons in southeastern Utah and northeastern Arizona, Canyon de Chelly may be the easiest to appreciate. It doesn't overwhelm; it enchants. Sculpted to a scale that we humans can comprehend, with a touch of history and just enough clear running water, Canyon de Chelly is gentle and accessible. When autumn arrives and the cottonwoods that grace the canyon floor turn yellow-orange against the towering red cliff walls, Canyon de Chelly seems otherworldly in its beauty, yet also somehow familiar. Unlike the weird, desert-baked canyons to the northwest, or the massive Grand Canyon due west, Canyon de Chelly is welcoming and intimate, colorful and comforting in autumn.

The geology of the Southwest's canyonlands region reveals millions of years of dramatic change. Mountains rose and were slowly leveled; ancient seas deposited layers of sandstone, shale and limestone. In this land of infrequent rain and sparse vegetation, the process of erosion has eaten away the rock to reveal bizarre formations at places such as Canyonlands National Park, Arches National Park and Capitol Reef National Park. Canyons, mesas, scarps—all of the massive and wondrous rock that dominates and defines this area of the Southwest can be explained by the simple but lengthy processes of sedimentary deposition and erosion. And these deposits were set down in a variety of ways.

The Colorado Plateau is an erosional feature, formed at one time or another by oceans, lakes, swamps, deltas, enormous floodplains, streams and tidelands, mountains and, of course, deserts. The plateau, the high region encompassing southern Utah, northern Arizona, southwestern Colorado and northwestern New Mexico, was created roughly sixty-five million years ago as a massive uplift occurred on this part of the continent. The Colorado River cut into the plateau as it rose, eventually revealing millions of years of history in the Grand Canyon, while tributaries and washes ate away at the sandstone in other areas to create canyons and dramatic formations. Thus it is water, interestingly enough, that has sculpted the most fascinating places in the desert. Moisture—ice that hardens and expands in fissures, summer rains that relentlessly pelt smooth sandstone or rapid rivers and washes that tug at rocks—breaks up the land and carries away sand and silt. Gravity finishes the work already begun: gorges become canyons as rocks and cliffs tumble into the water below.

The color of this land is at its best in autumn. The cottonwoods that often line the streambeds, rivers and washes of canyons turn a soft orange, contrasting with the magnificent red sandstone so characteristic of the Southwest. Canyons are cooler and crisper in fall, allowing the visitor to enjoy their color without the glaring summer sun that seems to blister the sandstone. Canyon de Chelly, where cliff dwellers, Hopi and Navajo have all lived and where ancient ruins and rock art abound, offers the best of a canyon in fall: towering cottonwoods, a sandy wash, sheer red cliffs over 1,000 feet tall. Small washes from out of the Chuska Mountains to the north and east carved the rocks of this national monument, which, while far from containing the deepest or widest of all canyons, has an undeniably unique peacefulness and beauty. Navajos, who were once rounded up by the U.S. Army here, still live and farm in parts of the canyon (they own the land here; the National Park Service only administers it), maintaining cornfields and peach orchards. Most of the monument, which consists of two canyons, Canyon de Chelly and Canyon del Muerto, can be viewed only from the rim. People do live here, after all. But take the White House trail to the canyon floor to experience the area at its best. The trail snakes down through smooth "dunes" of sandstone, graceful and deeply red rock that seems to have been hardened in some ancient kiln. Cross the sandy, slowly trickling wash at the bottom, bounded by enormous cliff walls, to the cool cottonwoods on the opposite side. The White House ruin, one of the most beloved and most photographed spots in the entire Southwest, lies nestled beneath an overhang in the cliff streaked with a smooth, natural varnish. Color, history, solitude, beauty—it all converges on an autumn day in canyonland.

NOVEMBER

61

Golden Eagles

Certain Native American tribes of the West, some of whom have long used golden eagle feathers in fans, headdresses and other sacred paraphernalia, once employed an ingenious method to catch the great bird. A hunter would dig a sizable pit, crawl inside, cover the hole with branches, then place a dead rodent atop the trap and wait. When a hungry eagle landed, the hunter would burst through and strangle it, almost certainly receiving more than a few scratches in the process. The bird, which, according to some native legends, could pass through a hole far up in the sky and then return to this world bearing messages from another, had been caught.

The golden eagle may be more impressive than its bald cousin. While its uniformly brown body is not as dramatic in coloration (the gold feathers on the back of its head and neck give the bird its name), its bill is less coarse-looking and smaller than the bald's, its feet are in better proportion to its body and its form is sleeker overall. A golden eagle presents a body very much like that of a hawk's, though with a greater wingspan. In habit, too, the golden is a bit finer than the bald eagle. Its wide circles that graze the clouds; its skillful, falconlike hunting; the way it soars over ridges before diving down quickly to snap up a jackrabbit or scurrying rodent—all of this puts the bald eagle's lesser hunting skills to shame. The golden eagle even nests nobly, generally selecting high, craggy mesas or cliffs in remote areas. No wonder it was once the only bird flown by European royalty during falconry's heyday. The golden was known as the "King of Birds," an apt description that still fits today.

Immatures have white at the base of their outer wings, with a white patch above the dark band on their tail that, in time, becomes a light area on a faintly banded tail. There is the notorious confusion in differentiating an immature bald eagle and a mature golden eagle (see chapter 2); goldens gain their adult plumage after three or four years. A golden eagle's wingspan on average may be just a touch smaller than a bald's. Its wide, blunt wings give it tremendous lift. It can ascend at low speeds, lugging some chunky cottontail, perhaps, and can soar powerfully, "leaning" against the wind for a long while without a single stroke of its wings.

The golden eagle is a true creature of the West, having been fairly well driven out of the East, where it is seen only during migration or perhaps briefly in winter. In the West, golden eagles are found year-round and are very common in some foothill, mesa and mountain regions. In November, when cold weather sets in, golden eagles are more active and more visible than in most other months. While rabbits and rodents comprise more than 90 percent of a golden's diet throughout most of the year, carrion may account for over half of its food in winter. Golden eagles can often be found at lower elevations in winter, scanning fields from perches rather than just soaring at distant heights.

Golden eagles are not endangered in the western United States, though they may no longer be captured as they once were. Nowadays, all dead eagles are sent to a repository in Oregon, where federal law mandates that they be examined. After clearance, native people can apply for permission to use the feathers in traditional ceremonies. A strange, though perhaps necessary, measure for such a spectacular bird.

HOTSPOTS

New Mexico, with its combination of high mesa lands and open plains, is ideal for golden eagles settling in for winter. Try

State Road 120 west out of **Wagon Mound** (see chapter 57) or
Maxwell National Wildlife Refuge (see chapter 2), where three
or four dozen may move in when cold weather begins. Another
great area for golden eagles lies along the road to the west of
Maxwell. Rather than turning east back to I-25, take State Road 505
west for 9.9 miles to its junction with US 64. This road is
unmaintained and worn away to dirt in some spots. Scan the sky
as you drive, particularly as the road draws closer to US 64. Turn
south onto 64, passing the Valle Vidal turnoff (see chapter 49) at
6.9 miles, to reach the small town of Cimarron after another 5.4
miles. The entire route from Maxwell is grassland and juniper, with
cliffs and foothill areas to the north. North of Carlsbad Caverns,
between **Carlsbad and Artesia** (see chapter 34), the telephone
and power poles along US 285 are frequently used as perches by
golden eagles.

In Arizona, try the drive through the **Sulphur Springs
Valley** (described in chapter 67) for golden eagles scanning fields
from utility poles or soaring high above. This is one of the most
consistently rewarding spots for golden eagles in Arizona by late
November. At about the same time of the month, golden eagles
may be found in relatively good numbers at Utah's **Bear River
Migratory Bird Refuge** (see chapter 56).

Mesa Verde National Park in southwestern Colorado is
an ideal spot for golden eagles, and the Anasazi ruins nestled in
its cliff caves are an added bonus. A great hump of land rising
above the rolling hills below, Mesa Verde is laced with snaking
canyons and covered with piñon and juniper. Eagles, held aloft on
stiff winds, sail above the vast mesa land's rugged cliffs and
canyons, hunting for prey. Virtually any overlook or pullout in the
park gives tremendous views, with Park Point, at an elevation of
8,571 feet, offering the most panoramic. The Knife Edge Trail near
the Morefield Village area is considered the best place in the park
for spotting golden eagles. To reach Mesa Verde National Park,
head east on US 160 for 10 miles from the town of Cortez and look
for the park entrance on the south side of the road. There is an
entrance fee of $5 per vehicle.

Both the **Arizona–Sonora Desert Museum** (see chapter
31) and **Living Desert State Park** (see chapter 34) have golden

eagles in captivity. Whatever your feelings about displaying animals in cages, this is the best chance a bird-watcher will ever have to see these magnificent birds up close. To look a golden eagle in the eye from 10 feet away is to deeply appreciate the bird's imposing presence.

62

Snow Geese

A species' scientific designation generally holds little poetic magic. Yet the original scientific name for the lesser snow goose, *Chen hyperborea*, reveals some of the mystery and wonder this bird has always elicited in the human imagination. "Goose of the north wind," this name means, and like tangible bits of the wind, autumn finds these graceful, brilliantly white geese returning south from their summer breeding grounds in the extreme northern reaches of the Canadian tundra.

The lesser snow goose (the greater snow goose is the slightly larger eastern version) is unmistakable in the field. White-bodied with black wing tips, snow geese migrate in flocks of several hundred at 1,000 feet or higher above the earth. With their loud, nasally "ouck-ouck" call and their U-shaped or oblique lines in flight, snow geese are a distinctive harbinger of approaching cold.

Snow geese begin arriving in the Southwest by the middle of October, having left their Arctic nesting colonies by mid-September. They follow the Pacific and Central flyways, some continuing south into Mexico for the winter. Interspersed with the white snow goose is its darker form, the so-called blue goose, once thought to be a separate species but now recognized as the same bird with a grayish body. The blue form of the snow goose has the

The light of the morning sun greets a flock of wintering snow geese at a southwestern lake.

same white neck and head as its pure white and far more numerous brother, and both have the distinctive black lips that seem to affix a permanent dry grin to their bills. (The black lips as well as the slightly larger body and longer beak allow the snow goose to be distinguished from the Ross's goose, another white bird with black primaries occasionally found along with the snow goose throughout the Southwest.)

Snow geese winter in wetlands, marshy areas along rivers or lakes that have an abundance of cottonwood and willow trees for night roosting and nearby open fields for daytime feedings. Several of the Southwest's national wildlife refuges, where snow geese can number in the tens of thousands during autumn and winter, grow corn and alfalfa and other crops or enlist nearby farmers to do so to provide each bird with the 60 or so pounds of food it will need before returning north in mid-February. These vast fields draw the geese to feed throughout the day. In fact, the most dramatic views occur at dawn and dusk when, during the "fly-outs" and "fly-ins," long, noisy lines of geese depart from or return to their night roosts. You can see massive congregations of birds in their feeding grounds throughout the day as nearby large fields turn into jittery oceans of dense white.

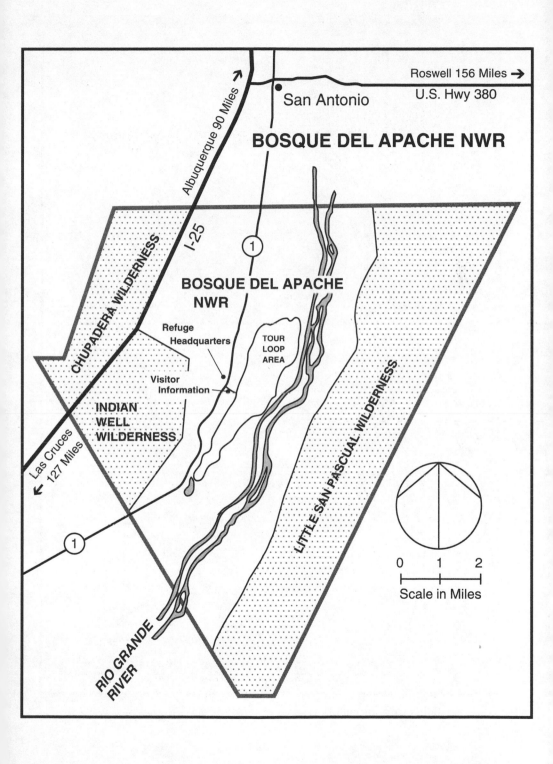

Roswell 156 Miles →

San Antonio

U.S. Hwy 380

BOSQUE DEL APACHE NWR

Albuquerque 90 Miles

I-25

① 1

BOSQUE DEL APACHE NWR

CHUPADERA WILDERNESS

Refuge Headquarters

TOUR LOOP AREA

Visitor Information

INDIAN WELL WILDERNESS

LITTLE SAN PASCUAL WILDERNESS

Las Cruces 127 Miles ←

① 1

RIO GRANDE RIVER

0   1   2

Scale in Miles

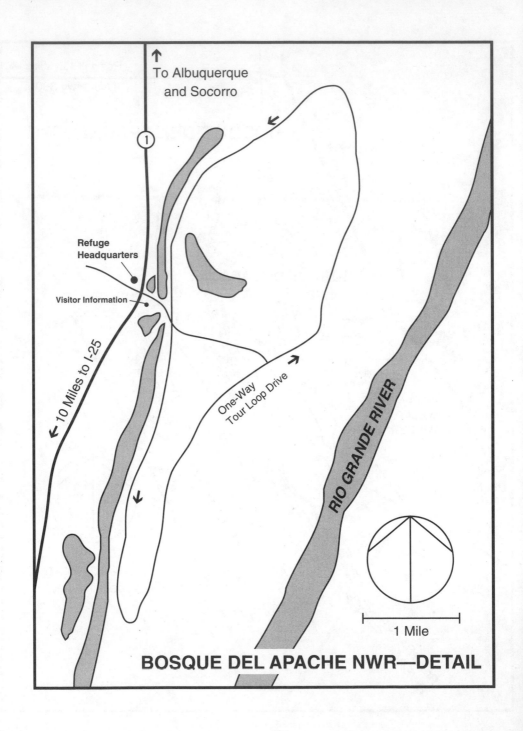

To Albuquerque
and Socorro

1

Refuge
Headquarters

Visitor Information

10 Miles to I-25

One-Way
Tour Loop Drive

RIO GRANDE RIVER

1 Mile

BOSQUE DEL APACHE NWR—DETAIL

November is a fine time for viewing snow geese through-out the Southwest, as many flocks pass through Utah and Colorado and then settle in primarily along the Rio Grande in New Mexico and the Colorado River along the California–Arizona border. By the end of November, some areas are home to tens of thousands of geese. In 1985, Bosque del Apache National Wildlife Refuge in central New Mexico reached a peak of over sixty-five thousand. Viewing in November, before much of the heavy snowfall has arrived, also allows a fine look at the crucially important contrast between the teeming, vibrant ribbons of wetland along the Colorado and the Rio Grande and the often barren lands that lie on either side of both rivers. With the trees losing the last of their foliage and the air tense with an approaching winter chill, it is easy to see why wildlife is attracted to the sheltering waterways and lakes of the Southwest's riparian habitats. Snow geese—known as *Chen caerulescens* these days, a name once used only for the blue goose—are beautiful reminders that wetlands sustain life even as the surrounding land begins its long winter slumber.

HOTSPOTS

Consisting of 7,000 acres of farm fields and marshland and 50,000 acres of desert uplands along 9 miles of the Rio Grande, **Bosque del Apache National Wildlife Refuge** in central New Mexico is one of the Southwest's premier sites for viewing wintering waterfowl. Snow geese begin arriving by about the first of November, with numbers beginning to peak by the end of the month. A well-managed system of dikes and waterways allows the refuge to create numerous water impoundments adjacent to fields of millet, chufa, corn and other supplemental crops. This conjunction of water, food, shelter and space creates an ideal wintering site for the more than forty-five thousand ducks, thirty thousand geese and seventeen thousand cranes that the Bosque supports.

Dawn and dusk are probably the best times to witness the more dramatic in-flight congregations of the geese, though they can easily be viewed feeding in the refuge's fields throughout the day. A 15-mile one-way loop affords a magnificent tour of the Bosque's wildlife. Along the southern portion of the loop—marshland with an abundance of cottonwood and black willow—one can find several species of ducks, mallard primarily, but also plenty of pintails, shovelers, teals and gadwalls. The loop's northern section, which has more open space, is where thousands of snow geese and sandhill cranes can be found throughout the cold winter days. Also look for northern harriers, red-tailed hawks, American kestrels and bald eagles. Coyotes can also occasionally be seen anxiously scanning the fields from the surrounding fringe of trees. On a late autumn day, with lines of honking geese strung across the sky and the jagged range of the Chupaderas as a backdrop, Bosque del Apache is about as lovely as the Rio Grande gets.

To reach Bosque del Apache, take I-25 approximately 85 miles south from Albuquerque to Exit 139, and take the east off-ramp directly into the small town of San Antonio. Signs direct you to State Road 1 heading south. Enter the refuge boundary at just over 3 miles; the refuge visitor center is at the 8-mile mark. The tour loop road (self-guided and open 365 days a year from one hour before sunrise to one hour after sunset) is on the east side of the highway, directly across from the visitor center, which is open seven days a week but closes on some holidays.

Las Vegas National Wildlife Refuge, just outside of the town of Las Vegas, New Mexico, is another good spot for snow geese. Situated on the flat highlands of the northeastern portion of the state, the refuge combines marshland and a sizable lake with grassland and agricultural fields. On a nice day in November, large numbers of snow geese can be found on and around the lake. To reach the refuge, take I-25 about an hour north out of Santa Fe, and at the town of Las Vegas get off on State Road 104 headed east. After a mile and a half, turn right onto State Road 281 and continue to the refuge headquarters 4.4 miles ahead. A half-mile farther is the Fred Quintana Overlook of Crane Lake, a bluff above a small lake where sandhill cranes may be seen. Three miles farther up the road is Lake McAlister, which offers ample parking and large numbers of easily seen ducks and geese.

Another outstanding site for snow geese is the **Bitter Lake National Wildlife Refuge**, adjacent to the Pecos River in southeastern New Mexico on the fringe of the Chihuahuan Desert. This refuge's wetland habitat is ideal for waterfowl. There are actually three sections to the Bitter Lake refuge, but the main section and best area to see snow geese can be reached by taking US 285 just north out of the town of Roswell, then turning east on Pine Lodge Road. Follow this road for 7.1 miles to reach the refuge headquarters. From here, begin a 7.4-mile loop drive on a gravel and dirt road that passes through marshland and open fields. The Salt Creek Wilderness area north of the main refuge area and reached by taking US 70 is also a fine spot for wildlife viewing, including mule deer and more waterfowl.

Two more spots that generally have large populations of wintering snow geese are **Imperial National Wildlife Refuge** and **Cibola National Wildlife Refuge,** both in southwestern Arizona (see chapter 1).

63

Sandhill Cranes

Like the American bison, the sandhill crane was once common across the plains of the Midwest, its rich, buglelike trill a familiar sound, particularly during its autumn and spring migrations. Also like the bison, though, sandhills proved attractive to game hunters and were slaughtered by the thousands. Couple this with the cultivation of the plains, effected by draining prairie swampland, and cranes became not only shotgun targets but the possessors of a diminishing habitat. For a time this mighty prairie scout seemed to be headed toward an all-too-common demise.

Today, with protected habitats and abundant food sources, primarily in strategically located refuges and sanctuaries, flocks of sandhill cranes fill western skies with their graceful forms and their loud, rolling calls. Sections of the Platte River in Nebraska see gatherings of up to four hundred thousand sandhills in early spring as they prepare to return to their summering grounds, the northern prairies of the United States and Canada and the Arctic tundra. And where do these birds come from? Many have departed from their wintering sites in the Southwest, where wetlands and food sources have sustained them from October through February.

Autumn migrations of sandhills are dramatic and easily viewed. Since thousands of these great birds are heading to southern Arizona and New Mexico and destinations ever farther

Silhouetted against the sunset, a small flock of sandhill cranes glides through the winter air.

south, it is possible to view them in large numbers in Utah and Colorado at the very beginning of November and then in even greater congregations farther south by the middle of the month. At 3 to 4 feet in height and with wingspans of over 6 feet, these slate gray birds are hard to miss. About the only species they might be confused with is the great blue heron, a bird of about the same size and shape but one that flies with its neck pulled in, a distinct contrast to the outstretched neck of the crane. Up close, sandhills display equally unmistakable features. Look for the striking patch of red on the crown; the slightly bluish coloration (immatures are brown), often with hints of rust; the long, delicate legs; and the tuft of feathers that hangs down from the rump like an untucked shirt.

Sandhills in flight have a certain heavy grace, particularly when just taking to the air. There is the slight scooping of the head, the extreme extension of neck and legs and the upward flick of the wings. But this apparent fragility belies what can be a fierce aggressiveness if provoked. John James Audubon, in an often-told story, was once attacked by an angry sandhill and forced to leap into a river to avoid being stabbed by the bird's pointed, jabbing bill. Audubon, incidentally, made a second and more lasting error with regard to the sandhill, claiming it was merely the immature form of the whooping crane and not a distinct species.

Many of the Southwest's sandhills—the greater sandhills, that is, as opposed to the lesser sandhills who pass through Nebraska on their way to northern Canada—summer in the fields and marshes of Idaho and Montana and up into southern Canada. Here is where their notoriously wild mating dances occur—the loud, frenzied hopping and racing; the noisy, wing-flailing congregations of birds that gather in open areas at dawn and exhaust themselves in their mating ritual. November viewing of sandhill cranes may be less exciting, but seeing lines of these huge birds in flight, winging their way to grainfields during their daily feeding "migrations," can be equally rewarding. The best time to see these wary birds up close is during their lengthy feeding sessions throughout the day in the open areas surrounding the marshlands that attract them. Whereas in their summer breeding grounds sandhills take much of their food from marsh waters, in winter they feed primarily on grasses and grains, maintaining their strength for their imminent return north. It is a cycle that has recurred annually for as many as ten million years. Sandhill cranes, unlike some of their less fortunate brethren in the American wilderness, show every sign of persevering.

HOTSPOTS

Sandhill cranes winter in some of the same spots as snow geese, often making it convenient to see both at the same time. **Bosque del Apache National Wildlife Refuge** (see chapter 62) has thousands of wintering cranes as well as geese and is one of the finest spots in the Southwest to view sandhills. **Bitter Lake National Wildlife Refuge** is similarly populated, as is **Las Vegas National Wildlife Refuge** (for both, see chapter 62).

Perhaps the best place to see sandhills in Colorado is **Monte Vista National Wildlife Refuge** in the arid San Luis Valley of the south central portion of the state. Though the valley receives scant rainfall, nearby towering mountain ranges provide enough water flow to supply the region's vast farmland acreage. Wetlands and grainfields being the two crucial elements that attract the cranes, the San Luis Valley is an important stopover point for the migrating birds, though they may depart from Monte Vista as early as the first week of November. The refuge may be reached by heading south from the town of Monte Vista for just over 6 miles on State Road 15. The refuge headquarters is immediately east of the road and is well marked. A 2.5-mile dirt-road loop winds through the ponds and dikes of the 14,000-acre refuge, allowing easy viewing of not only the cranes but also a variety of waterfowl. The loop road rejoins State Road 15 0.7 mile south of the refuge headquarters, the point where the loop road began.

In Arizona, sandhill cranes may be found at **Cibola National Wildlife Refuge** (see chapter 1) and, more prominently, near the **Willcox Playa,** an enormous dry lake bed south of the town of Willcox just off I-10. This "lake" in southeastern Arizona fills with water only after heavy rains, but it provides a roosting site for sandhill cranes in winter and allows them proximity to the grainfields of the nearby Kansas Settlement area. Willcox is roughly 80 miles east of Tucson on I-10. To reach the Kansas Settlement region, head southeast out of Willcox on State Road 186 for just over 6 miles and then turn south onto the Kansas Settlement Road. Four miles south on this road is a signed wildlife area with parking space, and a hike west at this stop allows a view of the playa. You are more apt to see sandhills, though, by staying on the road for another 2 to 5 miles and examining the area's farm fields.

64

Rocky Mountain Bighorn Sheep

The violence two bighorn rams inflict on one another during their mating season battles—the precise and powerful charges, the jarring head crashes that echo like rifle blasts as much as a mile distant—is not only spectacular but somehow humbling. If their fights weren't so entirely instinctive, they might be lessons in ritualized, restrained violence, neatly devoid of the malice or vengeance that often taints conflicts within our own species. Nature has a knack for revealing our own excesses, and few of her shows are more instructive or more exciting than the late autumn bighorn battles, enacted on snow-frosted stages amid some of the lower forty-eight's loftiest and most rugged terrain.

By any measure, the Rocky Mountain bighorn sheep, the largest wild sheep in North America, is an impressive animal. Stockier, more muscular and darker than its less populous cousin, the desert bighorn, the Rocky Mountain bighorn, particularly at close range, looks as sturdy and solid as the mountains it inhabits. The prominent white patch on the rump is the only bodily mark that might draw attention away from the most obvious and dramatic of the bighorn's features, its massive horns. While ewes have slender, sickle-shaped horns with only a slight curve, rams grow a thick pair of C-shaped ones that curl back and then circle forward alongside the face. A 7- or 8-year-old ram's horns may have grown through a complete circle, leading the sheep to "broom" or break off the horn tips so that they do not obstruct his peripheral vision. Unlike bony antlers, which species such as deer and elk grow and shed seasonally, the sheep's horns grow throughout his lifetime, much like claws or hooves, reaching weights of more than 30 pounds. Definite ridges form along the horns after they undergo their most rapid growth during spring and summer, creating rings that, like a tree's, reveal exactly the ram's age.

From early spring through late autumn, male bighorns band together in small groups—"bachelor societies"—and live apart from the larger herds of ewes, lambs and immature males. Both herds summer in remote alpine regions, often at elevations of over 9,000 feet, feeding on mountain grasses and sedges and replenishing a strength depleted during the harsh winter months. As autumn begins, the herds move down to valleys more than a mile lower than their summering grounds, where running water can be found and sagebrush and willow can be nibbled on throughout the long Rocky Mountain winter.

By late November, the rams join the larger herds of ewes at various rutting sites. Males of roughly equal horn size begin challenging one another, slightly at first—kicking, bumping, prodding—and then, if a nearby ewe is in estrus, more seriously. While it is more common to see bighorn rams merely tussling with one another, the rare sight of two in full battle is unforgettable. The rams will move away from one another, perhaps 10 yards apart, though usually much closer, and then, as if on some mysteriously synchronized cue, will simultaneously rear and charge, legs driving as the two animals smash heads with a terrific noise. Many fights last for only half a dozen charges, though some may last the better part of a day. One of the rams eventually gives up, while the winner breeds the ewes and tries to keep other rams away.

Watch for this sort of nervous, protective activity throughout the rut, which lasts into mid- or late December. Small groups of sheep, with a dominant ram and perhaps one or two straggling males, will divide up for winter foraging. A ewe in estrus will scamper about and feed absently, skittishly avoiding the eager ram who hovers behind her like an unrelenting bad date. He moves to her; she prances away. They engage in a lengthy, almost comical courtship, until eventually she allows him to breed her, something that entails far less posturing if she is at the peak of her receptivity.

While bighorn sheep are not considered an endangered species today, earlier in this century their numbers had diminished to alarmingly low levels. Once relatively abundant throughout parts of western North America, with a population of perhaps two million, bighorns, which include Dall sheep, stone sheep, desert bighorn and other subspecies, now number about fifty thousand in the United States and Canada, up from a low in the 1920s caused by hunting and human encroachment. Since that time, with banned and restricted hunting and state transplant programs designed to reintroduce sheep to some of their historic range, the Rocky Mountain bighorn—the wild sheep found most abundantly in the high mountain states—has thrived. In Colorado alone, where the bighorn is the state animal, approximately seventy herds contain roughly six thousand of these majestic animals.

Despite their success, bighorn sheep still are in retreat from human advances, inhabiting the more remote and isolated regions of the western mountains. According to some wildlife experts, bighorns once dwelled more in the valleys and foothills than in the high mountains. If this is true, it is ironic that the habitat we instantly conjure when picturing the bighorn is possible only because we have pushed the animal up into it. They have retreated in response to us; their "normal" habitat is a recent adaptation.

HOTSPOTS

While the desert bighorn sheep, an inhabitant of some of the most desolate and arid land in the United States, is intriguing in its own right, the Rocky Mountain bighorn is the larger of the two cousin species and more easily viewed. And while the desert bighorn, the so-called North American camel, remains elusive through its ability to go as many as three days without water, some of the better spots to find the Rocky Mountain sheep during their late autumn ruts are near their frequently visited water sources.

The Arkansas Headwaters Recreation Area, a 45-mile stretch of Colorado's Arkansas River along US 50 between Cañon City (35 miles west of Pueblo) and Salida, affords prime bighorn viewing. There are numerous turnoffs and established recreation sites, including Five Points and Parkdale, along the route. This is classic bighorn canyon country: the river courses through a cut at the bottom of steep cliffs on either side, with abundant piñon and juniper trees covering the surrounding hills. Look for sheep all along this route, particularly from Parkdale to Cotopaxi and from Howard to Salida, as they come down to the Arkansas to drink. The road travels parallel to the river on its south side, and though bighorn can be seen on both slopes of the canyon, they are more likely to be seen across the river on the north side, often at very close range. Have your binoculars ready, and be careful when pulling on and off the road, even at the established turnoffs. If the sheep don't get spooked by the train that occasionally puffs through the canyon, it is possible to watch them drink, feed and frolic—and perhaps even fight—for long stretches of the crisp afternoon.

Probably the easiest spot for viewing bighorn is right off I-70 in the town of **Georgetown,** roughly 45 miles west of Denver. Hemmed in by steep mountains on all sides, the area around Georgetown provides outstanding wintering habitat for bighorns. A herd of about two hundred, one of the larger gatherings in the state, inhabits the area, and with a sharp eye it is even possible to spot them just off the interstate as you drive by. A better idea is to take Exit 228, go 1 block south, then follow the frontage road east for about three-fourths of a mile to a viewing area along the edge of Georgetown Reservoir. Signs point the way, and within the immediate area of the town, radio frequency 530 AM plays a recorded message about bighorn viewing. A small observation tower with spotting scopes is at the viewing site, and you must scan the steep slopes across the interstate to see the sheep. Looking for the generally wary animals as vehicles race past is a strange sensation, but this area offers one of the best and probably most accessible opportunities for bighorn viewing in Colorado.

The Colorado Springs area offers some good prospects for sheep watching. From Manitou Springs, just a few miles west of Colorado Springs, a short rugged drive leads up **Rampart Range Road,** an area where bighorns often descend to the lower reaches of the steep Rampart Range during late autumn. In Manitou

Springs, take the Garden of the Gods Road. A half-mile past the entrance sign to Garden of the Gods Park, renowned for its magnificent rock formations, look for Rampart Range Road to the left. This is a dirt road and can be muddy or, at best, bumpy, even if it is not covered with snow. The road climbs quickly up through wide-open slopes, offering broad vistas of rugged piñon–juniper terrain. Use binoculars to look for bighorns on the slopes above you. This rugged road goes on for almost 25 miles to the town of Woodland Park, though the sheep will most likely be seen—if they're going to be seen at all—within the first 5 to 10 miles.

Another spot fairly close to Colorado Springs is the area near **Mueller State Park.** This lush, forested region is home to a small herd of bighorns that can best be seen south of the main entrance to the state park, though the most heavily visited portion of the park is a fine wintering site for deer and elk. To reach Mueller State Park, head west out of Colorado Springs on US 24 for 25 miles to the town of Divide. Turn south on State Road 67 and at just under 4 miles, look for the entrance to Mueller State Park on the right; or continue for 1.5 miles and take the right fork of the road. This dirt road is County Road 63 but is also known as Fourmile Road. Travel along it, stopping to scan the meadows or hills to the east. Or park in the parking area down a steep grade just at the 2-mile point along County Road 63. From here it is possible to hike through bighorn country all the way to Dome Rock (it's a long, icy hike in winter). Dress for snow, and look and listen for sheep through the spruce and fir that abound here.

65

November
Shorttakes

Finch Flocks

Finches gather in large numbers during the colder months of the year and can be found in many montane areas of the Southwest. House finches, of course, are most common, but Cassin's and rosy finches are also found in abundance in some regions, as are pine siskins and grosbreaks. For an excellent chance to find all of these species, try the drive up to **Sandia Crest** (see chapter 25) in New Mexico. There are several established picnic areas on the way to the top where masses of finches can be found; look for rosy finches at the crest. Also in New Mexico, try **Bandelier National Monument** near Santa Fe and the nearby **Pajarito Mountain Ski Area** (see chapter 20). In Colorado, try **Mesa Verde National Park** (see chapter 61), **Golden Gate Canyon State Park** (see chapter 8) and **Rocky Mountain National Park** (see chapter 49).

66

Breakout: Whooping Cranes

Birding manuals from a century or more ago often described the whooping crane in tones alternately awestruck and amused. There seemed to be something almost inexpressibly delightful in encountering such enormous and dazzling birds who appeared to revel in their own existence. From the frenetic bouncing and swinging of their mating dances to the grace of their cavorting white forms glistening in the great heights of a summer sky, few observers have been unimpressed by these creatures.

They never existed in very great numbers: perhaps a few thousand bred from Hudson Bay over to the Yukon in Canada and down into the heart of the American Midwest. Even after they were pushed out of much of their previous range, they were still listed as occasional visitors to parts of New England and farther south on the East Coast into the mid-1800s. Hunting, primarily, depleted the great bird's ranks, as did human destruction of its habitat. By the middle of this century there were a dozen or so still in existence. The bird whose great migrations were once likened to the passings of loud and resolute armies was all but wiped out; several authorities declared the bird extinct.

But the whooping crane had not, as they say, gone the way of the whooping crane. Conservation efforts sustained the continent's last remaining wild flock, a group of whoopers that

A whooping crane in a field. Pairs mate for life, and, in courtship behavior, dance near their nesting site.

migrated 2,500 miles between Wood Buffalo National Park in northwestern Canada and Aransas National Wildlife Refuge along the Texas Gulf Coast. Slowly, the birds made a very modest comeback. Still, as a federally protected endangered species whose numbers were no more than a few score by the early 1970s, there was always the fear that some natural disaster might wipe out many, even all, of the remaining whoopers during their arduous annual migration. Cranes were being bred in small numbers in captivity, when the idea of creating a viable second flock in the wild grew.

In 1975, the U.S. Fish and Wildlife Service, together with the Canadian Wildlife Service and a few other agencies, began transplanting some whooping crane eggs from the Wood Buffalo flock to the nests of sandhill cranes in southern Idaho. Since female whoopers generally care for only one of the two eggs they usually lay, there would be no diminishment of the existing flock. The theory—or hope—was that the sandhills would hatch and raise their whooper cousins and teach them how to survive while imprinting on them their own migratory route between Idaho's Grays Lake National Wildlife Refuge and central New Mexico's Bosque del Apache National Wildlife Refuge. The project's apparent success—by the winter of 1984–85 there were thirty-three whooping cranes making the annual 800-mile migration—was, if not entirely surprising, a gratifying example of science's ability to restore what humans have nearly destroyed.

Whooping cranes can still be found with the sandhill cranes as they both migrate through Utah and Colorado and then settle in at Bosque del Apache for the winter. The birds move with a slow, heavy flapping of their enormous, black-tipped wings. At a height of about 5 feet, they are North America's tallest bird. Their white bodies, wingspans of over 7 feet and red skin patches on their crown and cheeks make them as impressive as they are rare. And, of course, there is their trumpeting call, a tremendously loud whoop that explodes from out of their 5-foot-long windpipes with a shrill blast that can be heard as far as 3 miles away.

Unfortunately, though the sandhill cranes have done an admirable job as foster parents, none of the mature whooping cranes have successfully mated. Despite all the high hopes, the egg transplant program was discontinued in the mid-1980s when it became clear that the Grays Lake whoopers simply were not forming pair bonds. Perhaps the only consolation to be derived from the project's failure is that future plans to reintroduce whooping cranes to the wild will benefit from this initial experiment. The Wood Buffalo flock has grown to about 150 birds and about 100 exist in captivity. The future looks bright, even if it may not be in the Southwest.

For now, a November visitor to Bosque del Apache has the rare opportunity to see the last of the whooping cranes in the West. And there is a new spectacle, also. A hybrid crane—half-whooper, half-sandhill—made its first appearance at Bosque del Apache in autumn of 1992 and returned again in 1993, making it the first known crossbreed ever found in the wild. Whether others will follow and for how many years this one may be seen remain unknown. It is enough, certainly, to know that whooping cranes will visit New Mexico for at least a few more years and are growing in number in other parts of the country. For a time it seemed certain that they would disappear forever, like a lone white crane circling higher upward in the glare of an autumn sun until it could be seen no more.

DECEMBER

67

December Birding
in Arizona

When it comes to winter birding in Arizona, particularly the southeastern portion of the state, limiting suggestions to only a few spots is as difficult as it is in any other season. There are so many outstanding sites that half a dozen—in fact, virtually any of the Arizona birding hotspots already listed in this book—might take the place of those listed here. However, given the generally less dramatic nature of winter birding, the potential for snow and cold (even in southern Arizona, winter weather can turn nasty) and the reduced number of daylight hours, the hotspots listed herein attempt to combine proximity with variety, of both species and habitat.

In December in southeastern Arizona, temperatures vary between the mid-30s and the high 60s, though warmer weather is a good possibility. Still, many first-time winter visitors to the area are surprised to find there are snowcapped mountain ranges visible on the horizon. Birds, of course, thrive in the moderate temperatures, and while many wintering species, for example, lark buntings and chestnut-collared longspurs, are in the region only during this time of year, others, such as Gambel's quail and pyrrhuloxia, are year-round residents. It is this pleasant mix of the uncommon with the familiar, the plain with the colorful, that makes birding in Arizona so enjoyable. And besides, it is an almost guilty pleasure—what with winter raging to the north—to stand in short sleeves and watch hawks soar above a plowed cornfield, or stroll amid towering cottonwoods as songbirds brighten the air.

HOTSPOTS

It is possible in little more than a day and a half to see a very fine representation of southeastern Arizona's desert grassland and riparian woodland, habitats for many of the region's wintering birds. Everything from the tiny winter wren to the majestic golden eagle and a number of waterfowl also can be found in this diverse landscape of farmland, mountain, forest and desert.

A great starting point, and one of the best-loved birding sites in the Southwest, is the **Patagonia–Sonoita Creek Preserve**, a 350-acre riparian wonderland administered by the Nature Conservancy. Dominated by massive Fremont cottonwoods, the preserve contains a representative slice of Sonoita Creek, a perennial stream whose woodlands harbor as many as 250 bird species during a typical year. The Patagonia preserve even smells alive during December, the cool air beneath the trees ripe with wet freshness. Wander the trails, including the berm of a long-vanished railroad line, and look for northern cardinals, sapsuckers, ground doves, Gambel's quail and a variety of sparrows and wrens. The creek trail affords a wonderful opportunity to see a range of songbirds, and the open sky above the grassy fields at the preserve's center may reveal a gliding red-tailed hawk.

Like many other popular birding sites, this registered Natural Landmark is in danger of being loved to death. In just a decade, the number of people visiting Patagonia–Sonoita Creek has grown more than tenfold, with numbers now topping thiry thousand annually. The Nature Conservancy's logical response? Shortened hours and fewer days open, 7:30 A.M. to 3:30 P.M. on Wednesday through Sunday to be exact, thereby reducing the stress on local birds. If you come, tread lightly, stay on established trails, and dress warmly. It is much colder amid the cottonwoods and willows on either side of the creek than it is in the scrubland below. To reach the preserve, turn west onto 4th Avenue in Patagonia and go 2 blocks to Pennsylvania Avenue and turn south. A gravel road begins straight

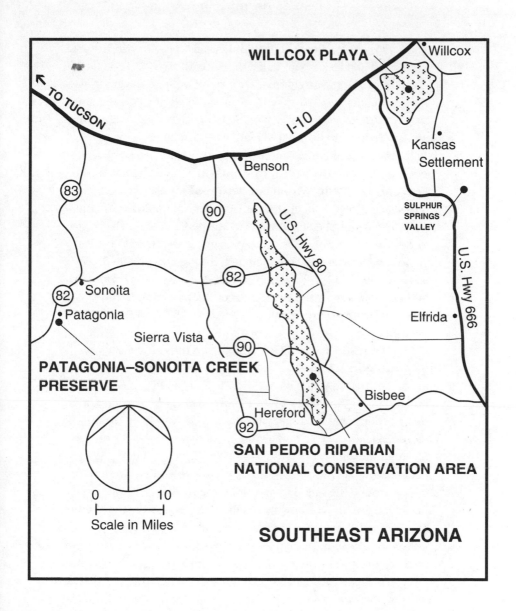

WILLCOX PLAYA

Willcox

TO TUCSON

I-10

83

90

Benson

Kansas
Settlement

U.S. Hwy 80

SULPHUR
SPRINGS
VALLEY

U.S. Hwy 666

82

82

Sonoita

Patagonia

Sierra Vista

90

Elfrida

PATAGONIA–SONOITA CREEK
PRESERVE

Bisbee

Hereford

92

0   10

Scale in Miles

SAN PEDRO RIPARIAN
NATIONAL CONSERVATION AREA

SOUTHEAST ARIZONA

ahead, crossing the creek almost immediately, with a parking area and fenced entrance about half a mile ahead. The preserve is just off State Road 82 in Patagonia, with easily followed signs.

After a stay at Patagonia–Sonoita, head north to the small town of Sonoita, continue east on State Road 82 for 19 miles, then turn south on State Road 90 to reach the rapidly growing town of Sierra Vista. From here you have easy access to two of the finest spots in one of Arizona's newest and most spectacular birding sites, the **San Pedro Riparian National Conservation Area** (SPRNCA). A 56,000-acre strip of riparian and grassland habitat, the SPRNCA stretches northward from the United States–Mexico border for nearly 40 miles, neatly hugging the San Pedro River and, not so incidentally, creating a charming and pristine birding paradise. It is little wonder that the Nature Conservancy has dubbed this conservation area, most of which was acquired by the Bureau of Land Management as recently as 1986, one of the "Last Great Places."

The first place to visit after passing through Sierra Vista is the **San Pedro House**, an information and parking area on a turnoff just before State Road 90 crosses the San Pedro River. Take State Road 90 7 miles east out of Sierra Vista to a well-marked turnoff, follow it a quarter of a mile and park in front of the San Pedro House, once a ranch house and now a bookstore and information center open only on weekends. Check the bird feeders for sparrows, finches, quail and thrashers. The cotton-woods around the building harbor kestrels. Next, follow the trails that meander east to the river. With virtually every step the tall grass seems to become animated by some skittish creature—a towhee or thrasher, perhaps—as birds quickly take to the air or burrow into thicker brush.

The San Pedro is a clear, slow-flowing river lined with cottonwoods and willows. Listen for mallards or northern shovelers taking wing as you approach the water, or look for them on the two small ponds adjacent to the river. A variety of hawks and a multitude of passerines can be found by wandering along the river's edge, an enthralling way to spend a winter afternoon. As in any streamside area, dress warmly, though the mesquite grassland area nearer the San Pedro House may be considerably warmer.

Similar species can be found at another SPRNCA spot, the **Hereford Road Crossing**, where the parking area is directly adjacent to the river. To reach Hereford, backtrack from the San Pedro House on State Road 90 west for just over 2.5 miles and turn south on Moson Road. Follow it for 7.5 miles and turn east onto Hereford Road for just under 5 miles. The parking area is immediately east of the single-lane bridge. The river here is thick with vegetation and cool air. Look for vesper, Brewer's, white-crowned and lark sparrows, a variety of flycatchers and warblers and even a great horned owl or two, as well as some of the species seen near the San Pedro House. This is also a good place to see green kingfishers.

Other access points to the SPRNCA are—south to north—Palominas on State Road 92, Charleston Bridge on Charleston Road, Fairbank on State Road 82 and Land Corral south of St. David. The Bureau of Land Management headquarters is at Fairbank and is a good first stop for information and directions.

After Hereford, a short drive leads to one of the outstanding wintering raptor sites in the country. Though not an official refuge or preserve area, the **Sulphur Springs Valley** is a vast expanse of farmland, grassland and plains that attracts such a variety of easily seen raptors it's a good idea to have a separate guidebook just to sort them out. *A Field Guide to the Hawks of North America* in the Peterson series is a good choice for the serious birder.

To reach Sulphur Springs Valley, continue on Hereford Road for 5 miles until it rejoins State Road 92. Then head east about 10 miles to Bisbee. Get on State Road 80 heading east, and at about 4 miles outside of Bisbee turn onto Elfrida Road, following it 7.4 miles to Central Highway. Turn north and the adventure begins. Hawks of nearly every type—rough-legged, ferruginous, Harris's, Cooper's, sharp-shinned and red-tailed—as well as northern harriers, kestrels, bald and golden eagles and prairie falcons can be seen perching on utility poles along the roads or soaring above the fields in this farmland region. If you've ever wanted to hone your hawk-watching skills, this is the place to do it. And what is the attraction here for these mighty birds? The farm fields that dominate the valley abound with rodents and sparrows, creating a plentiful prey base for wintering raptors. Loggerhead shrikes, the black and gray songbirds who, it almost seems, have learned their fearsome hunting skills from neighboring hawks, also dot the utility lines along the road. Pull off nearly anywhere and watch sparrows, quail, even roadrunners dart about.

After 15 miles the road connects with US 666 at the town of Elfrida. Follow US 666 as it winds north, then through more of the raptor-rich fields, turning off the road to go north through Kansas Settlement about 15 miles past Elfrida. Similar terrain leads to a connection with State Road 186. Head west on 186 for just over 5 miles and you are in Willcox. Even here, though, just before getting on I-10, there is one last treat for the winter birder. Turn up the Willcox golf course road and, after a brief 1-mile drive, find a small lake, one of the northernmost water depressions in the vast Willcox Playa (see chapter 63). The bumpy drive around the lake is only a mile or so long, but look for coots, mallards, phalaropes, geese (perhaps even a Ross's) and an occasional great blue heron. Check the adjoining golf course, too, before heading for the interstate. Such a variety of species within such a compact region—Patagonia–Sonoita to San Pedro to Sulphur Springs—is available in few other areas at this time of year.

68

Christmas Bird Counts

It doesn't get a lot of press, and not many people outside the circle of birding enthusiasts know much about it, but the National Audubon Society–sponsored Christmas Bird Count (CBC) is one of the highlights of the year. As its name would suggest, it is a sort of holiday: a year-end treat for experienced and beginning bird-watchers alike, a chance to get together with other nature lovers and count birds.

To understand what the CBC is, it is best to understand its history, which goes back to 1900. In that year, Frank Chapman, editor of *Bird-Lore* magazine, organized a group of bird counters to tally species on Christmas Day. Chapman sought a more humane alternative to the now thankfully forgotten "side hunt," a traditional, holiday-season contest—slaughter, really—in which teams of hunters would compete to see which side could kill the greatest number of animals in a single day. With the first count in Englewood, New Jersey, Chapman's group recorded eighteen species, about one-fourth the number found on that count nowadays.

From its modest beginnings, Chapman's CBC, which takes place within about the last two weeks of December, has spread to all of North America and even parts of Central America. It now draws over forty-three thousand people to more than sixteen hundred separate counts, and both numbers increase each year.

The guidelines for a CBC are simple: within a twenty-four-hour period, a team of birders, usually divided into groups of two or three, counts both the different species and the number of birds of each species seen within a preestablished 15-mile-diameter circle. Generally, all or almost all of the birding is done from dawn to dusk, good news for those in areas of the Southwest where winter differences in day- and nighttime temperatures can easily be 40 or 50 degrees.

A friendly competition has built up between birding groups in some parts of the country, while in other areas birders are content simply to have fun and sharpen their birding skills. Perhaps even more important, counters contribute to a more exact understanding of bird habits and patterns nationwide. The CBC, the results of which are published each year in a special edition of the Audubon Society's *American Birds* magazine, constitutes one of the greatest contributions to the world of science made solely by nonprofessionals.

There is a small fee—$5, at present—required to take part in a CBC, and depending on locale, a potential counter should be prepared to stay out all day regardless of the weather. A certain Audubon machismo seems to prohibit most CBC participants from retreating from even severe winter weather. Not too many years ago, in fact, a lone birder in Prudhoe Bay, Alaska, braved a frozen day to record but three common ravens. Southwestern birders, of course, have the option of heading to relatively balmy climes, such as Phoenix, where the number of recorded species can number in the 150s, or braving the cold in places such as Denver, where counts can reach 100 or so. Wherever the local count is, it's bound to be fruitful. For the beginner, there's almost no better way to learn about birds, and you needn't feel that lack of experience will make you unwelcome. It's almost a cliché among Christmas counters to say that an extra pair of eyes, no matter how unskilled, can make a count all the more successful. Merry Christmas!

HOTSPOTS

To find out about the nearest Christmas Bird Count, call the Audubon chapter in your area by at least the middle of December, or call one of the regional offices listed in the appendix.

69

Coyotes

There is an abundance of Native American folktales in which the coyote plays a central role. In some it is a sort of creator or Promethean teacher, in others the personification of evil and mayhem and in still others a cunning trickster or simply a dupe. This range of representations, from the revered and powerful to the feared and malevolent, might seem odd with any other animal. The coyote, however, is singular and singularly multifaceted. Just as it dominates many of the primeval stories of the Southwest in a variety of guises, so today it proliferates across the continent through a variety of uncanny adaptations, its character as varied as it ever was. Alternately loved, abhorred and admired, it remains, in this corner of the country, the archetypal animal, its lofting howl the song of the Southwest.

The coyote has followed a path different from most species, growing rather than diminishing in number, expanding in range rather than retreating. It's estimated that there are ten times the number of coyotes at present as in the days of Columbus. And there is no doubt that it is more widespread. Primarily a creature of the West just a few decades ago, coyotes now reside in every part of the continental United States, though only scantily in the Southeast. Despite widespread slaughter of coyotes through a variety of methods—poisoned baits, cyanide traps, air hunting—

A solitary coyote crouches behind a dirt berm. Coyote pairs are monogamous; the female bears five or six pups each spring.

they continue to thrive alongside humans, adapting to fit changes wrought by civilization. They've been seen begging for food at national parks, and, in a highly publicized and anomalous incident not long ago, they killed a young girl in her backyard in suburban Los Angeles after gun-banning regulations had made the local coyotes progressively less skittish.

Adept at living off the scraps and refuse of their natural environments, coyotes seem equally adept at taking advantage of civilization's leftovers, as they are familiar visitors to the fringes and even interiors of large cities. And although ranchers are loathe to admit it, coyotes are maddeningly cunning, able to cross fences and kill livestock with a skill that seems to defy explanation. It has been said that many a livestock man who has foreclosed on a mortgage or been unable to send his children to college has held the coyote unequivocally responsible for his financial woes.

As with many other modern environmental dilemmas, the proliferation of the coyote was at least partially created by the humans who decry it. The killing of the coyote's natural predators, such as wolves and grizzly bears, left the coyote with no real predators outside of humans. Antitrapping and antifur movements, whatever their intrinsic merits, left greater numbers of coyotes—for better or worse—alive.

But it cannot be said that humans are solely responsible for the present situation. Coyotes are exceptionally smart, they reproduce quickly, they will eat almost anything and they have shown a rare ability to alter their ways to fit their environment. Whereas wolves were destroyed in large numbers because of their habit of running in packs, the coyote, who also used to be more of a pack animal, has become more solitary, working with one or two others to hunt, perhaps, but generally avoiding large groups. It is wily and opportunistic, not above subsisting on the sick or the weak, and it is a well-known and perhaps repugnant fact that coyotes will eat a creature while it is still alive, taking chunks from a doe's leg, say, as she struggles to escape.

This adaptability, this stealthiness and ruthlessness, has made a deep impression on all those who have lived in close contact with the coyote. "God's Dog," the Aztecs were believed to have called him; "Little Brother" is the Navajos' respectful term for the creature who shared their land and helped itself to their sheep. Mexicans said it could speak, and many of the Indian tribes of the Southwest held it to be a sort of witch or devil. Often in the legends, it seems to be a sort of symbolic representation of humankind, the potential for goodness or mischief its defining trait.

And beyond the varying opinions and the multitude of disguises lies the coyote's song, one of the most clichéd, yet beautiful, representations of the West. Almost anyone who has spent time in the deserts and mountains of the Southwest has heard it, usually at night or early morning, a series of yaps leading to a high, mournful howl. It may be answered by another coyote from some other point on the horizon, a chorus of song that serves—to communicate? to announce dusk or dawn? to signal a change in the weather? Perhaps we will never know. It has been said that coyotes sing to allay their loneliness or simply to express their pleasure at being alive or to greet the brightening moon. Maybe it is all of these. With a growing legion of these animals spreading across the land, the coyote's song seems destined to become the most widespread serenade on the continent.

HOTSPOTS

Coyotes are much easier to hear than they are to see, though December is a particularly good time to spot them as the colder weather makes them more anxious to find food. The "gray ghost" can often be found wandering nonchalantly in backyards in cities such as Phoenix or Tucson—where they have become downright brazen—or waiting patiently in mountain farm fields for birds or rodents; a late afternoon hike through many wilderness areas in the Southwest during winter can turn up a coyote or two. One trick of the hunter, an inexpensive call that mimics the sound of a distressed rabbit, can bring coyotes rushing, often amazingly fast. For the wildlife viewer, it is one of the surest ways of getting a good look at a coyote.

Perhaps the best way to locate coyotes is to contact any of the various Fish and Wildlife Services or Game and Fish Divisions listed in the appendix and ask one of their agents where the best coyote hunting is. This may be an odd suggestion, but for the outdoor enthusiast interested in viewing rather than shooting, there is no better way to see the elusive coyote than to visit those spots where hunters have found success. Armed with a call as noted above, even a beginner can bring the wary coyote within sight.

Some of the better places already listed in this book to find coyotes are **Rocky Mountain Arsenal** (see chapter 2), **Trough Road** (see chapter 71), **Apishapa State Wildlife Area** (see chapter 20) and **Monte Vista National Wildlife Refuge** (see chapter 63) in Colorado; **Bosque del Apache**, **Bitter Lake** and **Las Vegas National Wildlife Refuges** (see chapter 62 for all three) and **Maxwell National Wildlife Refuge** (see chapter 2) in New Mexico; **Imperial** and **Cibola National Wildlife Refuges** (see chapter 1 for both) in Arizona; and **Hardware Ranch** (see chapter 8) in Utah.

70

Mule Deer in Rut

Compared to its more numerous and more wide-ranging white-tailed relative, the mule deer—the western deer—gets no respect. Less aggressive than the white-tail and more apt to linger and examine whatever may arouse its curiosity, muleys have struck many an eastern woodsman as just plain stupid. This is, of course, an unfair assessment. The mule deer simply has remained more fixed in its elemental habits, proving perhaps less adaptable to civilization's advances than the white-tail while retaining the simple, rugged charm that has made it one of the most beloved animals of the West.

"Mule deer" is actually the generic term for a number of subspecies that roam from west Texas up to the Dakotas and over to the Pacific. In the southwestern states, mule deer can flourish in virtually any type of habitat, from desert to mountain, though they generally avoid open areas that offer little protective cover. Does and fawns summer in small groups, while males may go it alone or seek the company of a few other bucks. In fall and winter, they gather in herds for the rut and often move to lower elevations to avoid the heavy mountain snows.

December is the time to see a variety of intriguing deer activity, all spurred by the annual breeding frenzy. Bucks become less wary, forsaking caution in their search for does. They may spar with saplings or small bushes or scrape wildly at the ground as a

Gary Zahm

A large mule deer buck and two does disappear into the dry grass.

means of working off some of their nervous tension. Because does are in heat for only a single day, a buck—or several bucks—may pester her until the time is right, breed her, then dash off to make a new conquest. This has been called serial polygamy, as fit bucks try to breed as many does as possible and have little interest in gathering and maintaining a harem.

Predictably, the whole affair brings bucks into conflict with one another, though usually without as much of the fierce violence of elk or bighorn sheep. Does are simply not that scarce, nor are bucks as inclined to battle as their white-tailed cousins. Still, fights do occur, and if you're fortunate enough to witness one, it can be rousing. After progressing through the more common threatening displays—the lowering of the head, the show of antlers—two bucks will lock antlers and, in a sort of cramped shoving match, attempt to lower one another's head to the ground. After a time, usually within just a few minutes, one buck will retire, allowing the winner more freedom to pursue the doe he desires. Another interesting sight, rarely observed and then only as the rut ends, is that of an unbred doe trying to entice a tired buck into breeding her—a sort of egalitarianism in rutting.

HOTSPOTS

Mule deer usually are active only during the early morning and late afternoon, preferring to bed down during most of midday. December, however, finds them up and about at any hour, so although these animals are admittedly difficult to see, it isn't absolutely necessary to limit attempted viewing to the beginning and end of the day. Even so, and despite their less cautious ways during the rut, there is no certainty that mule deer will be seen, even in an outstanding viewing area. Look for signs of them, such as aspens chewed about their lower reaches by desperately hungry deer or small trees stripped or broken by a frenzied buck.

Because mule deer are so plentiful, it is difficult to limit suggestions to only a few spots. Almost any sizable state park or recreation area or refuge, or any drive through forest land, holds the opportunity for December viewing. Seeing mule deer becomes a hit-and-miss affair, though some areas have much greater potential than others. The following is a listing of one outstanding site in each of the four southwestern states, with suggestions for other possible viewing.

Mule deer are scattered throughout Arizona, though often in small pockets or in areas inaccessible after winter storms. One place—a long, long drive—that offers a good chance of seeing mule deer is US 666 between the towns of Clifton in the south and Springerville in the north. This demanding 125-mile drive, best known as the **Coronado Trail**, winds through the mountains of the Apache–Sitgreaves National Forest and is definitely not for those in a hurry. Steep, slow travel is the rule here, as the road seems to climb endlessly through the mined hillsides beyond Clifton and the nearby town of Morenci, then ascends into snowy pine forests. Switchbacks pass through scrubland, stream and meadowland, aspen, fir and grassland. There is an especially good chance of seeing wintering mule deer near the Hannagan Meadow area north of Nutria. There are several picnic sites and camp-grounds along the drive, and if there have not been recent snows, the road will be quite clear. Avoid this drive in bad weather; the deer won't be around, anyway, and the trip will be miserable, if not dangerous.

Also in Arizona, try the roads north and west out of **Prescott** in the Prescott National Forest about 100 miles northwest of Phoenix or the **Cochise Stronghold** area of the Coronado National Forest west of US 666 south from Exit 331 on I-10.

Mule deer can be found in most parts of Utah, though less prominently in the Great Basin area to the northwest. One intriguing and fairly reliable spot to find them is in the canyonlands area of the southeastern part of the state, a land of rugged sandstone rock and blistering heat in summer that provides good wintering range for deer. The **Squaw Flats Scenic Byway**, also known as State Road 211, begins 14 miles north of Monticello on US 191. Turn west on 211 and drive through sage scrubland for about 8 miles before entering piñon–juniper forest and then descending to the creek that flows through Newspaper Rock State Park, 12 miles from the US 191 turnoff. Deer are visible all through here, often on or right off the road. Newspaper Rock, where there are Indian petroglyphs (recently vandalized, unfortunately), is worth a stop, but be sure to continue through the deep, red rock canyon for more deer viewing. The road continues all the way to a campground and drive into Canyonlands National Park, a total distance of about 34 miles, though the best deer viewing is along the first 15 or 20 miles. This a quiet and little-visited spot in winter, with abundant mule deer.

Other good spots in Utah include the area between the towns of **Cedar City** and **Summit** along I-15, just north of Zion National Park; US 89 north out of the town of **Fairview**; **Steele Ranch**, accessible from the first exit south of Santaquin on I-15, 20 miles south of Provo; and **Fremont Indian State Park**, just off I-70 about 17 miles east of where it intersects with I-15.

Colorado is a great state for mule deer, and one of the finest viewing sites is, surprisingly, the **U.S. Air Force Academy**. The enormous grounds of the academy lie along the west side of I-25 just north of Colorado Springs and provide a vast and secure haven for a variety of wildlife. Mule deer are plentiful, even passing through the visitor center parking lot in morning hours. The academy contains grassland, ponderosa pine foothills, a riparian habitat along Monument Creek and, aside from the roads and various air force facilities, is an idyllic wildlife setting. Enter the grounds at Exit 156-B and proceed to the visitor center about 5 miles ahead for a map, or drive the grounds on your own. The main drive through the academy curves south and will put you back on the interstate at Exit 150-B, or you can loop back up to the main entrance. The Santa Fe Regional Trail, which follows Monument Creek down to the southern boundary of the academy, offers an outstanding streamside hike. A parking area for the trail is just before the entrance gate at Exit 156-B at a point called "North Gate Trail Access." The academy is open from 9:00 A.M. to 5:00 P.M.

Mule deer can also be found in Colorado at **Great Sand Dunes National Monument** (see chapter 24); along the Colorado River southwest of the town of Kremmling near the **Radium State Wildlife Area** (see chapter 71); and 11.4 miles north of the town of Ridgway (see chapter 55), where the **Billy Creek State Wildlife Area** offers particularly good deer viewing.

New Mexico also has plenty of mule deer, and some of the best places to see them in winter are in the **Sangre de Cristo Mountains** in the north central part of the state. From Taos, head east and north along US 64 to high, windswept Eagle Nest Lake. Continue east on US 64 for 12 miles to the Cimarron Canyon State Park area, or 11 miles past this to State Road 121 and 4 miles south to Philmont Scout Ranch (see chapter 46), both good places to look for deer. All of US 64, in fact, from Eagle Nest through Ute Park and past Cimarron—a total of about 30 miles with spectacular scenery through a red rock canyon—is good deer habitat, though the two sites mentioned both have turnouts and parking areas.

Bandelier National Monument near Santa Fe also has wintering deer, and, once again, the wildlife oasis of **Bosque del Apache National Wildlife Refuge** (see chapter 62) has many easily seen mule deer.

71

December
Shorttakes

Elk

Elk congregate in their largest numbers in winter, and there are many fine places to see them. In New Mexico, it is possible to view an enormous herd of elk by driving US 285 north to the Colorado border from the town of **Tres Piedras**. San Antonio Peak lies to the east of the road, and the sagebrush areas and meadows between it and the road are outstanding for elk, particularly on an early December morning.

In Colorado, try the **Holy Cross Ranger District Office** just off I-70 west of Vail. A covered viewing area with interpretive signs and a spotting scope directs the visitor's attention to the snowy slopes to the north where scores of elk can be seen on any given day. Sometimes the animals even march through the small community of Dowd right by the ranger office. The established viewing buildingis located right off the interstate at Exit 171. County Road 1 southwest out of Kremmling (see chapter 57), also known as **Trough Road**, follows the Colorado River for approximately 30 miles through some of the state's best wintering elk range. The route, which passes the Radium State Wildlife Area, ends at State Bridge on State Road 131, 15 miles north of I-70. This area is roughly 40 miles north of the Holy Cross Ranger District Office.

72

Breakout: The Desert in Winter

Pull off the road in December as you drive through southern New Mexico, get out of the car and walk. Nothing could seem more bleak and lifeless than this place at this time of year. Most mammals and reptiles are hidden; many of the birds are miles to the south, having long since departed for warmer climes. It may even be cold. In fact, most of what is thought of as American desert land hardly fits the image in winter—aside from the fact that it truly is deserted. Sagebrush country, for instance, the Great Basin Desert that blankets Nevada and reaches out to pull in the northern and southern strips of Utah, is frozen for months out of the year. Even the Sonoran Desert in southern Arizona, the most diverse and colorful of the Southwest's deserts, seems dull and quiet in December. It must be a peculiar sight to the newcomer, especially if he or she is expecting an ocean of sand dunes and shimmering oasis visions, to drive south toward Phoenix in winter and find vast spreads of Arizona's signature cactus, the saguaro, looming over the snow-covered desert like oddly stretched, haphazard tombstones.

The desert is confounding. Its initial allure, perhaps, lies more in what is not there than in what is. We are so accustomed to a beauty defined by water and greenery and trees and mountain peaks that the desert seems to offer only a foreboding brownness and uniformity. Aside from an explosion of spring wildflowers and flashes of water during the summer rains, there is little in the way of dramatic seasonal progression in the desert. Joseph Krutch, the perceptive desert observer, wrote that there was more of a "shift of emphasis" as the desert year passed, none of the full and definite transformations he had known in his native New England. Where we seek enclosing shape and color, the desert offers clear space and sky; instead of soft lines, we are given stark texture and bold shadows. The seasons merge imperceptibly.

Winter is the quietest time of all. The light seems less intense in the south, and the air can be fog shrouded in Utah. Down near Mexico the sky often seems supernaturally still and clear, allowing telescopic views of low mountain ranges 100 miles distant. A light snow or rain may fall for a few hours, even a few days in some areas. Winter winds usher storm clouds in from the Pacific Ocean in a more easterly and inland path during the cooler months. Winter sunsets are the best of the year, with a slowly falling luminous curtain of turquoise that melts into pinks and reds and golds. December in the more southerly parts of the Southwest, unlike much of the rest of the country, is not wholly different from July. It is just quieter, subtler: *less,* but pleasantly so.

Some reptiles will emerge from belowground on warm days. Less devoted to their winter sleeps than many mammals, heated air and midday sun may bring some of them, for example, the side-blotched lizard, aboveground for a few hours. Deer and jackrabbits and ravens and wrens might be about. The world opens gently on a winter's day.

It is true that there is little, or, rather, less, to see in the desert in winter. Utah's sagebrush land is cold and ice rimmed; New Mexico's Chihuahuan Desert is pale and dry; Arizona's cacti and Joshua trees endure wet and cold. But it is possible to stroll 100 feet off the highway in these, the least inhabited places in this part of America, and sense a stillness not found among pine trees or along a mountain stream. There is only openness here, and the wind and the clouds. A soul accustomed to the forests might find it too big and wide. But here, it is just right.

APPENDIX

NATIONAL WILDLIFE REFUGES

ARIZONA
Cabeza Prieta NWR
1611 N. Second Avenue
Ajo, AZ 85321
(602) 726-2619

Imperial NWR
P.O. Box 72217
Red Cloud Mine Road
Martinez Lake, AZ 85365
(602) 783-3371

Kofa NWR
356 First Street
P.O. Box 6290
Yuma, AZ 85364
(602) 783-7861

Cibola NWR
P.O. Box AP
Blythe, CA 92225
(602) 857-3253

Havasu–Bill Williams Delta NWRs
1406 Bailey Avenue
Needles, CA 92363
(602) 326-3853

COLORADO
Arapaho NWR
P.O. Box 457
Walden, CO 80480
(303) 723-4717

Monte Vista–Alamosa NWRs
9383 El Rancho Lane
Alamosa, CO 81101
(719) 589-4021

NEW MEXICO
Bitter Lake NWR
P.O. Box 7
Roswell, NM 88202-0007
(505) 622-6755

Bosque del Apache NWR
P.O. Box 1246
Socorro, NM 87801
(505) 835-1828

Las Vegas NWR
Route 1, Box 399
Las Vegas, NM 87701
(505) 425-3581

Maxwell NWR
P.O. Box 276
Maxwell, NM 87728
(505) 375-2331

UTAH
Bear River Migratory Bird Refuge
P.O. Box 459
Brigham City, UT 84302
(801) 744-2488

NATIONAL FORESTS, MONUMENTS AND PARKS, AND RECREATION AREAS

ARIZONA NATIONAL FORESTS
Apache–Sitgreaves National Forest
South Mountain Avenue,
    US Highway 180
P.O. Box 640
Springerville, AZ 85938
(602) 333-4301

Coconino National Forest
2323 E. Greenlaw Lane
Flagstaff, AZ 86004
(602) 556-7400

Coronado National Forest
Federal Building
300 W. Congress
Tucson, AZ 85701
(602) 670-4552

Kaibab National Forest
800 S. Sixth Street
Williams, AZ 86046
(602) 635-2681

Prescott National Forest
344 S. Cortez Street
Prescott, AZ 86303
(602) 771-4700

Tonto National Forest
2324 E. McDowell Road
P.O. Box 5348
Phoenix, AZ 85010
(602) 225-5200

COLORADO NATIONAL FORESTS
Arapaho and Roosevelt National
    Forests
240 W. Prospect Road
Fort Collins, CO 80526
(303) 498-1100

Grand Mesa, Uncompahgre and
    Gunnison National Forests
2250 US Highway 50
Delta, CO 81416
(303) 874-7691

Pike and San Isabel National
    Forests
1920 Valley Drive
Pueblo, CO 81008
(719) 545-8737

Rio Grande National Forest
1803 W. US Highway 160
Monte Vista, CO 81144
(719) 852-5941

Routt National Forest
29587 W. US Highway 40
Suite 20
Steamboat Springs, CO 80487
(303) 879-1722

San Juan National Forest
701 Camino del Rio, Room 301
Durango, CO 81301
(303) 247-4874

White River National Forest
Old Federal Building
Ninth Street and Grand Avenue
P.O. Box 948
Glenwood Springs, CO 81602
(303) 945-2521

NEW MEXICO NATIONAL FORESTS
Carson National Forest
Forest Service Building
P.O. Box 558
208 Cruz Alta Road
Taos, NM 87571
(505) 758-6200

Cibola National Forest
2113 Osuna Road NE, Suite A
Albuquerque, NM 87113-1001
(505) 761-4650

Gila National Forest
2610 N. Silver Street
Silver City, NM 88061
(505) 388-8201

Lincoln National Forest
1101 New York
Alamogordo, NM 88310-6992
(505) 638-2443

Santa Fe National Forest
1220 St. Francis Drive
P.O. Box 1689
Santa Fe, NM 87504
(505) 988-6940

UTAH NATIONAL FORESTS
Ashley National Forest
355 N. Vernal Avenue
Vernal, UT 84078
(801) 789-1181

Dixie National Forest
82 N. 100 East
P.O. Box 580
Cedar City, UT 84720
(801) 865-3700

Fishlake National Forest
115 E. 900 North
Richfield, UT 84701
(801) 896-9233

Manti–La Sal National Forest
599 W. Price River Drive
Price, UT 84501
(801) 637-2817

Uinta National Forest
88 W. 100 North
P.O. Box 1428
Provo, UT 84601
(801) 377-5780

Wasatch–Cache National Forest
8230 Federal Building
125 S. State Street
Salt Lake City, UT 84138
(801) 524-5030

ARIZONA NATIONAL MONUMENTS
AND PARKS
Canyon de Chelly National
Monument
P.O. Box 588
Chinle, AZ 86503
(602) 674-5436

Grand Canyon National Park
P.O. Box 129
Grand Canyon, AZ 86023
(602) 638-7888

Organ Pipe Cactus National
Monument
Route 1, Box 100
Ajo, AZ 85321
(602) 387-6849

Saguaro National Monument
3693 S. Old Spanish Trail
Tucson, AZ 85730-5699
(602) 296-8576

San Pedro Riparian National
Conservation Area
RR 1, Box 9853
Huachuca City, AZ 95616
(602) 457-2265

COLORADO NATIONAL MONUMENTS
AND PARKS
Great Sand Dunes National
Monument
11500 Highway 160
Mosca, CO 81146
(719) 378-2312

Mesa Verde National Park
Mesa Verde, CO 81330
(303) 529-4465

Pawnee National Grassland
O Street
Greeley, CO 80631
(303) 353-5004

Rocky Mountain Arsenal
U.S. Fish and Wildlife Service
P.O. Box 25486
Denver Federal Center
Denver, CO 80225
(303) 289-0132

Rocky Mountain National Park
Estes Park, CO 80517
(303) 586-2371 or 8506

NEW MEXICO NATIONAL MONUMENTS
AND PARKS
Bandelier National Monument
Los Alamos, NM 87544
(505) 672-3861

Carlsbad Caverns National Park
3225 National Parks Highway
Carlsbad, NM 88220
(505) 785-2232

El Malpais National Monument
P.O. Box 939
Grants, NM 87020
(505) 285-5406

White Sands National Monument
P.O. Box 458
Alamogordo, NM 88311-0458
(505) 479-6124 or 6125

UTAH NATIONAL MONUMENTS AND PARKS
Arches National Park
P.O. Box 907
Moab, UT 84532
(801) 259-8161

Canyonlands National Park
125 W. Second South
Moab, UT 84532
(801) 259-7164

Capitol Reef National Park
Torrey, UT 84775
(801) 425-3791

Flaming Gorge National Recreation
  Area
P.O. Box 278
Manila, UT 84046
(801) 784-3445

STATE AGENCIES AND STATE OFFICES OF FEDERAL AGENCIES

ARIZONA
Arizona Office of Tourism
1100 W. Washington Street
Phoenix, AZ 85007
(602) 542-8687

Arizona Parks and Recreation
  Association
3124 E. Roosevelt
Phoenix, AZ 85008
(602) 267-7246

National Parks and Monuments
  Office
202 E. Earll Drive
Suite 115
Phoenix, AZ 85012
(602) 640-5250

USDA Forest Service
517 Gold Avenue SW
Albuquerque, NM 87102
(505) 842-3292

U.S. Fish and Wildlife Service
517 Gold Avenue SW
Albuquerque, NM 87102
(505) 842-3292

Arizona Game and Fish
  Department
2222 W. Greenway Road
Phoenix, AZ 85023
(602) 942-3000

Arizona State Parks
800 W. Washington
Suite 415
Phoenix, AZ 85007
(602) 542-4174

Bureau of Land Management
Arizona State Office
3707 N. Seventh Street
Phoenix, AZ 85014
(602) 640-5547

Navajo Indian Reservation
Navajo Tourism Department
P.O. Box 663
Window Rock, AZ 86515
(602) 871-6659 or 6439

COLORADO
Colorado Division of Wildlife
6060 Broadway
Denver, CO 80216
(303) 297-1192

Colorado Tourism Board
1625 Broadway
Suite 1700
Denver, CO 80202
(303) 592-5510

USDA Forest Service
11177 W. Eighth Avenue
Lakewood, CO 80225
(303) 236-9431

U.S. Fish and Wildlife Service
P.O. Box 25486
Denver Federal Center
Denver, CO 80225
(303) 236-7904

Colorado Division of Parks and
   Outdoor Recreation
1313 Sherman Street, Room 618
Denver, CO 80203
(303) 866-3437

National Park Service—Rocky
   Mountain Region
Denver Federal Center
P.O. Box 25287
Denver, CO 80225
(303) 969-2000

Bureau of Land Management
Colorado State Office
2850 Youngfield Street
Lakewood, CO 80215
(303) 236-2100

U.S. Air Force Academy
Colorado Springs, CO 80840
(719) 472-2555

NEW MEXICO
USDA Forest Service
517 Gold Avenue SW
Albuquerque, NM 87102
(505) 842-3292

U.S. Fish and Wildlife Service
P.O. Box 1306
Albuquerque, NM 87103
(505) 766-2321

Museum of New Mexico State
   Monuments
P.O. Box 2087
Santa Fe, NM 87504
(505) 827-6334

Bureau of Land Management
P.O. Box 27115
Santa Fe, NM 87502-7115
(505) 438-7400

National Park Service
P.O. Box 728
Santa Fe, NM 87504-0728
(505) 988-6012

U.S. Army Corps of Engineers
P.O. Box 1580
Albuquerque, NM 87103
(505) 766-1729

New Mexico State Parks
P.O. Box 1147
Santa Fe, NM 87504
(505) 827-7465

New Mexico Department of
   Tourism
P.O. Box 20003
Santa Fe, NM 87503
1-800-545-2040 or (505) 827-7400

APPENDIX

New Mexico Department of Game
and Fish
P.O. Box 25112
Santa Fe, NM 87504
(505) 827-7911

UTAH
USDA Forest Service
324 25th Street
Ogden, UT 84401
(801) 625-5347

Utah State Office
Bureau of Land Management
324 S. State Street
Salt Lake City, UT 84111
(801) 539-4001

Utah Travel Council
Council Hall/Capitol Hill
Salt Lake City, UT 84114
(801) 538-1030

Utah Division of Wildlife Resources
1596 W. North Temple
Salt Lake City, UT 84116
(801) 596-8660

U.S. Fish and Wildlife Service
1745 W. 1700 South
Salt Lake City, UT 84104
(801) 524-5630

Utah Division of Parks
and Recreation
1636 W. North Temple
Salt Lake City, UT 84116
(801) 538-7220

STATE AND MUNICIPAL PARKS AND MANAGEMENT AREAS

ARIZONA
Catalina State Park
11570 N. Oracle Road
P.O. Box 36986
Tucson, AZ 85740
(602) 628-5798

City of Phoenix Parks
17642 N. 40th Street
Phoenix, AZ 85032
(602) 262-7901

Lost Dutchman State Park
6109 N. Apache Trail
Apache Junction, AZ 85219
(602) 982-4485

Picacho Peak State Park
P.O. Box 275
Picacho, AZ 85241
(602) 466-3183

COLORADO
Barr Lake State Park
13401 Picadilly Road
Brighton, CO 80601
(303) 659-6005

Durango Fish Hatchery
151 E. 16th Street
Durango, CO 81301
(303) 894-7778

Golden Gate Canyon State Park
3873 Highway 46
Golden, CO 80403
(303) 592-1502

Jackson Lake State Park
26363 County Road
Orchard, CO 80649
(303) 645-2551

Mueller State Park and Wildlife
Area
P.O. Box 49
Divide, CO 80814
(719) 687-2366

NEW MEXICO
Brantley Lake State Park
P.O. Box 2288
Carlsbad, NM 88221
(505) 457-2384

Living Desert State Park
P.O. Box 100
Carlsbad, NM 88310
(505) 887-5516

Oliver Lee Memorial State Park
409 Dog Canyon Road
Alamogordo, NM 88310
(505) 437-8284

Percha Dam State Park
P.O. Box 32
Caballo, NM 87951
(505) 743-3942

UTAH
Bear Lake State Park
P.O. Box 184
Garden City, UT 84028-0184
(801) 946-3343

Fremont Indian State Park
11550 Clear Creek Canyon Road
Sevier, UT 84766-9999
(801) 527-4631

Hardware Ranch
Utah Division of Wildlife Resources
1596 W. North Temple
Salt Lake City, UT 84116
(801) 245-3131

Newspaper Rock State Park
P.O. Box 788
Blanding, UT 84511-0789
(801) 678-2238

Willard Bay State Park
650 N. 900 West, #A
Willard, UT 84340-9999
(801) 734-9494

PRIVATE PRESERVES AND ORGANIZATIONS

Albion Basin–Snowbird Activity
Center
USDA Forest Service
324 25th Street
Ogden, UT 84401
(801) 521-6040

Arizona–Sonora Desert Museum
2021 N. Kinney Road
Tucson, AZ 86743-9989
(602) 883-1380

Boyce Thompson Southwestern
Arboretum
P.O. Box AB
Superior, AZ 85273
(602) 689-2811

Desert Botanical Garden
1201 N. Galvin Parkway
Phoenix, AZ 85008
(602) 941-1225

Dripping Springs Natural Area
Mimbres Reservoir Area
1800 Marquess Street
Las Cruces, NM 88005
(505) 522-1219

HawkWatch International, Inc.
P.O. Box 35706
Albuquerque, NM 87176-5393
1-800-726-4295

Kitt Peak National Optical
    Astronomy Observatory
P.O. Box 26732
Tucson, AZ 85726
(602) 325-9204

Patagonia–Sonoita Creek Preserve
P.O. Box 815
Patagonia, AZ 85624
(602) 394-2400

Ramsey Canyon Reserve
27 Ramsey Canyon Road
Hereford, AZ 85615
(602) 378-2785

Rio Grande Nature Center
2901 Candelaria NW
Albuquerque, NM 87107
(505) 344-7240

Tohono Chul Park
7366 N. Paseo del Norte
Tucson, AZ 85704
(602) 742-6455

Tucson Botanical Gardens
2150 N. Alvernon Way
Tucson, AZ 85712
(602) 326-9686

CHRISTMAS BIRD COUNTS

Audubon Society
Southwest Regional Office
2525 Wallingford, Suite 1505
Austin, TX 78746
(512) 327-1943

Audubon Society
Rocky Mountain Regional Office
4150 Darley, Suite 5
Boulder, CO 80303
(303) 499-0219

ARIZONA
Atascosa Highlands
Avra Valley
Buenos Aires NWR
Carefree
Elfrida
Flagstaff–Mount Elden

Gila River
Green Valley–Madera Canyon
Hassayampa River
Jerome
Kayenta
Kirkland
Martinez Lake–Yuma
Mormon Lake
Nogales
Patagonia
Pipe Spring National Monument
Portal
Prescott
Ramsey Canyon
Salt–Verde Rivers
Santa Catalina Mountains
Sedona
Sierra Pinta, Cabeza Prieta NWR
St. David

St. Johns
Timber Mesa
Tucson Valley

COLORADO
Barr Lake
Boulder
Colorado Springs
Cortez
Crook
Curecanti National Recreation Area
Denver
Denver (urban)
Douglas County
Durango
Evergreen–Idaho Springs
Fort Collins
Grand Junction
Great Sand Dunes National
    Monument
Greeley
Gunnison
Holly
Hotchkiss
Lake Isabel
Longmont
Monte Vista NWR
North Park
Nunn
Penrose
Pikes Peak
Pueblo
Pueblo Reservoir
Rawhide Energy Station
Roaring Fork River Valley
Rocky Mountain National Park
Summit County
Walsenburg
Weldona–Ft. Morgan
Westcliffe

NEW MEXICO
Albuquerque
Bluewater Lake
Bosque del Apache NWR
Caballo
Carlsbad Caverns National Park
Chaco Canyon
Clayton
Espanola
Farmington
Five Points
Gila River
Lakes Avalon–Brantley
La Luz–Otero County
Las Cruces
Las Vegas
Loving
Peloncillo Mountains
Roswell
Sandia Mountains
Santa Fe
Sevilleta NWR
Silver City
Zuñi/Aspen

UTAH
Bear River Migratory Bird Refuge
Cedar City
Dinosaur National Monument–
    Jensen
Fish Springs NWR
Heber Valley
Jordan River
Kanab
Logan
Moab
Ogden
Provo
Salt Lake City
St. George
Zion National Park

SELECTED BIBLIOGRAPHY

Benedict, Audrey DeLella. *The Southern Rockies—A Sierra Club Naturalist's Guide*. San Francisco: Sierra Club Books, 1991.

Benyus, Janine M. *The Field Guide to Wildlife Habitats of the Western United States*. New York: Fireside, 1989.

Brown, Lauren. *Grasslands—The Audubon Society Nature Guides*. New York: Alfred A. Knopf, 1985.

Brown, Jr., Tom. *Tom Brown's Field Guide to Nature Observation and Tracking*. New York: Berkeley, 1983.

Calvin, Ross. *Sky Determines*. Albuquerque: University of New Mexico Press, 1965.

Carr, John. *Arizona Wildlife Viewing Guide*. Helena and Billings: Falcon Press, 1992.

Caughey, Bruce, and Dean Winstanley. *The Colorado Guide*. Golden: Fulcrum, 1991.

Cole, Jim. *Utah Wildlife Viewing Guide*. Helena and Billings: Falcon Press, 1990.

Dalrymple, Byron W. *North American Big-Game Animals*. New York: Outdoor Life Books, 1987.

Davis, William A., and Stephen M. Russell. *Birds in Southeastern Arizona*. Tucson: Tucson Audubon Society, 1990.

Desert Botanical Garden Staff. *Arizona Highways Presents Desert Wildflowers*. Phoenix: Arizona Department of Transportation, 1988.

Dodge, Natt N., and Jeanne R. Janish. *Flowers of the Southwest Deserts*. Tucson: Southwest Parks and Monuments Association, 1985.

Findley, James S. *The Natural History of New Mexico Mammals*. Albuquerque: University of New Mexico Press, 1975.

Gray, Mary Taylor. *Colorado Wildlife Viewing Guide*. Helena and Billings: Falcon Press, 1992.

Holt, Harold R., and James A. Lane. *A Birder's Guide to Colorado*. Colorado Springs: American Birding Association, 1988.

———. *A Birder's Guide to Southeastern Arizona*. Colorado Springs: American Birding Association, 1990.

Insight Guides. *American Southwest*. Singapore: APA Publications, 1988.

Krutch, Joseph W. *The Desert Year*. New York: Viking Press, 1963.

———. *Voice of the Desert*. New York: William and Morrow, Inc., 1955.

Larsen, Peggy. *The Deserts of the Southwest—A Sierra Club Naturalist's Guide*. San Francisco: Sierra Club Books, 1977.

Levitt, I. M., and Roy K. Marshall. *Star Maps for Beginners*. New York: Simon and Schuster, 1976.

MacMahon, James A. *Deserts—The Audubon Society Nature Guides*. New York: Alfred A. Knopf, 1985.

Murie, Olaus J. *A Field Guide to Animal Tracks*. Boston: Houghton Mifflin, 1982.

National Geographic Society. *Field Guide to the Birds of North America*. Washington, D.C.: National Geographic Society, 1987.

Peattie, Donald Culross. *A Natural History of Western Trees*. Boston: Houghton Mifflin, 1950.

Peltier, Leslie. *Starlight Nights*. Cambridge, MA: Sky Publishing, 1980.

Stebbins, Robert C. *A Field Guide to Western Reptiles and Amphibians*. Boston: Houghton Mifflin, 1985.

Weber, William A. *Rocky Mountain Flora*. Boulder: University of Colorado Press, 1976.

Whitney, Stephen. *Western Forests—The Audubon Society Nature Guides*. New York: Alfred A. Knopf, 1992.

Zimmerman, Dale A., Marian A. Zimmerman, and John N. Durrie, eds. *New Mexico Bird Finding Guide*. Albuquerque: New Mexico Ornithological Society, 1992.

INDEX

NOTE: Boldface numbers denote directions and
italic numbers indicate maps

ABOUT THE AUTHOR

Ben Guterson is a high-school English teacher who lives on the Navajo reservation in northwestern New Mexico. His articles on the outdoors and Southwest culture have appeared in several regional publications, including *New Mexico* magazine and *New Frontiers*.